Stories Mediators Tell

Editors
Eric R. Galton
Lela P. Love

Cover design by Monica Alejo/ABA Publishing.

Printed in the United States of America.

18 17 16   8 7 6

Cataloging-in-Publication Data is on file with the Library of Congress

Library of Congress Cataloging-in-Publication Data

Galton, Eric, 1952-
Love, Lela, 1950-
Stories mediators tell / By Eric Galton and Lela Love
    p. cm.
Includes bibliographical references and index.
ISBN 978-1-61438-356-7 (alk. paper)
1.   Dispute resolution (Law)—United States.   2.   Arbitrators—United States.   3.   Mediation—United States.   I. Title.
KF9084.G35 2012
347.73'9--dc23

                                    2012003999

Dedications

I dedicate this book, with deepest appreciation, to my expanding family: Kimberlee, Justin, Seth, Noah, Kaela, Katie, Margaret, Jamie, and, of course, Emmy. You have enriched my life in so many ways. And also to those who trusted in the mediation process and had the courage and conviction to find peaceful resolutions when all appeared lost.

Eric Galton

This book of stories is collected in loving tribute to the characters who have made the story of my life so rich, so varied, so full of challenging obstacles and soaring flights over them—Peter Popov, my strong husband, Nicole Love Doppelt, my beautiful daughter, and Christmas, my noble horse.

Lela Love

Thanks

We thank Rick Paszkiet, of ABA Publishing, for skillful and dedicated editing of these stories; we feel exceedingly lucky that he took on this project. We are ever grateful to the ABA Section of Dispute Resolution for its leadership role in the dispute resolution field and to the Section's Publications Board, led by Daniel Bowling, for accepting this manuscript and furthering its publication. We also take a deep bow with great appreciation to the writers whose stories populate this book. They rose to every challenge that was presented to them by the project.

Lela thanks Glen Parker for his enthusiasm and his assistance with the manuscript. She also thanks: Josh Stulberg for providing lifelong inspiration as a mentor, mediator and story-teller par excellence; and Kim Kovach for being one of her first writing partners, celebrating what mediation can and should be and leading her to Eric and this collection. Josh and Kim are silent movers behind this book. Lela also thanks her sister, Spencie Love, an amazing oral historian, who taught her the power of stories to discover the past—and, in that way, while uncovering the past, to impact the future.

Eric thanks his fellow Lakesiders, Ben Cunningham and Greg Bourgeois, who are amazing mediators and even better friends. He has been greatly inspired by his professional family, the International Academy of Mediators and especially his dear co-trainer, Tracy and his Cousin Jeff.

Contents

Contents

Contents

Introduction

STORIES

What is the purpose of a book of stories that mediators tell?

Consider your favorite stories. *Once upon a time … My grandfather once told me … In the beginning … I had a farm in Africa at the foot of the Ngong Hills … Arma virumque cano ….* With these exciting words, we are transported into another world.

Stories entertain and while they do they explain the world, teach, inspire, enshrine community norms and bind a community together both with respect to current members and across generations. Stories are windows into other worlds—other times and places where the listener or reader cannot go without them.

There are numerous examples of peoples with oral traditions where stories provide the glue for a community, passing down, from one generation to another, wisdom and inspiration. The Native Americans in North America or the Aborigines in Australia, for instance, have stories that explain the earth—its creation and operation, so that each new generation can survive in an optimal manner, harmonious with the earth and each other.

The famous Uluru (also known as Ayer's Rock), for example, according to Aborigine story, was created in Dream Time by Creation Beings, and most of the rock formations have stories about the larger-than-human Creation Beings interacting with one another and thus forming particular caves, outcroppings and pools. Each Creation Being has a particular animal manifestation—an animal it is related to and whose form it takes. Legend describes one of the caves at Uluru being formed by a Creation Being, who is a relative of a burrowing animal, and who needed to welcome other Creation Beings to Uluru. The cave was made after many unsuccessful tries to burrow directly into the stone (so the actual stone at Uluru is pitted in this place) until finally the Creation Being discovered it was possible to burrow near the ground, under the stone, and make a wonderful cave. When the visiting Creation Beings came they were welcomed into an awesome new cave-home. For the visitors to Uluru and for Aborigines, the story is a lesson in hospitality, perseverance and ingenuity made vivid at the beautiful cave where the story is set.

Geologists at Uluru tell another story, how the rocks were compressed over millennium until the plates of the earth rubbing together thrust up the rock forms we now see. The science story too is mind-boggling and inspiring.

Both stories can be told side by side. Both can generate awe. Some of us won't remember the geological explanation but may remember the story of the burrowing creature, the pitted rock and the cave, and the advice it imparts about the effort necessary to welcome visitors properly. Others will remember the geological explanation.

In the United States, we have stories that are retold to every school child: George Washington chopped down a cherry tree to try out his new hatchet and afterwards could not lie to his father about his transgression. Whether or not true, our first president is used as an exemplar for truth telling. The story can educate and inspire listeners about right conduct, more than a lecture on morals. Stories about our leaders, like the stories of the Iliad and the Odyssey, or stories from the Bible or Koran, instruct us about bravery and honesty, goodness and personal sacrifice.

Sometimes fiction—or the exaggerations and distortions of any history—can illuminate more than a recitation of "facts". For example, another famous story, that is not true, has been told and retold in news media and novels and by word of mouth. It is the story of Dr. Charles Drew, an African-American physician who discovered how to use blood plasma for transfusions before World War II, and thus saved countless lives. During that war, a blood bank was created that refused to accept African American blood. Drew became a well-known figure protesting this insulting policy, particularly insulting since African-American soldiers were spilling their blood in the war effort. Drew was seriously injured in a car accident in North Carolina and taken to a near-by hospital, where, the story goes, he was denied treatment, including a blood transfusion, because the black beds were full, and as a result he died. That story was true for countless black patients (though it was not true about Drew who received the best care possible at a small hospital where he was recognized as a famous doctor), and it needed a figure like Drew to carry it as a myth. The story certainly played some role in touching hearts and changing public policy.

OUR MEDIATION STORIES

Some of the stories in this book are factual, an effort to recount precisely what happened in a particular mediation. Some are an effort of the writer to give an accurate account, but with the license of a fiction-writer who wants to convey the feel and tone and mood of a situation. This license is necessary in some cases to preserve confidentiality, and in others to help the reader step into the shoes of people in the story.

Unlike trial lawyers, who are permitted to tell "war stories," write about infamous trials, or use real cases to teach, mediators have been silenced because of the need to preserve confidentiality. Confidentiality is one of the safety nets that allow disputants to share their inner thoughts and feelings, trusting that their confidences will not come back to haunt them. Until now, with a few exceptions, the only way a good mediation case got told was in the form of a role play, which is a common training tool used to teach about the process or about a mediation technique. Roleplays are typically derived from real cases. Apprentice mediators "perform" the conflict as parties, while a trainee mediates, and, in so doing, they create potential resolutions. Despite nearly three decades of the modern mediation movement, this "storytelling" used in training has been largely focused on those who aspire to become mediators. This book brings these wonderful stories to a wider audience.

Our stories were not collected to glorify or to vilify mediation, but to make the process accessible to readers generally. We are motivated by the belief that mediation is not well understood—even its practitioners are often limited to their own experience, particularly given confidentiality strictures.

Recent public surveys regarding mediation demonstrate a very positive impression of mediation, albeit with certain misunderstandings. For example, the majority of the public believe one has to have a lawyer and be in a lawsuit to access mediation. Not true. Another misapprehension is that mediation is limited to resolving small neighborhood disputes. Also not true. Finally, the majority of the public believe a mediator must be a lawyer. Also untrue.

These misapprehensions demonstrate that while mediation has become "mainstream" in the United States legal community and many legal communities abroad, the modern mediation movement has not become even partially integrated into the American culture. We think this is regrettable. Families involved in conflict often find their troubles exacerbated in costly and extended litigation. Business relationships are severed. People lose jobs. Long term conflict adversely impacts health and quality of life.

Despite these misapprehensions and the serious costs of conflict, the relationship between mediation and the law has been successful. Mediation has unclogged court dockets and has allowed many lawyers to evolve into better problem solvers for their clients. The question remains, however, whether the public will come to understand how and when to use mediation. The earliest mediation intervention may produce the maximum financial savings and may enhance the preservation of relationships, allowing parties to access their creativity and discover alternatives that our justice system could not offer.

Some of the stories highlight the good that mediation can do. Some are funny. Some provide lessons in what mediators should not do. The stories stand as a contrast, a different route in conflict resolution, to the far more familiar route of litigation and adversarial contest. We believe that the "other path" needs to be illuminated by stories. In that sense, this book is important. We hope that it marks the beginning of a tradition where the omnipresent stories about litigation have side by side companions of stories of showing "another way" to address conflict.

Introduction

We thank the mediators who have contributed to this volume. We asked them to write their story because of the abiding respect of the mediation community for their work. The invitation that went to the current authors called for "a rich array of stories about moving, successful, unsuccessful, happy, sad and funny mediations or incidents in mediations. The goal is to shed light on the dynamics and realities of a process that is little known by the public and to share stories among professionals that might expand their sense of possibilities in the mediation process—or hidden dangers that are lurking there. The book's target audience is broad: users of mediation (the public), lawyers and other advocates in mediation, and mediators." The writers and mediators represented in this volume rose to that challenge!

On behalf of all the writers of these stories:

Readers should note that to protect the identity and privacy of mediation participants, the authors in many of the stories have changed the names of individuals and institutions, have "recreated" dialogue, and have changed details.

These stories were collected from many sources. Some already were written when we began this project, for example: the Sisters of the Precious Blood, Glen Cove and Mediation as Parallel Seminars. Others were solicited from committed and successful mediators who were likely to have important stories to share.

SECOND THOUGHTS:

After each of the authors submitted their story, we asked them for additional thoughts: Why did they choose to tell the story they told? What meaning did they find in the particular story? What lessons did the story speak for him/her After the end of each story, you will find a segment called "Second Thoughts" where each author reflects on their story. On the one hand, the stories stand on their own, and we will all glean different meanings. On the other hand, the reflections of the author enrich each narrative.

A word about the organization of the stories and the themes of the nine Parts. From our perspective, the stories organized themselves around certain central experiences shared by most mediators. We summarize them here:

PART 1. TRAGEDY, REVENGE AND RECONNECTION

We begin with the hardest cases. All of the stories in this part involve a tragic death or catastrophic injury and a subsequent action by the bereaved against those whom they believe caused the loss.

The stories vividly chronicle mediation's potential to advance healing and closure, even in situations of enormous grief, rage and hostility. The dramatic reconnection of parties in these stories—both with their own sense of positive purpose and with their counterparts— is brought about by mediation. Parties in these stories are enabled to turn their tragedy into something of value. The stories show how a mediator's attention to details—to the setting, to the co-mediation team, to insuring the presence of helpful participants, to the needs of the parties—can pay off by promoting life-changing shifts. These stories are a testament to the human spirit which can—with the help of thoughtful intervention—rise up and become generous, courageous and whole after great loss, and also a testament to the value of a skillful and patient mediator.

PART 2. SURPRISING CONCLUSIONS

Entering a mediation, the mediator never knows where a case will go. These stories show that outcomes can be surprising—and delightful— and sometimes result in further complications. And the central lesson? Go with the flow. Good mediators do not get in the way of party driven—and sometimes creative—outcomes.

PART 3. THE PRINCIPLE OF UNKNOWABILITY

The stories in this part highlight that "you never really know". You never know if someone who acts immovable will suddenly move. You never know why people are acting badly—or well. You never know when dramatic shifts have already occurred, under the surface, and are being masked by unreadable faces determined to "save face". The lessons you will find vividly illustrated in these stories are: be present, be attentive, keep listening, and don't become a judge. Above all, be humble about what you think you know.

PART 4. LISTENING FOR THE UNDERCURRENTS AND FINDING MISSING PIECES

One aspect of mediation is that it can reveal undercurrents and it can add the missing pieces of the puzzle to bring resolution. Conflict is influenced by things that happened decades earlier, by old alliances and enemies, by professional and personal orientations, by values and preferences, by youth and age, by the pressures of debt or the prisons of addictions, by personal needs of all types, such as the need for order and clear lines, and by connection and loyalty to certain people due to one's own history. All these things can aid or aggravate conflict resolution. All of these things, if understood and used, can provide a bridge to make the pieces fall into place—to generate understanding and options. These stories show how mediation can potentially weave the undercurrents and the missing pieces into a workable whole.

PART 5. STAYING IN THE MIDDLE WITHOUT JUDGMENT OR FAVORITISM

One of the supreme challenges for mediators is to stay in the middle. Not to lean toward that party who seems weaker, or with whom one identifies, or to whom one's sympathies and affections naturally flow. Can a feminist mediate a matter where a male chauvinist is on one side? Can the mediator stay with party choice even when parties don't choose the best course of action? These are not academic questions but are pressing challenges for the mediators in these stories—and in real life.

PART 6. MOMENTOUS SHIFTS

A mediator bumper sticker reads: "Shifts Happen." Conflicts bring together the danger of people who are angry, frustrated, and sometimes grieving, with the opportunity inherent in having gathered all players necessary to make a change. In that cauldron changes occur. Dogmas we believed as truth as a child can be revealed to be limited.

Borders of families can move to embrace new members. Ancient hatreds can be abated. Of course, not all shifts are "momentous". In almost every mediation, parties leave understanding more than when the mediation started. The momentous changes these stories describe stand as a reminder that where big things can happen, so can meaningful small things.

PART 7. SELF-REFLECTION AND REFLECTION ON PRACTICE

Whether practitioners of mediation grow and improve—or whether they repeat the same mistakes over and over—depends on reflective practice. The stories in this part show potential benefits of taking practice up a notch via thoughtful reflections. Analyzing each of one's choices as a mediator, each of one's attitudes, tends to reveal that other choices might have been better. Did the mediator make unwarranted assumptions? Did the mediator neglect something that could have advanced the mediation? This section will show master mediators finding fault with themselves, and, enriching their own capacities as they do.

PART 8. ADDRESSING ISSUES THAT LITIGATION CANNOT

Can constitutional issues be mediated? Why would you mediate a case with a central legal question which calls out for an adjudicated response? The answer is simple. The issues that mediation can address are very different from those that a court resolves. In Tony, for example, there is a question about freedom of speech that might have been adjudicated to a conclusion that would provide a public precedent. The mediation, instead, resolved issues of a high school student's graduation and eligibility for college scholarships and, on the other hand, the high school's ability to conduct a graduation without interference from protesters and picket lines. The reputation of the student and the school was on the line, as well as the student's career. These interests and issues are more important for the individuals and institution involved than the constitutional question of free speech.

These stories show what can happen when rights take a second seat to interests.

PART 9. BEYOND AGREEMENTS

So, in conclusion, it's not the agreement that's important. The final part offers a case where there is no agreement. In fact, the mediation session itself is almost entirely aborted. The story chronicles, however, that the framework offered by mediation can nonetheless advance important goals—a step up in self-knowledge and an advance towards a richer life.

A DISCLAIMER AND A CLAIM

Truly transformational mediations are rare. Routine mediations where parties exchange information and proposals and perhaps come to an agreement after back and forth negotiation are the norm and might seem unremarkable as stories. Similarly, though, a book of stories about run-of-the-mill litigations or medical procedures or a myriad of other things would not be enlightening. What the stand-out cases offer us is a window into what is possible and what pitfalls are lurking—"the best" and the avoidable errors. We need stars as guides. We need buoys to avoid rocks.

An attorney friend recently told us that devoting a career to mediation was a waste of time. After traveling from New York to Boston, he had just participated in a full day mediation involving a ship captain whose vessel had sunk due to the captain's own misjudgments. The captain was nonetheless suing the company for his allegedly wrongful termination from employment, alleging age discrimination. The relationship between the captain and the company spanned decades. The captain had suffered deeply from depression and post-traumatic stress after his vessel sank. The company actually liked the captain. Nonetheless, despite the long relationship between the parties— coupled with the complications due to the sinking of the ship—the entire session was conducted in caucus. Our friend reported that the sum of the mediator's work was to go back and forth between caucus rooms essentially saying "I need more money" or "You have to

Introduction

reduce your demand." The attorneys who were the spokespersons in the negotiation were deeply set in their positional stance, and the gap between positions was unbridgeable using this technique. The attorney friend who reported this found the mediator's efforts both depressing and fruitless. The captain and the company representative were marginalized during the mediation. And it was not surprising that very little happened. This case moved back into the litigation stream. So, while the stories in this book—the transformative ones—may be the exception, we hope they will inspire practice that makes every case a potential candidate for stories mediators tell. That captain and his company could have parted ways much differently thanks to a different sort of mediation.

We hope these stories invite you, the reader, to speculate about mediation in the light of the tales told by the master mediators in this book. Whether you are reading this as a sometimes party in conflicts or a mediator or an advocate, you should know that great things are possible in mediation.

Eric Galton and Lela Love

PART I

Tragedy, Revenge, and Reconnection

*The quality of mercy is not strain'd,
It droppeth as the gentle rain from heaven
Upon the place beneath: It is twice blest;
It blesseth him that gives, and him that takes.*

William Shakespeare, *The Merchant of Venice*

1.
A Meeting of Strangers

Eric R. Galton

GINNY

Christmas was coming to West Texas just like it always did, thought Virginia Stevens as she drove home from the H-E-B store with her Christmas dinner groceries. The harsh, cold winds from the west had already cloaked the unforgiving landscape with an extra layer of dust that Ginny had to sweep off her front porch at least three times a day—as if she didn't already have more than enough to do this time of year. In fact, driving was the one time during the day that she had an opportunity to do nothing but reflect.

Nothing much had changed in Odessa, Ginny thought as she glanced at houses with the same suspended holiday lights that she remembered from high school and maybe even from before that. How long ago was that anyway? Thirty years? Forty? No point in trying to recall exactly. As her doctor husband Bill would say, "Just a damn long time ago."

3

The old nativity scene sure could use a new coat of paint, Ginny also thought as her Saturn breezed by the Catholic church. And that manger looked droopy and nothing like the heavenly home she conjured up in October when she felt Christmas coming hard like a train rolling fast down the track.

Yes, West Texas was still pretty much the same. Sure, the inevitable and sometimes convenient Walmart, Applebee's, and even Target Superstore now dotted the landscape. But the landscape remained sorry, flat, and, yes, hopelessly dusty. The dust was such a problem for those baby doctors' wives from Dallas who Ginny, along with the West Texas Medical Recruiting Committee, tried to convince to settle and raise their families in Odessa instead of on those green lawns in Highland Park that seemed to hiss in the summers. For heaven's sake, the town fathers had even built a special subdivision to recruit doctors, with man-made lakes and artificial "rolling hills." Actually, they looked more like uneven mounds of dirt; but they called it "Pill Hill," and at least a few of the Dallas wives seemed to like it.

Most folks who loved this place, though, were born here, grew up here, raised their kids here, and were buried a few miles from the house they grew up in. Sometimes it felt like one of those dumb movies in which someone goes back into the past; but the past was the present, and it all ended up in one big stinking mess that was way too confusing to try to figure out.

When out-of-town folks conjured up stereotypes of Texas and came to Odessa, they were rarely disappointed. West Texas was a large place with an open sky, a place where big men still walked the land trying often to lasso oil from terrible holes in desolate country. Ten minutes outside Odessa, you could set the car cruise control on eighty-five and drive for over an hour and not see much of anything.

Friday nights were only about high school football. And, yes, when folks got divorced—and, yes, that happened way too much, in Ginny's humble opinion—they'd go to court and fight over the football tickets. To heck with the kids and where they'd live. Ginny's brother John, who had disgraced the family and become a lawyer, had spent two full weeks in court in Midland trying to convince twelve good citizens that Old

Man Williams was not in his right mind when he bequeathed the season tickets to his daughter Susie instead of his son Alex.

Saturdays were spent mostly at the Odessa Country Club. The men would golf, usually badly but lie about it; the women would start with tea and charity talk but migrate to gin and tonic while pondering who was having an affair with whom, blaming it all on whiskey, the modern destruction of proper society, and three well-known bars three miles outside of town.

Sunday was church. Visitors never had to trouble themselves about finding religion here. By last count, eighty-seven churches existed to support the needs of 57,523 citizens who had a whole lot of confessing to do and required an awful lot of forgiveness.

Yes, lots of things were predictable in Odessa. But Ginny also couldn't figure out why, at sixty-five years of age and the matriarch of a very large family, she was still responsible for Christmas dinner. Adding up the grandkids, her allegedly grown kids and their spouses and even ex-spouses, and purported family who claimed an invitation by about ten degrees of separation, Ginny was going to feed something near ninety bodies, all of whom came as if they had eaten their last meal on Thanksgiving—which, by the way, was also at her house.

But West Texans don't complain out loud much. They moan a lot to the Lord and maybe whimper a bit to their very best friend. And even in moments of terrible crisis, West Texans never wear their hearts on their sleeves. Life is tough. Life ain't fair. You just put on your boots, roll up your sleeves, and do what you have to do.

Just when Ginny was beginning to feel a mythical sense of resolve and developing the usual delusion that she would once again pull off Christmas dinner without a hitch, she remembered the three-bean casserole and the absolutely, positively necessary Campbell's cream of mushroom soup. She had been in the H-E-B for two and a half hours (thirty minutes of which was a brief conversation with Wanda Stewart about her unfortunate daughter who was trying to become a singer and had moved to crazy Austin) and had even brought a list, but she still had managed to forget something. Although she was almost home, Ginny

5

pulled into the Odessa Church of Christ parking lot, turned her Saturn around, and headed back to the market. You can't have Christmas dinner without three-bean casserole, Ginny thought. As Ginny drove back to the H-E-B, she let her mind wander to whatever else she had forgotten. Growing older had not been the joyride to grace that her mother—may she rest in peace—had promised.

SAM

Oddly enough, Sam Kitchens was driving to the same H-E-B. He was feeling very happy and spry, despite the fact—and unbeknownst to him—that his mission was much the same as Ginny's. Sam was getting the "fixins," as he was fond of calling them, for Christmas dinner, which he had been planning for weeks.

The funny part, at least funny to Sam, was that he didn't mind at all that after his beloved Christine had passed away seven years ago, he had become the master chef for his family. Heck, at seventy-two, Sam no longer was fit to drill in the fields. And, if the truth be known, he did not miss it one bit. Christine, bless her heart, used to smile after he walked in and say, "Sam, you stink worse than a hog on a bad day." But then Christine would smile, wash his clothes, send him off to the shower, and yell, "But I know how to put lipstick on a pig." He sure missed Christine and still thanked God that the cancer took her fast, but Sam had a mess of kids, grandkids, and former comrades from the oil patch who kept him hopping. Sam did think that he would be given a special place in Heaven for watching way too many Disney videos with his niece Gloria's kids, but it was a small price to pay for adoration and, more importantly, for an audience that would listen to him with rapt attention.

Sam didn't really realize how much his cooking had evolved. He had always been good at cooking large slabs of red meat to perfection on the grill. After Christine died, Sam violated one small promise he had made to her—he got cable. Immediately, he became a food channel junkie. Sam attributed this current obsession to Emeril, who Sam thought was a "man's man"; and even though he talked funny, he sure was enthusiastic about his work. Cooking was much like drilling for oil.

Sometimes, if you worked hard enough at it, amazing and wonderful things could come out of the ground or the oven. More often than you'd care to admit, though, you could work all day and end up with a total disaster. Sam actually wrote to Emeril to find out what went wrong with that veal dish that, when Sam got through with it, resembled beef jerky. Fortunately, only Sam had been there to eat it, and Sam very much liked beef jerky. He'd never had jerky with a veal-like flavor before.

Christmas dinner really was for Sam's four daughters: Ruby, Crystal, Jade, and Jackie, each of whom Sam loved beyond life itself. Jackie, though, was his favorite. Sam always wondered whether he was slightly closer to Jackie because she was the youngest or because she was the only child not named after some type of rock. Sam and Christine had never figured out where the rock thing came from, but once they started with it—well, you just don't fix things if they ain't broke. But for reasons that Sam could never understand, Christine had always worshipped Jackie Kennedy; and when the last one came along, Christine had said, "Let's stop doing rocks. She looks just like Jackie." And so the name stuck.

Sam understood completely, although he never said it out loud, that his daughters supported his cooking addiction and especially Christmas dinner because it "kept him busy." His daughters even ordered exotic kitchen utensils for him off the Internet from Williams-Sonoma. Half the time, Sam could not figure out what the device was for, but he religiously hung up each new one in his kitchen. Privately, Sam was hoping for a new sweater instead of the usual four new utensils.

None of this mattered at this special moment. The heater was working in his little Toyota, he was two minutes away from the H-E-B, and the only question was how was he going to navigate two full shopping carts.

THE ACCIDENT

Sam was thinking about his special oyster dressing for the turkey. He saw the light turn green and made it halfway through the intersection.

What else had she forgotten? Ginny wondered as she glanced down at her list on the passenger seat. As she glanced back up, she saw that her light had turned red, but she was already through it.

Everything happened quickly then—and yet in slow motion. She saw the car just ahead, a small one; and a man, a full head of white hair. There was a horrible, jarring smash and the sound of crashing metal and breaking glass. Ginny hurtled toward the windshield, but her seat belt held. She thought she saw the man's face before everything went black. She thought she heard sirens and someone asking her questions.

Hours later, Ginny woke up in a hospital bed, her husband and children around her. Bill, her husband and one of the few remaining good family doctors in Odessa, was holding Ginny's hand and jumped up when Ginny's eyes opened.

"You gave us all quite a scare," Bill said. "How are you feeling?"

Ginny tried to manage words, but she realized she was almost choking on tears that were seemingly rolling down her throat.

"You don't need to speak, Ginny," Bill said. "You're banged up some, but you are going to be all right."

Ginny summoned whatever strength she had and gently tugged Bill closer to her.

"The man?" she breathed. "The man?"

"He didn't make it, dear. He didn't make it," Bill said.

Ginny heard the words and prayed that this was some terrible dream. Mercifully, Ginny fell back asleep. When she woke again the next morning in the same hospital bed, Ginny realized that it was not simply a terrible dream and something deep inside told her that the nightmare was just beginning.

TWO YEARS LATER: GINNY

Ginny reflected on that terrible December day today, two years later, as she glanced at Bill, who was driving her in their Navigator to Austin. Reflecting back was pretty much all Ginny had done before, during, and after physical therapy. The fact that it was December probably made it worse. Ginny had come to almost hate Christmas and felt its cold press upon her starting around Halloween. Christmas was, as always, speeding down the rails, but now she was lying on the tracks like in one of those old movies with no hope of escape. Sure, she had met her share of heroic rescuers. The best psychologists, pastoral counselors, and potent antidepressants had done their level best to unbind the ropes and save the day. The mighty Christmas train had her in its sights, though, and Papa Noël wasn't blowing any whistle.

Objectively, if Ginny had any capacity to be objective, she was a complete and total disaster. She had not been behind the wheel since what everyone now referred to as "the accident" and could barely get in a car, even when dependable Bill was driving. Ginny had dropped thirty pounds because depression, she had been advised, had robbed her of her appetite. Bill kept telling Ginny she looked great, but she had, without exception, refused him any hope of intimacy. She slept poorly but now refused the pills. Ginny had other new addictions. She didn't need the pills.

The need to reflect back on the accident seemed especially important today. They were driving to Austin to attend a mediation to end what was now referred to as "the lawsuit," which resulted from the accident.

Initially, Ginny felt modest relief that she wasn't going to jail, although the largest part of her spirit believed that is where she belonged. Ginny, like everyone back home, didn't like to sugarcoat things. The equation was terribly simple: She didn't pay attention. She ran a red light at an intersection that she had crossed a zillion times. She killed a man. She killed a very good, kind, vital man. What else was there to say?

And, today, at this mediation thing, she was going to see his precious daughters whom she had never met and had never spoken to even though they lived in the same place, probably less than four miles from each other.

That part of it was the most baffling to Ginny. After Ginny was in the clear, Ginny wanted to call and visit the family; but her lawyer brother and the lawyer that her insurance company had hired to represent her in the lawsuit told her there could be no contact with the other family. Ginny was reminded that there could be criminal charges and, even if not, that she would surely be sued. Anything that Ginny said could and would be used against her. Her lawyer brother seemed to almost enjoy reminding her, "You never listened to anyone before, but this time you just have to keep your mouth shut."

Ginny thought all that was indecent and certainly not very Christian, but everything about this had become indecent. Ginny had told her insurance lawyer that the company should give the family whatever they wanted. Her lawyer told Ginny that it just didn't work that way but that hopefully everything would get settled at mediation. Ginny's lawyer told her that he would do most of the talking at mediation and that the mediator was there to help everyone arrive at "a number" that would settle the lawsuit.

Talking about a number made Ginny sick. Regardless of whether mediation was about numbers or about something else, Ginny spent most her time thinking what could she possibly say to Ruby, Crystal, Jade, and Jackie, now collectively referred to as "the plaintiffs." Ginny tried to put herself in their shoes. What would they be thinking? Ginny knew what they must be thinking: "Some ditsy doctor's wife wasn't paying attention and killed our father, and she should pay for it."

Bill pulled the car into a space next to the mediation center by the lake. Ginny's lawyer was already there along with an insurance company representative. As Ginny was escorted into a private room that was going to be "their room," she peered through the glass and saw four women and a man—their lawyer, Ginny guessed—seated on one side of the conference table. "The daughters," Ginny said out loud as she felt her stomach tighten.

Two Years Later: Jackie

Jackie glanced up as Ginny walked by. She had been wanting to get a look at this woman. She needed to see the woman who had killed her beloved father.

Jackie was the involuntary spokesperson and decision maker for her sisters. Ruby had not wanted to file a lawsuit and had told her sisters, "Lawsuits don't raise the dead." Crystal and Jade hadn't felt much different, but all had succumbed to Jackie's plea: "We've got to do this for Dad. We've got to make this right." In moments of sadness and reflection, none of this felt exactly right to Jackie. Jeff, their lawyer and a certifiably good guy, had done a full investigation of Virginia Stevens. The report, in a tabbed and indexed binder, told the whole story: No drugs or alcohol on the day of the accident. No history of drugs or alcohol. Large history of charitable work—volunteer work in the schools, at a food shelter, and even at the rape crisis center. Regularly attends the other Methodist church. No prior traffic accidents. Two speeding tickets in the past twenty years (amazing by West Texas standards). No speeding when the accident occurred. Just missed the red light. Virtually admitted the mistake to the police. The mistake that killed my father, thought Jackie.

Jackie had been infuriated that Ginny had never tried to contact the family or even send a card. Then Jeff told her that her lawyers would advise against it and, in fact, almost certainly not allow her to do it. "Well, the law sort of stinks on that one, Jeff," Jackie said. Jeff just winked and shrugged his shoulders. Nice guy—never an unkind word about anyone.

As much time as Jackie had spent thinking about the mediation, she never felt less prepared and more uncertain about what she would do. Jeff had provided a full explanation of what mediation was and what might happen. But Jeff had also said, "Mediation is also really different, and sometimes weird things happen." Jackie actually liked the different part but found *weird things* to be somewhat unsettling. Jackie remembered saying a prayer on Sunday that things go well today. She didn't really know what *go well* meant. Christmas was coming soon, and each Christmas since Dad had passed seemed to weigh more heavily on her heart. It wasn't something that she could put her finger on precisely.

Jackie, and her sisters, too, still mourned the fact they did not have a chance to say good-bye to their father. Dad, according to the doctors, had died instantly—"sort of like a bug hitting your windshield when you're driving ninety," said one of the physicians. Crystal often commented that "at least Dad didn't suffer"; and Jade would remind them that "he led a vital, healthy life, and he went out strong." Sometimes Jackie found some consolation in such thoughts; but the plain truth was that Dad didn't need to die, and she hadn't been ready for him to die.

The oddest thing, at least by Jackie's way of thinking, was that even though Dad had been laid to rest years ago, she didn't feel as if he was buried. Letters from her lawyer, hearing dates, depositions, and now this mediation thing—all of it felt, especially when she opened some chatty letter from Jeff, like it was just happening. While Jackie ostensibly was back at work and back to being a mom and better-than-average wife, she felt like her life was somehow on hold. Jackie had little reason to believe that today would make things different, but she really hoped that might be so.

Dad used to call Jackie "the hope of our family." Sometimes he used the word *glue*. Jackie liked *hope* better; but she understood that for reasons she couldn't fully explain, her father had bestowed captain-of-the-family-ship status on the youngest. Dad said it had everything to do with her heart. Jackie was hoping at this moment that she could find it.

THE MEDIATION

The next thing Ginny remembered was that somehow she must have sleepwalked into a large conference room. She was sitting at a table with her husband and lawyer next to her. The daughters were less than three feet across the table from her with their lawyer. She could almost reach out and touch them. She wanted to look each of them straight in the eye, the West Texas way, but she could only glance from time to time.

I made a presentation. The tone was comforting to Ginny, but she did not hear many of my words. Next, the daughters' lawyer spoke very briefly. He seemed kind, almost nice. Ginny wanted to hear the four women speak. I encouraged them to speak, but they didn't. Ginny's counsel told her that their lawyer would tell them not to speak, but Ginny was disappointed anyway. Even if their words were harsh, cruel, or condemning, it would have been better. Ginny felt that she had it coming.

Ginny's thoughts were disrupted by hearing her own lawyer's words. She was sure she heard her lawyer say, "We're sorry." Ginny thought that such a sentiment must be said, but she almost resented her lawyer saying it for her. Then there were details about the accident. Ginny tuned out her own lawyer until she began to hear him talk about her suffering. "You know," her lawyer said to the four women, "my client has been clinically depressed since the accident, has been on medication, and has virtually become a recluse." Ginny's lawyer added more words and then stated, "Ginny has never been behind the wheel of a car since the accident."

Sometimes when the fortunes and fates are right in West Texas, the drill hits a special spot in which the physical force becomes so powerful that it blows away all in its black wake. Something like that welled up in Ginny's soul—an irresistible, unstoppable force of amazing clarity.

"This has nothing to do with me or whether I can drive or how badly I am feeling. How dare anyone talk about me!" Ginny blurted. The room fell silent.

"This is about what I did to your father," said Ginny, looking across the table straight into the eyes of each of the four women. "God forgive me," Ginny said. "I wasn't paying attention. I have wound and rewound what happened a thousand times. I keep asking myself why. Why was I thinking about Christmas dinner instead of driving? What was so important? Why did I look down? It was just for a half a second. And then the red light. I saw the white hair. I think I saw his face. It was all my fault. I didn't mean it to happen. I didn't want it to happen. I've never hurt anyone before. I've learned what a great and wonderful man he was. I am so very, very sorry. I would gladly trade places with your father if I could. I have caused your family such terrible harm. Not meaning or intending it is no excuse. But I'm sorry for all the pain . . . and all the unimaginable heartache I have caused you."

Ginny's words seemed to echo off the walls into the church quiet of the room. Sometimes silence is uncomfortable. Sometimes silence is necessary. The room felt like it had moved someplace else. Where it was, no one really knew.

Certainty and clarity, sometimes elusive, may find you at the strangest times. Something, something beyond labeling, found Jackie. Jackie looked at me and between her own tears asked, "Are Ginny and I allowed to be alone together?" I answered affirmatively, and Jackie got up, went around the table, and softly touched Ginny on the shoulder. Ginny got up and, guided by Jackie, went into a room and shut the door.

BEYOND MEDIATION

Jackie and Ginny were in the room alone for over two hours. With regrets to drama and theater, the words and feelings exchanged between Jackie and Ginny belong uniquely and solely to them.

There was no Spielberg music when they walked out, arm in arm; and for those who witnessed the moment, it did not feel maudlin. On this day, Jackie felt that her dad was finally at peace. Ginny had expressed sorrow and responsibility and without seeking or requesting it had received forgiveness. Two families had become inextricably intertwined because of a terrible moment in time. Sam's hope was that Jackie would always find a way to forgive, to heal, and to restore. Jackie always felt that obligation applied to her own family. But today, for reasons that Jackie felt made no objective sense, her family had grown somewhat larger. Ginny and Bill would have Christmas dinner with Jackie's family this year. And Jackie, with Ginny's help, would cook some of her dad's favorite recipes and use all those utensils that had now found their way into Jackie's kitchen.

In a way, this was an ending and a beginning. There was still much healing to be done. Not everything was neat and tidy and safe, and maybe it would never be completely so. But just as the West Texas weather can turn on a dime and change on you, something in that large West Texas way had changed—something that would likely grow in the retelling.

When they came out of the room, all Jackie said was, "We're going home."

Ginny looked at Jackie and said, "That's right, we're going home."

So, the two women left and headed west. Christmas was coming, and it would be here soon.

SECOND THOUGHTS:

"A Meeting of Strangers" was actually the third case that transformed my view about the potential of the mediation process. Although I mentioned the presence of an insurance adjuster, I left out the monetary details of the mediation. Yes, liability was undisputed. Yes, a significant chunk of a $1 million insurance policy was paid. But the economic aspect of the mediation was the least significant part of the process from the parties' perspective, so it is not the focus of this story. Rather, the focus is the parties' descriptions of their lives and their words because after ten "successful" years of mediation, I had finally learned to listen to the parties and respect what was important to them. It took that long. Why?

A year earlier, I was mediating a medical malpractice case against an obstetrician. The physician had delivered the couple's first two children without incident. The third child, a boy, was delivered and died nine hours later. This was an otherwise brilliant doctor's bad day. Liability was undisputed, and a mediation was set up shortly after the lawsuit was filed.

I conducted my usual joint session. The lawyers made presentations. I did not invite the parties to speak, I made some encouraging remarks about the process, and we quickly adjourned to private caucus. Five hours later, the mediation was a "success" as a settlement was reached. I drafted a memorandum of agreement and delivered it to the doctor's room.

As his lawyers were reviewing the document, the doctor told me that he was pleased with the settlement but had been hoping for more out of the process. The doctor, a devout Catholic, asked if he could meet with the family and apologize. His counsel immediately advised him that this was not necessary, but the doctor insisted that I ask the family.

I went to the family's room and passed on the doctor's request. The parents, also devout Catholics, said that they would very much like to meet with their doctor. The family's lawyer interjected that the meeting was not necessary, but the parents insisted.

As I brought the doctor into the parents' room, all the lawyers moved to the back of the room. For a few moments, nothing happened. But the mother then stood up and held out her arms. The doctor went to the mother and held her and repeatedly apologized. The father joined the group and they stayed together for a few minutes. The parents seemed to be consoling the doctor. The lawyers watched from afar and appeared astonished.

Six months later, I was mediating a sexual harassment case in which two highly paid administrative assistants had been undisputedly and viciously harassed by a senior doctor. The two women had been with the practice for ten years and had watched a string of female employees harassed, terminated, and paid a generous "severance." Finally, the senior doctor turned his attention to these two women. The claimants went to the junior doctors for help; but, fearing reprisal, the junior doctors did nothing. Finally, the women were forced to quit and filed suit.

The two women, their husbands, and their counsel were on one side of the mediation table. The two junior doctors, their lawyer, and an insurance representative were on the other side of the table. The lawyers gave low-key presentations.

I noticed one of the husbands flinch after defense counsel made a certain remark. It was not my practice to ask parties questions at joint sessions, but I decided to throw caution to the wind. I looked at one woman and asked, "Do you have anything to add?" She put her head down and said, "No." So why not ask the same lame, useless question again? I did so with the next woman and one of the husbands sitting next to her, all with the same response. I then looked at the husband who had flinched and said, "I noticed your face changed when defense counsel was talking. What was going through your mind?"

And the husband spoke! He started describing what this had done to his wife and their marriage and his disappointment with the young doctors. Then, without a question, the next husband spoke, and then both women related their experience. As the last woman concluded, one of the young doctors got up, apologized, and said that he should have done something to stop the conduct. Sparks seemed to be flying throughout the room. The lawyers were in a daze. So was I. So I called a time-out and rushed everyone into their rooms.

In the plaintiffs' room, the parties told me that even if the case did not settle, the mediation had been successful.

Then I went into the defense room. The defense lawyer asked, "When did you start doing this talk show, Oprah style of mediation?" I was crushed. My career was over, I thought. He would go on the defense counsel website and let 5,000 lawyers know that I had lost my mind.

But a funny thing happened. The case settled. Everyone was happy, including the defense lawyer, who said, "I don't understand it, but it worked." And I still had a career.

And then, like a freight train, Ginny and Jackie's case came to me, and I was finally ready for it. I was, for the first time, really mediating.

I suppose this is a confession of sorts. It took a long while before I heard the parties' voices or bothered to respect what they wanted or expected out of this amazing process.

I do not force transformation. The easy truth about what mediators do is that each case is different and what the parties want or expect out of mediation is different in each case. A one-size-fits-all approach will not work and squeezes the life out of a flexible, fluid process.

But many people do want more out of the process. They want to be creative. Parties sometimes value things that their lawyers do not. And I want to be ready to hear that and provide a process that delivers that opportunity to them. I want to be open, aware, and available.

For a long while I was not available. I am happy to report that I am now, and that is why I wrote this story.

2.
Noah's Gift

Debra Gerardi

NOAH'S PARENTS

The cool spring air and bright warm sunshine made this an unusually beautiful day. The trees were filled with a diffuse light dancing off of the newly emerged leaves, and the yard was dressed in brown with bits of green grass promising a recovery from the winter's snow.

I walked up to the front porch of the ranch-style home and took a deep breath. It was my first in-person visit with Noah's parents. I paused for a moment and then rang the bell.

Megan Donnelly was younger than I imagined. She welcomed me into the house, and we exchanged the usual pleasantries. We wandered into the kitchen. Her young daughter ran by, curious about my arrival. "This is Noah's older sister, Jennie. She is four and a half years old," Megan told me. Jennie and I shook hands. Then Megan took me into the kitchen and introduced me to her husband. We greeted each other. "Call me Tom," he said as he reached for my hand. He looked uncomfortable, and I acknowledged that this was a hard situation and that I was sorry we had to meet under such circumstances.

We sat down at the kitchen table. Megan, always caretaking, asked if I wanted anything to drink. She made some tea and I took out my notebook. This was the first time that they had participated in mediation, and they didn't really understand how it worked. I gave them a general description of the process: facilitated conversations with key individuals to see the possibilities for moving forward together. We'd had more detailed conversations by phone, so I kept my focus on developing trust with them; we were going to need every ounce of it for the days ahead. They seemed to be reassured as I explained that they would be a part of decision making throughout the process, and I reinforced that we would work together to ensure that they felt supported along the way.

"So tell me about your son, Noah," I began. Tom dropped his head. Megan said that the best way to get to know Noah would be for me to see his baby book. She got up from the table and grabbed a small blue and white book from the counter. She opened to the first page: Noah Donnelly, born March 27, 2003. I felt tears welling up already. How do you prepare to go through a baby book with grieving parents knowing that the photos end when Noah was a mere ten weeks old?

She turned the page and we began. For the next two hours, we cried together as they told me the story of how Noah died in the hospital and what they hoped could come from mediation.

NOAH

Several weeks after he was born, Noah Donnelly was admitted to the hospital with an electrolyte imbalance and fever. His admission was uneventful, as health professionals say, meaning that there were no complications from care. However, no definitive cause was found for his condition. He was discharged home with his mother, Megan, three days later. She was given discharge instructions that included bringing him back to the physician's office if he started to deteriorate again. Several days after his discharge from the hospital, Megan noticed that

Noah did not look good, and she made an early morning call to his primary care physician's office. She was told to bring him in to the clinic to be examined. After a quick glance at Noah, the pediatrician told her that she was going to readmit Noah to the hospital.

The nurses on the medical floor admitted Noah and per protocol, took him to the procedure room upon his arrival so that they could assess him and start an IV. Inserting IV catheters into small babies is an art, and it is particularly difficult when the baby is dehydrated, which causes the veins to flatten and burst when the needle is inserted. Several nurses made multiple attempts to start the IV without success.

The nursing staff called the specialist on duty that day, Dr. Chang, to see if he could get the IV started or, if not, to initiate a central line, i.e., a large IV inserted into a major vein using a sterile technique. Dr. Chang came promptly, and he also tried to get an IV into Noah. Both of his attempts failed as well. The nurses began to prepare Noah for the central line insertion by getting the supplies and necessary equipment while Dr. Chang tried to reach Noah's primary care physician to update him and let him know what they were planning to do.

Although not obvious to the nurses and doctor, Noah's condition was deteriorating and his subtle changes were only apparent to the one person who could detect them—his mother. Noah's body was unable to sustain itself, and he stopped breathing. The team initiated emergency procedures and began their resuscitation protocols. Sadly, without an IV, there was nothing anyone could do to reverse the situation. Noah died at just ten weeks of age. It broke the hearts of everyone in the room and everyone who heard his story over the days and weeks to come.

NOAH'S DOCTOR

I walked down a corridor of the tenth floor of the medical center looking at room numbers to locate Dr. Chang's office. He agreed to meet with me that morning between his clinic visits and his shift in the ICU. Scheduling time with physicians is always a challenge, and I was happy that he was able to find an entire hour for us to talk.

I have been in hundreds of hospital hallways, having worked as an ICU nurse myself for over fifteen years before becoming a mediator. Hospitals feel more like home to me than any other place. They are familiar and predictable to those of us who have spent days, nights, weekends, and holidays working to care for the ill and injured. We forget, though, how foreign these hallways are to those who pass through as patients and family—hopeful that all will go well and that the trust they have in the care they receive will not be violated. I found the correct office and wondered how the conversation would go.

Physicians are compassionate and hardworking people; and when faced with a situation in which a patient under their care is harmed, a deep and profound wound occurs. *Primum non nocere*… first do no harm, is a tenet that undergirds the ethics of all health professionals and one that is taken quite seriously. Nothing is as painful to clinicians as knowing that harm has occurred to someone who has come to them for help and that they may have contributed to it in some way. And when that harm is to a child and results in the death of that child, the resulting feelings of regret, shame, and self-doubt are magnified. Such inevitable human responses are often carried inside as a silent penance for years. Even with the belief that everything possible was done, the reliving of such an event can be devastating to a clinician. Participating in a process that is designed to help address those feelings can alleviate the burden.

Having an opportunity to make amends and directly address a situation in which an adverse event occurs is often not available to clinicians due to legal procedures, hierarchical conventions, and liability concerns. Such barriers, however, only serve to exacerbate the pain that everyone feels and often block system wide changes that could prevent future harm. And even when there is an opportunity for a clinician and the patient's family to sit and talk together, the natural defenses of blame, attribution, and justification create a wall of resistance that is hard to penetrate without assistance from someone who can stand outside of the situation and convene a safe conversation. Despite the challenges, navigating through these barriers is necessary if there is to be healing for all involved.

Dr. Chang welcomed me into his office; we shook hands, and he offered me a chair. He was clearly distraught and eager to get to the point. He affirmed that he wanted to do what needed to be done but asserted that he did not kill the child even though in his mind, Megan Donnelly believed that he did.

Dr. Chang was in his early thirties and very mild-mannered. I was impressed by how compassionate and open he was—just what a person would want in a pediatrician. They are also the qualities a person would want in someone whom you ask to sit down with distraught and grieving parents. He was very willing to make the situation right, and yet he did not want to be the blamed for the situation. He was worried about meeting with the parents, in part because of the concerns of his boss, the chief medical officer, who described Noah's mother as inconsolable.

We talked about the possibility of him sitting down with the parents in a conversation. It was something that the parents wanted—to be able to talk with him directly and ask questions face-to-face. Prior attempts by the hospital administrators to share information in a group setting with the parents did not go well—sometimes those meetings happen so early in the conflict that it is hard for everyone to listen openly. Dr. Chang was nervous and reasonably so. The chief medical officer was not supportive of the idea of him meeting with the parents but was leaving it up to Dr. Chang.

The hospital administration was eager to move things forward. After a year of working with the parents to make improvements in how the hospital staff cared for babies, they were unsure of what more they could do. They were committed to change but were at a loss for what more could be done. Everyone was doing the right thing: looking to prevent this from happening to another child. And yet there remained unresolved questions, layers of fear and anger, a desire to honor Noah's life—all wrapped in a patina of suffering that impacted their collective ability to move on.

"I am willing to do this and I want to do this, but I don't want to be attacked or blamed for Noah's death," Dr. Chang stated. "I was not the only person involved that day." I assured him that the conversation would have a structure to it that prior conversations had not had, that it remained a voluntary commitment on his part and not a requirement, that he could stop the conversation or leave at any time, and that I would intervene whenever I thought the conversation was no longer working for everyone. We agreed to set a time and place, and we agreed to talk about what he needed from the conversation so that he could move on as well. It had been a long time for him to carry such a heavy burden.

PREPARATION FOR THE MEDIATION

I called the parents to set a date for the conversation—everyone agreed to meet on Friday morning. Recalling a date in the baby book, I asked the parents if they were sure they wanted to meet with the physician on what would be the two-year anniversary of Noah's death. We talked it through, and they assured me that they did—they saw it as a tribute to Noah. Dr. Chang was not so sure that this was a good idea given the importance of the date, but he agreed anyway.

I felt good about getting this far, and I began the process of preparing all of them for what was bound to be a difficult but much-needed conversation. Over several days' time, I talked with the Donnellys and Dr. Chang. We talked about what they each needed from the conversation, what they were concerned about, what they wanted from me, and any topics that were off-limits.

We talked about a location to meet, and they all settled on a conference room in the hospital. It worried me to have the parents come into the hospital for such a meeting, but they agreed to the location without reservations. My intention for such conversations is to provide the safest place possible for a compassionate and honest dialogue.

As a nurse, I am accustomed to hard conversations and ways of supporting others through them. As a mediator, I am always hopeful that people will rise to their best selves—where they are able to listen fully and connect as human beings regardless of whether they are ever able to agree on the details of the past or their desires for the future. I find that from this deep and authentic space, everything becomes possible. It is this connection and relationship with one another that creates hope and inspires forgiveness.

LAST-MINUTE ANXIETIES

It was 6:00 p.m. the evening before the scheduled mediation session. As I was driving, I received a call on my cell phone from a very upset Dr. Chang. He was beside himself with anger and frustration. "I am not going through with this tomorrow," he said. "I just got home from work, and do you know what I had in my mailbox? A letter from the state licensure board! I am being investigated! I have to leave town next week for a conference, and I have to respond to this letter within seven days. I can't go through with this."

I assured him that of course he could change his mind about meeting with the parents and that, in light of what had happened, it made perfect sense. I asked him if he knew when the complaint was filed; it could have been months ago given how slow regulatory agencies are at responding to these things. I asked if he was certain that it was even related to this case. He did not know, nor did it matter to him in his current emotional state. I asked him what he would like to do, and he said that he needed to sleep on it before he could make any decisions.

I agreed to meet him in his office at the hospital at 7:00 a.m. to talk about what came next. I continued to hold out hope that the meeting with the Donnelly family would still happen while trying to surrender any attachment to a particular outcome—a delicate balancing act experienced by every mediator.

At 7:00 a.m., Dr. Chang and I met and talked through his concerns. He was still upset and rightly so. An investigation by a licensure board is a nightmare for any licensed professional, and receiving this letter on the eve of a meeting with the parents was devastating to his trust in them and in the process. The chief medical officer was also present during our conversation. He was still leaving it up to Dr. Chang as to whether he wanted to meet with them, and he advised his colleague to just leave the meeting if it did not go well—a clear projection of his own discomfort and fear.

An hour and a half later, Dr. Chang resolved to meet with the parents in an effort to do the right thing.

THE CONVERSATION

I prepared the conference room for the conversation, arranging water, tissues and chairs so that it felt a little less threatening. I moved the chairs so that we could all sit together at the end of the long table. Noah's parents arrived, nervous but ready. I brought them into the room as Dr. Chang arrived. He looked nervous and tired but purposeful. They acknowledged each other briefly and we began. I set the stage, describing this as a conversation of possibility, and I gave them a structure that reinforced respect and open listening.

Dr. Chang started the conversation and said, "I want to talk with you today as a parent, not as a physician. I want you to know that not a day has gone by during this past year that I have not thought of your son." The tension in the room lessened.

The next few hours were the most heartfelt and respectful in which I have had the honor of participating. Each of the participants was able to ask questions and give answers in ways that were heard—without rebuttals, justifications, or attacks. Details were clarified and intentions were explained. A connection was made among them that enabled them to talk about the most difficult of situations and what they wished could have been different. The mood in the room ranged from somber to sad. Intermittent frustration and regret was followed by moments of clarity and waves of relief—a grieving process enacted in real time.

Megan asked Dr. Chang to explain his decisions that day. Through their dialogue, he came to understand that their questions to be more than a request for a medical explanation, but rather a mother's plea for understanding. Megan acknowledged that she wanted him to hurry that day and wondered why he didn't see that Noah was not doing well and help him. "I wanted you to hurry, but I didn't want to be seen as a hysterical family member," Megan told him. Recognition crossed his face as new meaning came to light and he recognized the subtle signal that he missed that day in the midst of all of the clinical chaos—her repeated suggestions were her way of telling him that Noah was not doing well.

Dr. Chang explained how he had changed his own practice because of Noah. "I entered the room that day as a technician and not a physician. And I will never do that again," he said. Tom Donnelly needed to hear that—not only did something change for the better as a result of Noah, but also responsibility was taken. Dr. Chang empathically reassured them that they should not blame themselves for what happened that day. They both needed to hear that. As they worked through the issues together, they all wondered why they hadn't had this conversation earlier. What had kept them from sitting down in this way and speaking honestly so that they did not have to wonder and worry for so long?

With some of the gaps filled in, the conversation moved away from the events of that day and toward what the hospital could do to support families when there has been an adverse outcome. The Donnellys said that although almost everyone at the hospital had been supportive and available and had worked with them to make changes in nursing practice and clinical protocols, the medical staff office had created a wall of resistance to her continued requests. Megan described her frustration as feeling shut down and indicated that she did not know what to do to instill further improvements in medical practice.

I acknowledged how frustrating that must have been for her and asked what she had done. "I wrote letters to everyone who might be able to take action," she replied. "I just wanted to get someone's attention, and a friend advised me to file formal complaints with review boards and accrediting bodies because that would be the only way I would be heard." The unexpected arrival of the letter was thus clearly explained.

We went on to discuss what it was like for a clinician to receive such a letter, what could be done differently in the future to enable parents to be heard fully, and how to support clinicians who desired a direct conversation after harm had occurred to a patient. Agreements were made as to how to move forward, what could be shared with the hospital administration, and next steps in the process.

LASTING IMPACT

More important than the agreements that day, there was the beginning of resolution—a healing process that enabled them all to move forward knowing that they had done what they could to make things better for the next hospitalized child and that they all had fully honored Noah's short life. Courage made way for understanding, and authentic human connection dissolved fear. The meeting ended with all three of the participants having shared tears, fears, and a joint desire to always remember the impact that Noah's life had on them.

What they couldn't imagine was the impact that his life also had on mine. . . .

SECOND THOUGHTS:

ALIGNING VALUES

Narratives are a powerful window into the complexity that comprises another human being—a reflection of our beliefs, hopes, fears, values and ideas. Every story we choose to tell to another projects what matters most to us, and reflects what we want others to understand about how we make sense of the world around us. *Noah's Gift* is indeed a reflection of all of these things for me.

My practice as a conflict specialist is centered on working with healthcare organizations and the essential work that health professionals do to provide care to communities of people. Noah's story reflects not only why this work is important to me but also the foundational values that inform my own professional practice. My mediation career emerged from my practice as a critical care nurse. I came to the world of dispute resolution from an ethical frame of "do no harm" and with a belief in the need for a holistic approach to human endeavors. I have intentionally integrated mediation and my other conflict work in a way that extends the work I have done over several decades as a health professional. With an emphasis on the importance of relationship and the healing nature of conflict engagement, I have crafted a niche in which I am able to align my values as a nurse with my knowledge of the law and my understanding of the principles of dispute resolution.

For me, Noah's story captures the need to expand the concept of mediation beyond the traditional frame of settlement negotiation toward a frame of conflict engagement. Such an approach is iterative and places an emphasis on facilitating engagement rather than driving toward resolution. Conflict engagement creates a bridge between what people truly need and the legal system that often blocks them from getting those needs met. In the clinical setting, adopting a conflict engagement approach provides the creative freedom to navigate the paradoxical pressures and moral dilemmas embedded within complex organizations while protecting or restoring the therapeutic relationship between clinicians and those whom they serve. The meeting between the Donnellys and Dr. Chang represents conflict engagement at its very best in the form of a courageous conversation within a supportive environment that is designed to optimize the greatest human potential. In this light, conflict engagement becomes a healing process.

Noah's case had many more twists and turns than are presented in the story, and there were a number of other participants with various issues that were addressed along the way. As in all mediations, there is a limit as to what can be achieved during the process. Much of the "work" of mediation occurs long after the mediator has concluded the process. I personally defined success in Noah's case as crafting the best opportunity for a conversation between the physician and the parents. In my mind it was this aspect of the case that would have the greatest impact on them and their ability to move forward. I guess this could lead to all kinds of debate on the meaning of "neutrality."

Noah's case illuminates the potential generated from a process that integrates the basic human desire for connection, trust, respect, fairness, and compassion while also addressing the broader obligations associated with accountable health care, risk management, effective advocacy, patient safety, restitution, and professional licensure. The story is a snap shot that exemplifies the growing movement away from an emphasis on claims management and self-protection following patient harm, toward a culture that supports conflict engagement as a means of restoring relationships and healing after harm.

As an attorney, I understand the severe constraints of the legal system and its limited ability to provide a humanistic approach when broken trust, shame, grief, and professional reputation are often at the crux of a dispute. This story reflects my belief that a more integrated approach is needed if we are to adequately serve others through both the legal and the health professions.

NOAH'S LEGACY

I was asked recently at a workshop to describe what I do in one sentence. "I create possibility in the midst of conflict," I said. I tell Noah's story because it is representative of what is possible in the midst of even the most difficult of conflicts. Noah's parents exemplified the courage and determination that always precedes major shifts in human consciousness. Noah's story also reflects an attempt by representatives of both the legal and healthcare systems to approach their work differently through creation of a process that could bridge the transition from a legalistic, rights-based approach to patient harm to one that restores human connection, instills safer practices, allows for healing, and generates hope.

Noah's legacy is more profound than the story above describes. The larger story is one of clashing paradigms manifested by the collision of outdated legal processes that emphasize distributive justice premised on a linear cause-and-effect civil code, with emerging principles of complexity science that reinforce the emergent and nonlinear nature of providing patient care. It is becoming apparent that clinical outcomes emerge from an underlying network of relationships and interactions, not from proscribed protocols. Noah's story underscores the need for alternative processes that better reflect the emergent and unpredictable nature of healthcare and conflict. Noah's case demonstrates such an alternative response.

During any mediation, it is hard to know what the lessons will be. With this case, lessons continued to emerge long after the mediation ended. Several months later, while speaking at a meeting for nurse executives, I recognized in the audience the chief nursing officer from Noah's hospital. She came up after my presentation to thank me for my help with his case and said that they had learned a lot from the process, in particular she mentioned that they determined that they should have called me a lot earlier. They gained insight into the benefits of having a conflict specialist facilitate the kinds of conversations that they had attempted early on with the Donnelly family but that required a facilitated structure. Their efforts had elements of success, and they learned more about how they could improve their approach in the future.

The Donnellys' attorney, hired to review any legal agreements that they might sign as an outcome of the mediation, worked collaboratively with me and the hospital attorney to craft a quality-improvement plan as a part of the final agreement between the Donnellys and the hospital, an aspect of his legal practice that was new to him given his litigation background and its emphasis on monetary damages. He later referred another client who was seeking quality improvements rather than monetary damages and he learned how to better negotiate for system change as part of his legal advocacy.

The Donnellys themselves learned more than they wanted to about both the healthcare and the legal systems and the limitations of each. They also appreciated the opportunity that mediation gave them to gain access to the information they needed and to obtain the system changes that assured them they had done what they could to improve care and prevent future harm. They promoted mediation with other patients who came to them for advice following their own adverse events.

And the insurance defense attorney representing the hospital's malpractice carrier acknowledged in a phone call to me a few months later that perhaps such cases were not just about money: he had called to request mediation services for a physician client who was being sued and who desired a face-to-face conversation with those who were attributing blame to him for an adverse outcome.

I continue to work with this hospital and its physicians from time to time. They are making affirmative efforts to improve the capacity of the organization to effectively engage in conflict, and the hospital leadership is looking into the possibility of hiring an internal conflict specialist to expand the expertise available to them. I often think of that spring day when I came to know Noah's story and the opportunity it provided for me to test my own limits and better learn how to create possibility in the midst of conflict. His story creates a ripple effect that continues to reflect the ongoing impact of Noah's gift to us all.

3.
The Other Sarah

Ben J. Cunningham

ROADSIDE TRAGEDY

Sarah was forty-two years old when she died on a lonely stretch of country road in West Texas. An avid bicyclist, Sarah was five miles away from the finish line of the fifty-mile breast cancer survivors' fundraising event when a pickup truck tried to pass her on the road. At 11:05 a.m., Sarah was alive. At 11:06 a.m. (depending on which competing expert report one might believe), either the defendant negligently struck Sarah's bike or Sarah had made a fatal mistake by suddenly swerving to her left, turning into the right front bumper of the defendant's truck. At 11:23 a.m. on that day, Sarah—with all of her history, future, triumphs, disappointments, and hopes and dreams for all of her tomorrows—was dead.

It took this roadside tragedy two years to arrive at my mediation office. I had gleaned a lot about the facts, as both sides viewed them, from the excellent pre-mediation submissions I'd received.

ART

I watched as Sarah's father, Art, walked through the door, accompanied by his lawyer. The father's face showed the strain of a long grieving. Art's lawyer pulled me aside and whispered to me, "This is going to be a tough one. He's out for blood."

Art had raised his daughter from the age of three after Sarah's mother succumbed to cancer. Art was the father who'd held Sarah's small hand as he walked her up the school steps on her first day of kindergarten almost forty years before, the father who had taught Sarah how to ride a bicycle, and the father who had driven her and her "boyfriend" on their first "date" to their middle school graduation party when she was almost fifteen. Art, Sarah's "Papa," had watched with deep pride and misty eyes as she graduated from college and embarked on her life as an adult. No father, Art told me, had "ever in the history of the entire world loved a child as much" as he'd loved his Sarah.

Art noted that Sarah was a great cyclist. "She was careful and cautious," he said, asserting that the driver of the truck certainly killed her by passing too close to her and clipping her. He ranted that the driver was probably one of those people who hated cyclists and was lying about Sarah veering into her lane. "My daughter is dead and this woman needs to take responsibility for my daughter's death," said Art. "I'm well off, Mr. Cunningham. This is not about money. It's about owning up to the truth."

"I hear you, Art, and I'm sorry you're going through all of this. And, please, call me Ben."

The other party had not yet arrived. I invited Art and his lawyer into one of my conference rooms that had a beautiful view of the lake by our offices. Outside, it was one of those gorgeous October mornings; inside, there was already an air of tension, the feel of something a bit deeper and darker. The look in the father's eyes revealed not only pain, but a mission. He was the last one left in the world to clear the record and establish that his daughter's death had been caused by the driver and that this negligence (or more) had struck down an irreplaceable woman—his Sarah. Art wanted two things, he said, and wouldn't ever settle for less: he wanted the driver to admit to killing his daughter; and he wanted her to pay dearly out of her own pocket, above and beyond what her insurance coverage might be. And, he added, if "that woman" could be sent to prison for the rest of her life, he would be very happy.

Art's lawyer piped up, "I've explained the mediation process to my client. I've told him this isn't exactly like the courtroom, and there are no criminal proceedings related to this case."

I explained to Art that his lawyer was right: the mediation process doesn't really include putting the parties on a witness stand, and as the mediator I wouldn't make any decisions about who was telling the truth or about who won or lost. I then suggested that we take a few minutes after we settled in to discuss the process and get a sense of what we could accomplish during the process.

The lawyer spoke up again. "I told Art that the only thing we can get here today is money, if they put enough on the table."

"Maybe *si* and maybe *no*," I said. I explained that no one could predict how the day would unfold and what might be learned, which was one of the valuable little things about mediation. I suggested that we get coffee and breakfast muffins and talk about the mediation process, what my role was, and how we might try to work through everything to see if we could get some bit of closure to this lawsuit.

"And, Art," I said, "just so you know, I've got children. And while I can't begin to understand the grief that goes into losing a child, I can imagine that the loss could never possibly go away, no matter what happens today or in the courthouse if the case goes to trial next month."

Sarah's father looked at me for a full minute, no doubt taking my measure. As I spoke, I saw his lip begin to quiver, but he quickly recovered. His sixty-five-year-old eyes showed the strain of two years of a wounded heart and the search for vengeance for what he perceived to be the murder of his daughter. I didn't need to be clairvoyant to see that this was going to be a very, very long day.

NORMA

The driver of the pickup truck was a woman in her late thirties named Norma. Her eleven-year-old daughter had been in the truck with her at the time of the accident. They were on their way home after a shopping trip in a nearby town. Norma had never been in an accident before, not even a fender bender. The cyclist, according to Norma, had swerved into the driver's lane and clipped the right front bumper of the truck. The police accident report was ambiguous and did not assign fault in the fatal event.

When Norma and her lawyer arrived, I showed them to another conference room and offered them some coffee. Norma accepted the coffee with shaking hands. I got them settled in and took a minute fussing with the blinds in the small conference room so that they could see the lake outside.

"Let's talk in private for a few minutes," I said, sitting down and sipping my own ubiquitous mug of coffee.

The lawyer spoke first, a bit stridently. "First, I don't know how you usually do things, but absolutely and under no circumstances will I allow my client to be in the same room with that guy. I took his deposition, and the man is on a jihad."

"We'll talk about that," I said. "But first, why don't you give me your impression of the plaintiff. Sounds like the depo was a bit tense."

According to the lawyer, the father saw the world in an eye-for-an-eye way. The lawyer explained that the plaintiff was "angry as hell" and refused to believe, according to the defense version of the accident, that his daughter was riding her bike on the shoulder of the road and that as the truck was approaching, she turned her head to look back, which caused her to veer into the front right side of the truck. It was an accident, the lawyer said—a tragic one, but it wasn't his client's fault. He didn't want to give Sarah's angry father the opportunity to directly confront his client, who was frightened of the father and emotionally devastated by having been involved in an accident that had caused a death. "We're willing to pay some money, obviously, but nothing we can do is going to give the plaintiff what he wants, which is to bring his daughter back," said the lawyer.

Norma's lawyer and I then discussed the potential benefits of having all of the parties present in an opening session. I explained that it would be an opportunity for me to get a sense of the dynamics and have counsel for both sides address each other to clearly state their view of the world. It would also assist me in beginning to understand the issues that needed to be addressed, I added.

"I don't see where it can help," replied Norma's lawyer. "I've got to protect my client."

As I was talking to Norma's lawyer, I glanced at Norma often. She was dabbing her eyes with a tissue that she had taken from the box on the conference table. I asked her how she was doing. With quivering lips and tears in her eyes, she shook her head and said quietly, "I'm so sorry. I'm so, so sorry."

Norma's lawyer became angry, noting that a joint session was a bad idea because Norma was so emotional. He was worried that she would break down in the session or say something that could be used against her later. I assured him that the decision was his to make with his client but that the process would have value for his client and that I would keep a lid on things. I reminded him that the mediation process encourages some candor and openness and that what is discussed between the parties in mediation is covered by confidentiality provisions that provide the parties freedom to express themselves in a way that can't be used at trial.

Norma's lawyer turned to his client and told her that they would "play this little mediation game because it's court-ordered" but that he didn't want her to say a word. "I don't want any interaction between you and Mr. Revenge in that other room. Do you understand?" he asked. The lawyer was worked up, taking on the anger that he wanted Norma to muster.

At that point, I asked Norma if I could "borrow" her lawyer for a minute. He and I walked outside the offices, standing on the deck overlooking the lake and surrounding hills. We stood for a minute or two looking at ducks bobbing on the water. In the middle of the lake, there was an old man in a tiny boat fishing for bass. "You've got your work cut out for you today, Ben," said the lawyer, sighing. "They aren't here to settle this case. The plaintiff is here to harass my client. He wants payback. He wants to destroy my client's life. I'm not going to allow that."

I assured him that I understood and that I would protect his client from any kind of harassment. I then asked him to keep an open mind about how the day would unfold. Although he thought he knew, I explained that not even I had the faintest idea how things would play out. However, part of my job as mediator, I noted, was to design and facilitate a process that would provide the best opportunity for the parties to reach a resolution, if that was possible. I then asked for his cooperation. "Because I'm going to be the only one in the place today who knows what's really going on in the opposing rooms, I want you to help me if I think a little flexibility will assist the process for everyone's benefit."

"What do you mean, exactly?" he asked.

I told him that I wanted him to stay open to listening and considering any harebrained idea I might have to bring this sad case to some finality. "You are completely in charge of how you want your client to participate," I said, "but I don't want to see you get in a position where you've drawn lines in the sand that will be hard to back away from. I want you to remember that because I'm working with both sides privately, I might have a different perspective of what's needed to keep the process moving toward resolution." I assured him that I wouldn't reveal anything to the other side that he didn't want me to reveal; that I would honor and respect his judgment about how he wanted to handle the case and what level of interaction, if any, there might be between his client and the other side; and that I would give both sides as much information as I could, subject to confidentiality limits. I wanted him to be an ally in trying to get the case resolved so that his client wouldn't have to endure a trial.

A new flash of anger in his eyes, the lawyer said that he was pretty sure this would go to trial—the only thing the plaintiff was interested in, he said, was raking his client over the coals because he thought that his client killed his daughter. The lawyer said that unlike the father, he was here in good faith but that the entire exercise was about how much money, if any, his client would be willing to pay.

Again, I assured him that I understood his position and that we would just move forward and see where we were at the end of the day.

BACK IN THE PLAINTIFF'S ROOM

I then returned to the plaintiff's room and had a similar conversation there. I discussed some ground rules with the lawyer and Art, explaining what would and what would not be valuable to the process during an opening session.

The lawyer looked at his watch and remarked that it was already 9:40 in the morning. He was anxious to "get the show on the road." I smiled amiably, making a mental note that lawyers and parties sometimes have a skewed view of when a mediation actually commences. A lot of work had already been done, but the "players" were focused on their idea of "the game," which entailed some version of an adversarial fray. They hadn't yet realized that the mediation had "commenced" when I first read their submissions the day before and that it had begun in earnest the minute they had walked through my doors that morning.

THE JOINT OPENING SESSION

I could tell that the lawyers were chomping at the bit to get going, to do battle on behalf of their clients. I always spend time privately with the parties before any joint session for the obvious reasons: it gives me an opportunity to decide whether to have a joint session and, if so, what it might be like. It also gives me the chance to start educating the parties (and sometimes their attorneys) about the mediation process, confidentiality, etc. These pre–joint session meetings are also valuable in building some rapport and (most importantly for a mediator) trust.

I commenced the joint opening session, making a point (in a quiet, slow, and measured tone) of going over every item that a mediator should cover with the parties. I wanted to make sure that everyone was paying attention to me instead of each other for a few minutes, and I wanted to look back and forth at each party and its counsel as I was addressing the matters of confidentiality, explaining that I thought that the most valuable layer of confidentiality in a mediation is the confidentiality that parties have with the mediator when privately caucusing. I explained to the parties that this level of confidentiality not only allows us to speak freely but also puts the mediator in the position of being able to identify issues and problems that need to be addressed. More importantly, I told the assembled group, it puts the mediator in the position of being the only person in the mediation who knows whether or not progress is being made toward resolution. I explained that if things looked hopeless, I would honestly assess whether we were making progress. If not, I would decide when it was time to stop. If we were making progress, I would work as long and as hard as it took to resolve the dispute with certainty and some finality.

After my opening remarks, I turned the floor over to the plaintiff's counsel, who made a predictable quasi opening statement for "the jury," with a PowerPoint, photographs of Sarah's life, and schematics produced by the plaintiff's accident reconstruction expert. The defense counsel responded accordingly.

However, I wasn't primarily concerned with their position statements, which tracked their mediation submissions; my main interest in this opening session was to observe the parties, Art and Norma. Art glared in Norma's direction; Norma stared down at her hands, occasionally dabbing her eyes with a tissue. At one point, she looked up, and both Art and Norma stared at each other for a few tense seconds, but there were no fireworks at that time. Norma was frightened; Art was angry and in pain. I didn't suggest that the parties speak to each other, at least not then. If I wanted that to happen, I'd need a lot more "mediator capital" than I possessed at that moment.

SEPARATE ROOMS

I split the parties up and returned them to their respective rooms. My evaluation after the opening session was that the lawyers were focused on a resolution strictly in terms of dollars and cents. Art was focused on getting Norma to admit that she had been responsible for his daughter's death. Norma was frightened and guilt-ridden and wanted to be any place in the world other than where she was at the moment.

There were a number of moving parts, and no one was on the same page with anything. It was time for me to get to work. I got the defendant and her lawyer resettled in their room, with a request from Norma's lawyer to "get their opening demand so we can see if they're here to do any serious business." I turned to Norma, asking if there was anything we needed to discuss. Norma began crying again, saying over and over again how sorry she was. Her lawyer interjected, telling her that anything she said would come back to haunt her.

I left to go to the plaintiff's room to see if they had a demand. When I got there, Art was the first one to talk, proclaiming that she was probably scared that his lawyer "was going to get her to tell the truth." "She looked guilty as hell, didn't she?" he asked.

I explained that I wasn't there to get beyond the only truths with which everyone could agree: that Sarah died a tragic death on a Texas highway; that she was a good woman and a great daughter; that she didn't deserve to die, no matter whose fault it was; that Art would have to live with her death the rest of his life; that Norma would have to live with that day for the rest of her life, too; and that there was nothing in this world that any of us could do to undo what happened on that day two years ago. "We can't go back; we can only go forward," I said.

"It's just not right," said Art, his voice cracking. "Damn it, it's just not right. . . ."

"No, it's not. It's sad—all the way around. . . ."

Art excused himself, saying that he had to step outside for a few minutes.

I turned to Art's lawyer, who was making doodles on a legal pad, and asked if he had given any thought to some kind of opening demand. The lawyer, acknowledging the futility of it, said that Art wanted to demand the policy limits plus a million dollars more from Norma. The lawyer knew that Norma, divorced and raising a daughter, worked as a waitress in a little café. The lawyer didn't want Art to blow an opportunity to resolve the case before it went to trial. Her insurance policy limits weren't that high, and the lawyer felt that the carrier would tender policy limits before trial. He felt that both sides' experts were good but a little ambiguous. Push come to shove, a jury was going to decide this, the lawyer said. If they liked Norma and believed her, his guy would lose. If they believed his guy or didn't like Norma or both, his guy would win, but all he would get would be what he could probably get in mediation, which was somewhere within the insurance policy limits.

The lawyer said that he didn't think that his client cared about the money; all that Art really wanted was for Norma to suffer because he was suffering—in other words, Art wanted to go to trial to force Norma to sit in an open courtroom and face the humiliation of trial. And, the lawyer added, Art hoped that she would tell a different story than what she told in her deposition.

The lawyer and I agreed that Norma and her lawyer would bolt if I took Art's demand back to them. I said that there was a bit more work to be done before we started hurling numbers back and forth.

Art came back into the room, looking better than when he had left. I told Art that before we started talking money, I would try to see if I could get what he really wanted: information, something to satisfy the big question marks that he'd brought with him.

As I walked back to the defendant's room, Art and his lawyer were headed out to stare at the lake—and no doubt try to figure out what in the world a mediator did to deserve getting paid.

Back in the room with Norma, I asked her questions about where she grew up and what she did for a living and asked her to tell me about her daughter and how she was doing. The questions about her daughter opened the floodgates. I listened as Norma poured out her heart for forty-five minutes about the effect all of this had had on both Norma and her daughter. The bottom line: Norma's world was devastated by the accident, her daughter was afraid to ride in cars, they both had continuing nightmares about that day, and Norma lived with the guilt of having been involved in the death of another human being. It was apparent to me that Norma was hoping I'd convey some of this to the man in the other room who was suing her. She reiterated for about the tenth time in the past couple of hours of mediation how sorry she was and how she wished that Art understood that.

Lunchtime came and food was delivered. The lawyers were a bit antsy that we weren't "negotiating," but I was satisfied with the way things were going. I spent all my time talking with the parties and dancing around the fact that there wasn't yet any money talk. I talked privately, and separately, with the lawyers and explained to them that in my view it was premature to be negotiating. I gave them my general observation that their clients needed to work through a lot and that we'd get to the money issues a little later. The lawyers, both good lawyers, saw the wisdom in this, each admitting that they were beginning to see that their clients had issues that couldn't be addressed by money and that maybe the process might at least let them "vent" a little. One of the lawyers dryly commented that he wasn't sure whether this was a mediation or a therapy session.

I spent a lot of time with Art, getting him to talk about his daughter and the history of her life, of their life together. The focus was on her living memory, not that moment of her death that had been consuming him for two years.

Likewise, I spent time with Norma, talking a lot about her daughter. I kept learning new things, getting to know these people in both rooms better in a few hours than some who had known them for years. The problem in this mediation was not money; it was pain and suffering, on both sides. At least that was my working premise at that juncture.

GETTING THE OKAY

One of the mediator's greatest tools is information, and the art and science of mediating requires (on a good day) that the mediator know not only how to mine and absorb information but also if, when, and how to use the information obtained. By 3:00 p.m., it was clear to me what the actual underlying issues were. Addressing those issues was the problem. What the plaintiff needed was to hear Norma personally tell him about that moment that his daughter died. What Norma needed was to explain to Art how sorry she was and what effect this "accident" had had on her and her daughter. Putting them together in a room was a gamble: it could turn rancorous, emotionally explosive, even disastrous. Norma's lawyer had my promise that she would be protected from "Mr. Revenge," but that was no guarantee that he'd ever agree to a suggestion that they should be put together. However, my gut told me that it needed to happen.

I knew that Art's lawyer would welcome what I had in mind, so I decided to talk to Norma's lawyer first about putting them together. I did this in private. We had spent hours together and gotten to know each other a little, and he was impressed that I was giving his client special attention, that she seemed more relaxed and calmer. I believe it also made a difference that I talked things over with him, that I wasn't ramrodding things down his throat, and that I honored his role as lawyer and protector of his client. I explained to him that I thought the joint meeting would be the only thing that would stand a chance of clearing the air enough so that the money issues could be discussed rationally by both sides. There would be ground rules, I told him. The joint meeting would be an informal opportunity for questions, answers, and (I hoped) discussion between the parties without overzealous input from the lawyers. This was a dangerous and delicate tactic, especially for lawyers a month out from trial in a forum in which they might not feel they have total control. I assured Norma's lawyer that I would be in charge of keeping the peace in the room, but if there was a question posed that he absolutely didn't want his client to respond to, we would simply move on.

"I think you're crazy," said Norma's lawyer, "but what the hell. Okay."

"My wife thinks I'm crazy, too," I said, "but she hangs in there all the same." Finally, some progress: the first small smile of the day from Norma's lawyer.

THE SPECIAL JOINT SESSION
This special joint session lasted more than an hour. I guided the session gently, with small questions or, when necessary, with some bit of redirection to keep things on track. I asked Art to speak first,

to explain to Norma his loss and to ask her any questions that he wanted answered. "Play nice, folks," I added. "This is grown-up talking time."

Art spent some minutes talking about Sarah and her life, much as he had done with me. Norma listened. Both had tears in their eyes. I had a question that I wanted to ask—one of the bits of information I had gleaned during the day sat in a corner of my mind, the smallest of things, something that had apparently gone unnoticed or at least unremarked—but something told me that the time wasn't yet right. Art caught himself beginning to get red-in-the-face angry, but he looked at me and then sat for a moment gathering himself, his long anger of the day mostly spent. He looked across the table at Norma, and in an almost gentle voice, he asked Norma to tell him what really happened out there that day.

Norma, wiping tears, began to talk. She spoke of how she and her daughter were coming back from shopping in town, how they had been slowing and passing bicyclists for miles, both talking about what a good cause the cyclists were riding for—it was big news in their little town. She said there was a paved shoulder on the road where the cyclists were riding. As she approached Art's daughter, Sarah was riding in the center of the shoulder, Norma recounted. Norma slowed a little but couldn't swing out into the other lane because of oncoming traffic. She thought Art's daughter was far enough off the road for her to pass by safely. "Just before I got even with her," said Norma, "she turned her head to the left, looking backward; and when she did that, her hands moved left, too, and she swerved a little and I couldn't jerk my truck away because there was another car that had come up from the other direction in the other lane. Your daughter's front wheel turned into my bumper, I guess. My daughter was screaming hysterically. I was in shock. . . ."

Norma was beginning to crumble. She began to weep into her hands. Art was listening and I think beginning to understand how bad Norma was feeling.

I decided that it was time for me to ask the question I'd been waiting to ask. "Norma," I said quietly, "I think you might have said, but what's your daughter's name again?"

"My daughter?" Norma's eyes showed a small revelation. "Sarah," she said. "My girl's name is Sarah."

"Oh my God," said Art. "Did you say your little girl's name is Sarah, too?"

"Yes, sir. And this terrible thing has ruined us both. For two years, we've been grieving, too, for your daughter. And until the day I die, I will be so sorry, sir, so very, very sorry for your daughter's death. . . ." Norma couldn't talk anymore through her sobs. For a full two minutes, except for Norma's quiet sobs, the room was silent. No one moved. I watched. Then Art stood and walked around the table and sat facing Norma; he reached out his arms, and Norma accepted his embrace. They were crying together, wordlessly. After a minute, he took Norma's hands in his own.

"Tell me about your Sarah," said Art.

An Unexpected Resolution

The mediation now belonged to its rightful owners, Art and Norma. I rose and motioned to the lawyers to come out of the room with me. The lawyers looked at each other for a second, then rose and followed me just outside the room into the lobby where we could keep an eye on things through the glass doors of the conference room. Norma and Art continued to talk, her hands still in his hands.

We talked about the money for a few minutes. The lawyers agreed—subject to their clients' approval—that the case could settle for two-thirds of the insurance policy limits.

When we reentered the conference room, Art and Norma were still talking. "She reminds me of my Sarah at that age," Art was saying.

With everyone back together in the room, Art and Norma sat side by side as the lawyers sat across from them explaining the proposed monetary settlement. I'm always waiting for the next problem, the unexpected. I was waiting for Art to go backward, to object to the monetary portion because it didn't require Norma to pay more in addition.

Art spoke up. "I'll accept, but with a condition. . . ." We all waited for the next shoe to drop. "I want to use the money to set up a college fund in my Sarah's name for your Sarah, Norma. Maybe use some of it for some counseling if she needs it." Norma put her face in her hands and wept.

Actually, there wasn't a dry eye in the room.

As I wrangled the lawyers while they worked on the language of the mediated settlement agreement, Norma and Art went out onto the deck, leaning over the railing and looking at the lake as they spoke quietly.

An hour later, the documents were done, the mediation was done, and to the surprise of every one of us who entered my offices so many hours ago, Norma and Art were still sitting on the deck talking about Norma and Sarah's future as if, I found myself imagining, Art and Norma were father and daughter discussing Art's new grandchild.

That evening, after everyone was gone, I sat outside looking at the rippling waters of the lake, feeling the last warmth of the fall sun on my face before the chill of night set in. All mediators who have experienced a similar day know that resolutions like this give the greatest satisfaction, defining us as peacemakers.

SECOND THOUGHTS:

Mediators as "game changers": Experienced mediators understand that their role goes far beyond a kind of mere shuttle diplomacy. The parties and their counsel often have a myopic view of not only the process but also the subterranean issues that must be addressed before any meaningful progress can be made. Mediators must be constantly attuned to the dynamics and must continually hone their skills (and intuition) in order to alter the game when it benefits the parties and the process. The red flags that a mediator must be watching for include out-of-control hostility, anger, and other destructive (and self-defeating) behavior by the parties and/or the participating representatives, legal and otherwise.

Even after all these years of the mediation process being a part of the dispute resolution landscape, many people (and here I do include lawyers) still approach mediation/negotiation as a zero-sum, win/lose game. It is often the task of a mediator to guide (usually with much subtlety and finesse) the process in a way that allows the people involved to maximize opportunities for something approaching a rational and (again, on a good day) collaborative negotiation that focuses not on winning and losing but on achieving critical interests on behalf of each party. Let's be frank here: It is often the task of the mediator to better instruct the parties about the mediation process and, mostly through skillful questioning, to obliquely impart some negotiation skills that fit into moving the process forward.

Obviously, developing skills as an active and empathetic (not sympathetic) listener is critical for any mediator in any mediation. It can't be reiterated enough that information is the most valuable tool of the mediator, without which most of the other tools in the mediator's "toolbox" are useless. A good rule: Ask, ask, ask; listen, listen, listen.

I do not want to dwell on this, but I see mediations in the context of my old martial arts training in aikido, which is known as "the peaceful martial art." In aikido, the goal is not to defeat an opponent (or win); instead, the object of aikido is to transform an opponent into an ally with the least amount of force. Aikido is the art of blending, timing, and working sometimes in circles. One might notice in the story above some of the moments of blending, not fighting head-on—good skills to contemplate as a mediator. Never engage in argument as a mediator and avoid all attempts by others to draw you—the mediator—into becoming the surrogate "opponent."

Be attentive to the physical and emotional needs of those attending the mediation. Little things count. Always try to provide the physical and emotional comfort required; without these needs being met, they transform into unspoken anger, hostility, or resentment. Many mediators (and lawyers) shy away from the emotional or irrational, but often it is necessary to "enter" into it, explore it, and allow that energy to dissipate or be transformed into a more positive behavior. The reasonable and rational mediations with people who are unemotional

48

and savvy negotiators are the easy ones (if *easy* is the correct word). The emotionally charged mediations are more complicated because the mediator must somehow incorporate the anger, hostility, aggression, and fear into the process in a way that facilitates their positive use or their transformation into something more positive. As mediators, we ignore the human qualities and personalities at our peril; we must work within the cauldron of the mediation as it exists, not as we wish it might be.

When attorneys are involved, always listen carefully to their concerns and their issues, whether those issues are with the opposition, the process itself, or with their own client(s). A mediator spends an enormous amount of time "fixing," identifying, or otherwise dealing with the smallest problems during the course of a mediation to avoid even larger problems at the end. I believe that a best practice in any mediation is to attempt to talk to the key players by telephone days before the actual mediation. There are things to be learned that can often allow the mediator to plan a more viable process and to have a certain foreshadowing of difficulties that might be inherent in the dynamics of that particular situation. This pre-mediation process doesn't end before the mediation; it is ongoing, and of course this goes back to the value of the mediator gathering information like a miner searching in streams for nuggets of gold. Find those little nuggets of gold along the way, put them in your metaphorical pocket, and choose the right time to trade those nuggets for something much more valuable—peace.

4.
Rosa and Gordon

Charles W. Crumpton

THE ACCIDENT

Rosa and Gordon were hardworking people, she with her church and at home and he as a commercial truck driver. They loved to take long rides together, often with good friends, on Gordon's Harley. On a trip with friends for a scenic ride around the island of Hawai'i, as they went around a sharp turn, part of the undercarriage of the motorcycle hit the roadway and they crashed. Rosa was paralyzed from the chest down, a T-2 paraplegic. Gordon, fortunately, had only minor cuts and scrapes.

THE LAWSUIT

Rosa and Gordon hired an attorney who investigated and filed suit against the motorcycle manufacturer and an aftermarket motorcycle parts manufacturer. The suit claimed that the motorcycle design and parts were defective in not leaving enough clearance above the roadway on sharp turns. The suit claimed that those product defects caused the accident, Rosa's paralysis and a mountain of related losses. Their expenses and losses were calculated by economic and life-care planning experts based on research, statistics and experience in such cases. The experts' estimates totaled several hundred thousand dollars for past and future bills for Rosa's medical treatment and rehabilitation therapy and for Gordon's loss of income for time he had to take off from his truck driving work to care for Rosa. In addition, the suit asked for several million dollars in compensation for her pain and suffering and the effects on their activities and enjoyment of life.

The manufacturers of the motorcycle and the parts claimed that the accident was caused by Gordon's negligent driving and denied any defect in the motorcycle and parts. The manufacturers also disputed some categories and amounts of Rosa's and Gordon's claims for losses, expenses and compensation.

DIVERGENT PERSPECTIVES

Recognizing that the suit would be extremely lengthy, expensive and difficult to prepare and take through trial, Rosa, Gordon, the manufacturers and their attorneys decided to try mediation to see if they could settle the case, and agreed for me to serve as the mediator. Before the mediation session, they provided their case descriptions and documents and we met in a joint session and separate sessions to get as accurate and complete as possible an understanding of the case information and the parties' interests, priorities and perspectives. Those meetings indicated that the parties were far apart on their settlement evaluations.

After a meeting with Rosa, Gordon, and their attorneys, their lead attorney told me confidentially that Rosa and Gordon were feeling overwhelmed, discouraged and unable to cope with the trauma of the accident; Rosa's permanent paralysis and limits on her life functions and activities; Gordon's having to take time off work to care for her and having to take over pretty much all of the home chores and work; the manufacturers' focus on blaming Gordon for the accident and trying to make it look like Rosa and Gordon were asking for more money than they deserved or needed; the length of time that the lawsuit seemed likely to drag out; the mounting expenses of the lawsuit that their lawyers were advancing but that would have to be repaid from any settlement or recovery they received, which would reduce their net recovery; the uncertainty of the lawsuit, which they thought might get them less compensation than they would need after their legal fees, experts' fees, and expenses were paid from any recovery; and their increasing feeling that they wouldn't be able to get through it all and that it might turn out badly for them. These factors put so much strain on them and their relationship that they had told their attorney privately that they thought they might separate and divorce if the case could not be settled soon in a way that would enable them to rebuild their lives.

For Rosa and Gordon, the case was intensely personal. The accident brought about severe change and dizzying damage to them as individuals and as a couple. They increasingly doubted whether they could cope any more, unless they got some positive help soon.

In contrast, the manufacturers looked at the case from a legal and economic perspective. They focused on legal fault for the accident, which they put on Gordon as the driver. They also believed that what they considered to be Rosa's and Gordon's objectively verifiable future medical care expenses and income losses were significantly less than those projected by Rosa and Gordon's life-care planner.

The gap between the parties' perspectives, settlement valuations and underlying interests and values seemed huge. The manufacturers didn't seem to see things from Rosa and Gordon's perspective or to understand (or care) what might enable them to rebuild their lives, individually and together. At the same time, Rosa and Gordon didn't understand the manufacturers' perspective and the legal system in which the dispute was mired. They did not recognize that the legal system's value of things they claimed might differ from their personal and emotional valuation of those claims.

THE DISABILITY CONSULTANT

To seek an experienced, neutral perspective that might help bridge the gap between the parties, I asked Rosa and Gordon if they would be willing to meet and talk with an experienced disability consultant, together and individually, in their home, about their situation. Rosa said she felt she had been poked and prodded and put under a microscope by too many experts and lawyers already, didn't feel that any of them really understood her or offered any real solutions that could work for her, and didn't really want to go through that again. I explained that the person I would like to have meet with them was himself a T-2 paraplegic from an auto accident and spent his life and his work working with people and businesses on adapting to disabilities. I also explained that his insights and recommendations might help the manufacturers better understand the effects of her injuries and what was needed to help her and Gordon rebuild their lives. Rosa and Gordon agreed to have the neutral disability consultant provide his evaluation, and the manufacturers did, too, so I arranged the meeting.

The disability consultant simply offered to do his best to understand, respect, and appreciate Rosa and Gordon's circumstances and talk with her and them about what opportunities and resources might help them rebuild their lives, individually and as a couple. He welcomed the opportunity.

After their meeting, their attorney called me and told me that Rosa had been very moved by it. She said that when she saw the disability consultant drive up to their house, get himself out of his truck and into his wheelchair, and roll up the makeshift ramp to their front lanai/porch, she said to herself, "Thank God, he's one of us," and tears came to her eyes. She said they spent hours talking about the things that had changed, the things that were most important to her and Gordon, and ways they might make their lives more what they wanted them to be.

The disability consultant did some research and checking and provided his report and recommendations. The plan was for them to start their own business, with Gordon becoming an independent commercial truck driver, Rosa learning the business accounting and computer skills to manage the business, and the business providing the health insurance to cover most of Rosa's future health-care needs and expenses. With input from the parties' experts, the disability consultant developed an estimate of Rosa's future health-care expenses that were to be covered by insurance and those that they would need to pay themselves. He also worked out a projection of the costs of the business and health-care plans. We provided those projections to the parties and their attorneys before the mediation session.

Rosa, Gordon and their attorneys came to the mediation motivated to try to achieve a settlement that would enable them to carry out the plans. The manufacturers and their attorneys came to the mediation motivated to achieve a settlement that would be a better choice than the risk and expense of litigation.

THE MEDIATION SESSION

At that stage, one of the manufacturer's attorneys said that they would like to bring in nationally acclaimed mediator Tony Piazza for the mediation. Fortunately, Tony and I have been good friends for years, have co-mediated cases, and everyone agreed for us to co-mediate the case.

The initial group mediation meeting focused on the tragic accident and the effects on Rosa and Gordon's life, which were respectfully acknowledged by all. All were also willing to consider starting the negotiations with the disability consultant's recommendations for Rosa's future care and their business plan.

With that starting point, the separate sessions then focused on what it would take to fund the recommended health care and business plan expenses, and on negotiating an additional amount for Rosa's and Gordon's general damages compensation. That helped get past arguments over legal claims and defenses. Rosa and Gordon came off as very credible and sympathetic in the group session, the disability consultant's recommended health care and business plan expenses were considered reasonable, and tentative agreement on an amount for that made it possible to work toward an agreement on general damages and a total settlement. In the mediation, the parties and counsel became increasingly collaborative and objective, their settlement valuations converged, and they reached a settlement.

When we gathered again in joint session to confirm and sign the memorandum of the settlement, Rosa, who was an ordained minister in her faith, asked everyone to join hands. She led a prayer of thanks to each and all for working together to help make a new life and hope possible for her and Gordon.

As Dana Curtis, a close friend and one of the best mediators I know, has put it, in a sense perhaps our calling as mediators is to practice the art of the possible in enabling people to find ways to connect with each other to move from misfortune and conflict to agreement and opportunity—even in a situation as devastating as this. As Rosa reminded us all to appreciate, the strength of the human spirit and its ability to connect us through mutual respect and understanding are often key to that art of the possible.

SECOND THOUGHTS:

Conflict resolution often involves breakdowns or gaps in relationships and communications, and power imbalances that the legal system may be used to increase rather than resolve. Mediation tends to work best when it becomes a shared learning experience for those involved to build mutual respect and understanding. For that to happen, it sometimes helps for the mediator to look not only at what problems, conflicts, interests and priorities there are among the parties and their representatives, but also at how a respected neutral perspective might help bridge those gaps and increase receptivity and motivation to reach a mutually beneficial agreement.

One lesson of this is that sometimes mediators have to be inventive in terms of what outside resources might be helpful to move things forward, whether it be, as here, a neutral expert on key issues, co-mediation, or another resource to promote understanding and motivation to reach agreement.

5.
Sarah McCrae

Susan M. Hammer

SARAH: FINAL HOURS

Sarah McCrae grew up in the Pacific Northwest, close to the Cascade Mountains and the evergreen forests. She had just completed her junior year in college and was working a summer job, waiting tables and serving drinks at the Seafarer, a local restaurant not far from her family home. It was a great summer job, and she especially loved the after-closing hours, a time when the staff of mostly twenty-somethings would drink, talk, and enjoy life together.

On August 7, when the first signs of rosy dawn outlined the mountains, Sarah left the Seafarer and headed home. She was happy all over, singing along to the radio and celebrating her good fortune in life. She had visions of a big breakfast of eggs and bacon. She just needed a quick stop at the grocery store and she'd be home.

As she turned left, across an oncoming lane of traffic, she was jolted by the crunch of metal against metal. The rest was a blur: insurance information, police, an ambulance. The other driver wasn't injured. Sarah, intoxicated, was cited for DWI and taken to the local trauma center, a quasi-governmental hospital called Community Health, to be checked out. She was sore and achy but appeared to only have a bruise from the seat belt impact.

Sarah was discharged and taken to the city jail. The city jail had a small medical facility that was staffed by nurses from Community Health. Taking vital signs upon admission was standard procedure, but the overworked nurse on duty looked at Sarah's chart, noticed that she had just been checked out at the trauma center, and decided to skip the protocols. Sarah seemed woozy and sleepy. The nurse put her in her cell to sleep it off.

Eight hours later, the nursing shift changed, and the nurse on duty made the rounds. Sarah was found dead in her jail cell.

SARAH'S PARENTS: FOREVER CHANGED

Sarah's parents, Joe and Mary, were notified of Sarah's death. Their beautiful daughter had gone from home to work, to a hospital, to jail, and, within twenty-four hours, to death. An autopsy identified the cause of death as internal bleeding. She had a lacerated spleen, probably caused by the impact of the seat belt.

Joe and Mary's lives were forever changed. Their wonderful, talented daughter, full of hope and promise—their life's work—was dead. Their feelings were beyond words. How could this happen in a civilized society? How could Sarah's big mistake—drunk driving—be cause for the death penalty? How could this happen at the hands of medical professionals? What kinds of savages were running their public institutions? How could life go on?

There were no answers. In response to their inquiries, Community Health and jail officials became quiet and distant. Administrators sent what looked like a form letter expressing condolences over the family's loss. Joe and Mary felt crippling grief, helplessness, anger, and, eventually, rage. They had many questions and few answers. Their marriage suffered as they went their own ways, into their private, inconsolable grief. A friend recommended a counselor, who recommended that they see a lawyer.

The Litigation Process Begins

Mary and Joe could not bring their daughter back, but they also could not let this travesty pass with no accountability. From referrals, they found attorneys Leslie Adams and Brett Winslow. Their primary goal was to find some answers that seemed unavailable without the tools of legal "discovery." Leslie and Brett filed a tort claims notice, just barely in time to preserve the claims against the public entities.

Mary and Joe were expecting that their lawyers would get answers and their suffering would diminish. They couldn't imagine that it could get worse, but it did. Community Health and the city jail secured legal representation, as did each of the individuals who had any level of contact with Sarah. The defendants resisted Leslie and Brett's inquiries and objected to many of their requests for discovery. Joe and Mary began to incur costs for subpoenas, depositions, and experts. Despite being barely able to face work every day, they had the added stress and cost of litigation. They took out a second mortgage on their house. They were determined to do whatever it would take to avenge Sarah's death. They needed answers, even if they were horrible answers.

After six months of litigation, there were little breakthroughs, starting with the jail surveillance films. It was clear that when Sarah was waiting to be "processed" she slid down against the wall to the floor. The video wasn't clear, but it looked as though the nurse kicked her while she was on the floor. Was this possible?

One of the jail employees who was off-duty when Sarah was incarcerated heard about the case and contacted Leslie and Brett. She reported that the nurse who "processed" Sarah was reputed to be careless and cruel and that there had been prior complaints about him. She also heard from the inmates that their complaints to the guards on the night of Sarah's death—that Sarah needed help, that she was sick and cold—fell on deaf ears.

Eventually, the pieces of the puzzle came together. Mary and Joe found that during the eight hours Sarah lay in a cold jail cell, she had only one thin blanket. She cried for her mother, cried out for help, screamed, moaned, and sobbed. The inmates yelled at the guards to help her and were told that she just needed to sober up. At some point, Sarah became quiet.

Joe and Mary, together with their lawyers, looked at the long road ahead—a few years of additional discovery, motions, litigation stress, and expense. Their biggest worry was that at the end of it all, the negligence claim would be subject to a tort claims cap and the attorney fees and costs would exceed the recovery. Even worse, maybe nothing at Community Health would change. Their only hope of increasing the recovery was a Section 1983 claim for violation of civil rights, one that would not be subject to the tort claims cap. Recovery was uncertain. Looking at the risks and costs of continuing, Leslie and Brett recommended mediation. They knew that the case was more about accountability than about money, although money was becoming increasingly important as costs mounted. They hoped that somehow there would be a way for Joe and Mary to find some peace before the whole thing destroyed them emotionally and financially.

THE FIRST MEDIATION

The first mediation was held about a year after Sarah's death. Brian Grey, a very experienced, compassionate, and insightful mediator, was asked to mediate the case. As Brian dove into the case, the multiple layers of complexity became apparent. He believed that settlement at this stage was highly unlikely but that it was worth a try. At the very least, it would a good first step in a multistep mediation process.

Despite Brian's best efforts, the case was just not ready for settlement. First, there were now nine defense attorneys involved, two for Community Health and seven representing the individual health-care providers. Each attorney was paid by a malpractice insurer, and each had a plausible defense and a reason to pass the blame to other defendants. None was apparently concerned about the cost of the litigation, and the insurer had not yet faced the reality of the defense costs. Second, the defendants were still withholding as much information as possible and counting on the protection of the tort claims cap to limit the recoverable damages. They were not willing to put a significant sum of money on the table. Finally, the "real people" who represented Community Health didn't come to the mediation; only the attorneys and insurance representatives, who were looking for an inexpensive, economic solution, were present. There was no psychological or procedural satisfaction for Joe and Mary. They were deeply angry and not ready to let go without being given a good reason.

Nevertheless, the mediation was a start. It brought focus and attention to the matter and engaged a professional mediator who would see the case through. Brian established rapport with parties and lawyers. The conversation had begun.

KEEPING THE LINES OF COMMUNICATION OPEN

Brian stayed in touch with the attorneys and kept abreast of legal developments during the next year. His years of experience told him that this tragedy could have a better ending than a jury trial. He also knew that if he didn't provide a focal point for resolution, the case would likely flounder and become enormously expensive, and the process would be even more painful for all parties.

Eventually, Community Health expressed an interest in coming back to the table. Brian had established an excellent working relationship with the lead counsel for Community Health. She was a big-picture thinker, and Brian encouraged her to take a leadership role. He saw that she had the capacity and motivation to engage in strategic thinking. She could become the "quarterback" for Community Health and counsel for the seven individual defendants.

Brian also developed a relationship of trust, confidence, and mutual respect with Leslie and Brett, the plaintiffs' attorneys. He worked on getting closer to Joe and Mary and even met with them at their home to discuss resuming the mediation. They were reluctant to open their wounds again without good reason.

Brian then set the stage for an informal meeting with all counsel. They agreed to take what they had learned from the first mediation and do better. The attorneys brainstormed ways to reflect their commitment to resolution and their seriousness about doing it right this time. They agreed upon a location for the mediation that was especially comfortable and convenient for Joe and Mary, although less convenient for the defendants. The defendants agreed to pay the entire cost of the mediation. They agreed to make an opening offer of $1 million, which exceeded the tort claims cap.

Joe and Mary's counsel had a glimmer of hope. This felt different. After long conversations with their counsel, Mary and Joe agreed to go forward.

CO-MEDIATORS

Brian also recommended that the parties engage a co-mediator to work with him. The attorneys had not worked with co-mediators before, and the defendants were hesitant to pay for two when usually one was enough. Brian convinced them that co-mediation was the right answer. The issues were complex, and there were many parties with divergent interests and many conversations that needed to go on simultaneously. There were both monetary and substantial nonmonetary matters to resolve. The plaintiffs and several of the defendants would need time to vent and process their feelings. There were difficult insurance coverage issues that would need to be worked through. There were the usual discussions with all parties about risk and cost. A single mediator could not do it all and maintain sufficient momentum on multiple fronts. Brian knew that this mediation would likely be the last chance for resolution before the litigation accelerated toward trial. It had to be done right.

Brian recommended me, a trusted friend and colleague. He vouched for my skill and established my credibility with the attorneys. He arranged for counsel to meet with me individually before the mediation. They liked me, saw the value that I would add, and followed Brian's recommendation.

Brian and I appreciated each other's strengths and were comfortable with the shared responsibility of leading the mediation. As we discussed the work that needed to be done, we easily moved into different primary responsibilities. We put together a plan. We thought through the pieces of the puzzle needed for a resolution. We decided who actually needed to come to the mediation and who needed to *not* come. We felt that there were too many people with lots to say but with little to contribute. We wanted each person who was invited to be there for a good reason. Our goal was to keep each participant involved, invested, focused, and moving forward.

THE SECOND MEDIATION

When the day of the mediation came, it was apparent to all that there had been careful planning. The mediation took place close to Joe and Mary's home at a comfortable business conference center. The location was an olive branch to the plaintiffs. It also represented an investment in the resolution. The facility was perfect: four large conference rooms, several small breakout rooms, and a lunch room that connected to all the conference rooms. Meals, drinks, and snacks were available throughout the day. Breakfast was served when the parties arrived. A nutritious and tasty lunch buffet was available at 11:45 a.m. Warm chocolate chip cookies and fruit appeared in the afternoon. The conference center was on a ground floor with easy access to the outdoors.

Brian and I began the day by meeting with the plaintiffs and their counsel. We laid out the plan for the day. Joe and Mary were cautious but seemed to appreciate that a lot of work had gone into the day. They approved the plan. Brian and I needed their buy-in and were satisfied that we had it.

Brian and I then had a brief introductory meeting with all defendants, received their buy-in to the process, assigned them "homework," and then returned to plaintiffs' room. I began the conversation. With little prompting, Joe and Mary poured out intense anger, grief, frustration, and feelings of retribution. I took it all in and acknowledged their feelings and their point of view. I said very little, knowing that whatever I said would seem wrong or trite to them. Mary chaffed at the very notion of settlement. Did they really think that her daughter's life could be reduced to money? This created an opportunity for me to inquire further about what she needed from the process and resolution. Mary and Joe had thought a lot about this. They wanted someone—some human being who was responsible—to hear their rage. They wanted to have reason to believe that this could never again happen to anyone else's daughter or son.

DEALING WITH THE ECONOMICS OF THE CASE

Brian and I then separated to meet with different groups simultaneously. Brian had previously laid the groundwork for the conversation that was about to begin. It included the insurance company representatives, defense counsel, and coverage counsel.

Brian was not sure that the insurance adjuster had focused on the fix he was in. He introduced the subject of payment above and beyond the tort claims cap. The insurer had exposure on a Section 1983 civil rights claim for compensatory damages, punitive damages, costs, prevailing party attorney fees, and experts' fees. Even without the Section 1983 civil rights claim, the insurer was paying for seven separate counsel for the individual health-care providers, each of whom was focused on getting his client dismissed, minimizing the damage, or shifting the blame. Each planned to hire an expert to vindicate his client. Paying attorneys to shift liability from one insured to another was costing the insurer a small fortune. Community Health would make some contribution. However, without substantial contribution from the insurer, the case could not settle. Although liability on the Section 1983 claims and the award of damages could be debated endlessly, the cost of litigation was more predictable. It was high.

MAKING A CONNECTION

I met with counsel for Community Health and its president and CEO, Dr. Barbara Williams. Dr. Williams was a warm, compassionate woman in her sixties who had devoted her entire professional career to public health, especially the care of indigent people. The purpose of the meeting was to prepare Dr. Williams to hear from Joe and Mary about their anger, their grief, and their loss and what they wanted from Community Health. This was a very important conversation. It could be the beginning of a resolution or the end of the mediation. Dr. Williams appreciated how important it was and knew that she was the only person who could do it.

I invited Joe and Mary into a conference room to meet with Dr. Williams. There were no attorneys present. Joe and Mary were full of trepidation, not sure how they would handle the flood of feelings they had toward Community Health and its leader. The initial moments were tense. I began by stating that I had talked with Joe, Mary, and Barbara separately and that all had agreed to meet and talk about the circumstances that brought them together. "This is intended to be a conversation between people, not a legal proceeding," I said. "I may guide the conversation, but mostly it is your opportunity to talk." I was well aware that each person had been mentally rehearsing this conversation for months, if not years, and had plenty to say. They just needed an opportunity, a little structure, and a safe environment in which to speak.

Dr. Williams then began by saying, "Please call me Barbara." She said that she was so grateful to have a conversation with Joe and Mary. She asked them to tell her all that they would like her to know and understand.

Mary's face flushed, her eyes tightened, and her jaw trembled. She said, "You killed my daughter." She went on to describe Sarah's excruciating death and recounted how Sarah cried out for her mother and no one cared. She said that Community Health was a "medieval organization" and that she thought the Holocaust was over until she encountered Community Health. She said that the loss of their daughter, plus the legal runaround they'd experienced for the last two years, had ruined their lives. They just wanted Barbara and everyone in her organization to feel some of the pain that she and Joe were feeling. She said that at this late date, the lawsuit was their only way to get revenge and to tell the whole world about the incompetence and cruelty of Community Health.

Barbara listened quietly but said softly, "I'm so sorry." And then again, "I'm so sorry." When Mary stopped, Barbara said that she too had a daughter, and she could barely imagine the depth of the pain they were feeling. Barbara had tears in her eyes. She reached for the tissue box in the middle of the table. She nodded as Mary and Joe expressed their feelings. She never contradicted their views.

As the conversation went on and the accusations became repetitious, I felt that they were reaching the point of diminishing returns. I attempted to intervene and move on but hesitated, not quite sure. Joe, who had been quiet for most of the conversation, said, "You're thinking this is becoming a waste of time, but it isn't. We have waited over two years to have this conversation, and we need this. This is good."

Barbara picked up on Joe's statement and said how truly sorry she was that two years had gone by and that she hadn't talked with them right after Sarah's death. She told them she wanted to change Community Health's practice so that there is a meeting with the family and/or patient immediately after a tragedy or an unanticipated outcome. Mary's face began to unfurl, her body relaxed, and her tone of voice changed. She saw that she was talking to the right person and that their lawsuit could make a difference to others.

One hour had passed. Barbara and Mary were in locked eye contact, both leaning forward slightly and nodding slowly when the other spoke. Joe reached under the table to hold Mary's hand. I felt the conversation winding down and fatigue setting in. I checked in, first by stating that I appreciated all that they had each contributed to the conversation. I asked if they would like to continue or take a break, get a snack, walk around, and think about the conversation they'd had. I clarified that there would be an opportunity to talk more later. Everyone nodded, agreeing that they had had enough for now. As they were leaving, Mary started to hug Barbara, then stopped herself. They all shook hands and thanked each other for the conversation.

OPERATIONAL CHANGES "SO THIS CAN NEVER HAPPEN AGAIN"

Mary and Joe were buoyed by their meeting with Barbara and set to work creating a long list of changes that they wanted to see at Community Health. After lunch they asked to meet with Barbara and present their list. I knew that many of the suggestions were impractical but felt that the benefit of having Joe and Mary involved in brainstorming solutions outweighed the risk of disappointment from having suggestions rejected. I prepared Barbara and her counsel for the conversation, coaching them to listen, take notes, and consider each proposal but not react to specific proposals during the meeting.

Refreshed by lunch and a walk outside, Mary, Joe, and their counsel returned to meet with Barbara and her counsel. I summarized the work that had occurred that morning, complimented the parties on their participation, and expressed optimism about the afternoon. Mary and Joe then began to present their ideas for operational changes at Community Health. Many of the suggestions amounted to the practice of medicine through a policy or micromanagement of medical providers. Their attorneys cringed but also saw the value in their clients having a say. I listened for the big-picture concerns, reframing many suggestions in more general terms. Barbara reflected that they were in agreement on several things: the need to retrain their providers on the protocols, the value of a periodic compliance audit by an outside auditor, and the need to discipline employees for violations. She asked for a little time to consider Mary and Joe's proposals. The meeting ended cordially.

With coaching from Brian and me, Community Health had given considerable thought to organizational changes prior to the mediation. Barbara had a number of meetings with the chief of the emergency room and the nurse in charge of the medical services at the jail. After talking with Joe and Mary, Barbara felt that she had a deeper understanding of the changes that would provide the most satisfaction, solace, and healing to the family and make the biggest difference in the quality of care at Community Health. She was ready to make a proposal to them.

PUTTING THE PIECES TOGETHER

There were many details remaining, but the pieces were in place. Mary and Joe's case settled on the afternoon of the second day. They were satisfied that their two-year fight had made a difference in the operations of Community Health. They came to agreement on the specific operational changes and were satisfied that the defendants had paid dearly for the loss of their daughter's life. They had hope that life could go on and that they had made a difference.

SECOND THOUGHTS:

This case presented a lot of lessons: the transformational power of deep listening; the value of co-mediation; the need to turn tragedy into something of value; the effect of a compounded injury; the decision regarding whom to invite and whom to leave home; the importance of leadership; the difference that food, comfort, and convenience can make; the opportunity to train for sainthood; and the rewards of being a mediator.

THE TRANSFORMATIONAL POWER OF DEEP LISTENING

Dr. Barbara Williams had a rare degree of emotional intelligence. She was able to absorb abusive language and exaggerated claims without reacting negatively. She had the good sense and self-discipline not to defend against or deny anything that Joe or Mary said. She listened with her heart and heard their feelings. She was the antithesis of a large, impersonal bureaucracy. She was a mother and a fellow human being. She related on a very human level, but she also was the person in charge, the one who was ultimately responsible.

As we (dispute resolution professionals, lawyers, parties) learn more about apology and forgiveness, we need to take some calculated risks. We must look for opportunities to break through the roles of adversaries and allow the parties to reclaim their essential humanity. This conversation did just that.

THE VALUE OF CO-MEDIATION

Co-mediation is a powerful, collaborative way to mediate a complex case. In this case, the complexity came from the number of parties and attorneys, the insurance coverage issues, and the highly emotional aspects of the case. Brian and I had very different histories with the case. Brian had been involved for over a year. He had built relationships with the attorneys and parties. I brought a fresh perspective and an infusion of creativity and optimism. Having a person of each gender seemed to be a plus. Brian and I had a high level of respect for each other and were colleagues and collaborators.

Mediators usually work alone and have few opportunities to learn by watching each other in real-life situations. The co-mediation was a unique opportunity for our professional development. Brian and I were able to create a plan together, execute the plan, and make adjustments as we went along. We learned from each other.

THE NEED TO TURN TRAGEDY INTO SOMETHING OF VALUE

Too often, when plaintiffs say that they "want to make sure this never happens again," defendants cynically think that it's really about money and that this is just a way to give a moral or ethical justification to the litigation.

Joe and Mary's counsel would not have allowed their clients to be manipulated or to sell themselves short in the litigation in exchange for noneconomic relief. Counsel had substantial costs and time invested in the case. Money mattered. However, their counsel understood that without the noneconomic terms of the agreement, the case could not settle.

Lawyers and mediators sometimes discourage discussion of changes in defendants' practices and procedures because plaintiffs will likely make suggestions that are not practical. They may violate a collective bargaining agreement or, as in this case, standard medical practices and procedures. We don't want to start conversations that will end in disappointment. As this case demonstrates, though, the "change" conversation can be more about interests than specific changes. Barbara Williams listened for big-picture suggestions: training, accountability, and discipline. She was able to convey a real desire for improvement and propose changes that resonated with the plaintiffs. They justifiably felt that they had gained a sense of control and that their lawsuit made a difference.

THE EFFECT OF A COMPOUNDED INJURY

Litigation can be a surprisingly brutal experience, compounded by the emotionally fragile state of the litigants. Television and movies, the source of most litigation education for parties, show very little about the costs of litigation, the sleepless nights, the second mortgages, and bankruptcy. They don't convey the effect of years passing without resolution or the emotional impact of feeling stonewalled in discovery. When Joe and Mary's anger, grief, and frustration were compounded, they felt that there was nothing left but revenge and the potential satisfaction of inflicting public shame and humiliation upon Community Health and its employees. Part of our job (mine and Brian's) as mediators was to understand and address the "process injuries" that Joe and Mary had experienced through the litigation.

THE DECISION REGARDING WHOM TO INVITE AND WHOM TO LEAVE HOME

This lawsuit had seven individual defendants, plus Community Health and even more defense attorneys. Few were invited and the others were told specifically, but nicely, to stay home. Crowd control can become an issue in a complex multiparty case. It is not economical or productive to have a large number of people with little to add sitting in conference rooms while the real players work. After a year of litigation, Brian knew who the real players were. He was in the best position to recommend who needed to attend and who should stay home.

THE IMPORTANCE OF LEADERSHIP

Mediators need to enlist help and leadership from the parties and attorneys. Brian identified the attorney for Community Health as the one who had the perspective, credibility, and experience to be a leader for the defense counsel. At the same time, he was careful not to appear to have "partnered" with her in a way that disfavored the others.

THE DIFFERENCE THAT FOOD, COMFORT, AND CONVENIENCE CAN MAKE

It is unlikely that this case would have settled in a traditional law firm setting. The comfortable conference center, the convenience to the plaintiffs, the amenities of the lunchroom, and the good food had a subtle and positive effect.

THE OPPORTUNITY TO TRAIN FOR SAINTHOOD

It has been said that the life of the mediator is one of training for sainthood. If so, Brian is a prime example. He provided the continuity and the communication link. He personified the potential for resolution by staying involved and looking for the right time for the second mediation. He was patient and committed to the case without knowing quite when or how he'd get paid.

THE REWARDS OF BEING A MEDIATOR

It is such a privilege to share in others' lives during their most challenging times. I appreciate the everyday heroism of people who struggle to deal with their pain, move on, and make sense out of it all. I am grateful for the opportunity to be a mediator.

PART II

Surprising Conclusions

Summum ius summa iniura. (The strictest following of law can lead to the greatest injustice.)

Cicero, De Officiis (On Duties)

6.
Duffer v. Mulligan: ¿Quien Es Mas Macho?

Ben J. Cunningham

HEADING FOR A BUSINESS "DIVORCE"

It was a common enough dispute: two business partners in conflict, grown so rancorous that one of the business partners, Carl Duffer, sued the other partner, Chip Mulligan, for $10,000 on claims arising out of breach of contract and fiduciary duties. Apparently, Chip had similar views about Carl's behavior, as set forth in Chip's counterclaim mirroring all of Carl's accusations. Chip also was seeking $10,000 from Carl.

The business continued operating during the dispute, though with some dysfunction as Carl and Chip were no longer on speaking terms. Both partners wanted the other out of the business, but neither partner wanted to depart. My separate pre-mediation discussions with the parties' attorneys revealed that their opinions were that what was really needed was a business "divorce," though neither partner had shown any interest in attempting to formally dissolve the lucrative business venture. The lawyers were on good terms, and each agreed that both Carl and Chip were "great guys" but that essentially they had "gotten crossways" and neither of them wanted to give an inch.

The feuding business partners and their lawyers showed up for a half-day mediation. Positions were simple, their partnership agreement required mediation, and neither side wanted to go to trial unless they had to. Both parties, however, were convinced that if the case did go to trial, justice would be served (to the other side, of course). The only way they would settle was if the other capitulated. Unless the opposing side put money on the table and exited the business, there would be no settlement and they would happily duke it out at the courthouse.

NEITHER SIDE BUDGES

The joint opening session was uneventful. The lawyers presented their clients' tepid legal cases, attempting to project as much enthusiasm as they could for their respective clients. The partners sat stonily during the session—not speaking, not looking at each other—one glaring at the ceiling while the other stared out the window.

I broke up the parties after the brief opening session, meeting first in private caucus with the plaintiff's side. I asked Carl what the fight was really all about. Carl said that Chip owed him money, wanted the company, and wanted Carl out. Carl was angry and said that Chip would pay for his disloyalty.

"And your opening demand is what?"

"It's not an 'opening' demand," said Carl. "It's what he needs to pay me or we go to court. Period."

I glanced at the lawyer, who responded with a kind of "I tried to warn you" look and a shrug.

"Well, you guys just sit tight, and I'll go ask the other side if they want to write a check for you so we can all get out of here quickly," I said.

The plaintiff missed my slight tongue-in-cheek tone, but thinking there might be a possibility of a quick acceptance by Chip, he added that he wanted an agreement that Chip would get out of the business.

"He cheats at golf, and he cheats at business!" added Carl. "I should have known better than to partner up with him. He can't be trusted."

In the defendant/counterplaintiff's room, the lawyer was seated at the conference table reading the newspaper; her client was standing up, pretending to be putting an imaginary golf ball into an imaginary hole. I watched for a second until he was done with his putt, wondering if this was like a new golf version of Air Guitar.

"Let's talk for a minute, guys," I said. "What's this case really about?"

"That bastard sued me before I had a chance to sue him first," said Chip. "He owes me. He's ungrateful and greedy. I'm the backbone of the company, and he's trying to cheat me out of the business I built." Chip said that he spent a lot of time marketing and was on the golf course at least three times a week with customers and potentials. Carl used to do some rainmaking, according to Chip, but lately Carl was leaving it to Chip because Chip was better at it. Chip felt that although he'd brought in all the business, Carl wanted the company for himself.

I told Chip that Carl wanted $10,000 and an agreement that Chip would exit the company. Chip's attorney looked up from her newspaper, rolling her eyes. Chip accused me of being on Carl's side.

I explained that I was just the messenger and wasn't on anybody's side. I reminded Chip that as I had said in the opening session, it wasn't my task to decide who wins or loses or who gets what—my task was to give Chip and Carl an opportunity to negotiate and see how they might resolve their differences so that they didn't have to keep paying for legal fees only to face the uncertainties of what might happen at trial.

Chip said that he didn't care about legal fees because he planned on getting all of his legal fees back when the case went to trial. "Doesn't sound to me like you know much about the law," said Chip. "What kind of lawyer *are* you, anyway?" he asked, with a slight smile to blunt the button-pushing question.

"That's a good question, Chip, but I think the jury's still out on that one." I smiled.

Chip told me to tell Carl that he wasn't going to accede to Carl's demand and that if Carl wanted to avoid losing at trial, Carl should fork over ten grand and get out of the company. "I've got a slam dunk case, and he knows it," said Chip.

"I've been practicing law for more years than is probably healthy," I said affably, "and in all that time I've seen maybe one slam dunk. Maybe."

The lawyer looked at her client as he spoke to me. "I wouldn't characterize this as a slam dunk exactly. We've got our side; they've got theirs."

I told Chip that it was time to talk about a response to Carl's demand. Chip said that he wanted Carl to pay him $10,000 and leave the company.

It was an hour into this mediation, and I probably could have declared an impasse; but I was having too much fun, and these guys had paid me a fee for a few hours to let them battle back and forth through a new intermediary. Plus, something told me that both Carl and Chip were having to work a little too hard at mustering up anger for each other. Some cases were just meant to be tried, though, and I was beginning to think that this might be one of them.

Back in the room with Carl and his lawyer, I conveyed the counterdemand. Carl felt that Chip was bluffing and was scared to death that Carl would win the case. We had a little discussion about slam dunk cases in the plaintiff's room, also, and about the notion of seeking justice in the courthouse in front of a judge and a jury of strangers. We talked about how it is always the case that when parties go to trial, they are each seeking their own special interpretation of that elusively defined term *justice*.

STAR TREK THEORY OF MEDIATION

Things were not really rolling right along, so I decided to explain the famous (or idiotic, depending on the audience) "Ben Cunningham *Star Trek* Theory of Mediation." I got out my black marker pen and went to the easel board in the room. I drew a long horizontal line. At one end, I designated the plaintiff (Carl), and at the far opposite end I designated the defendant (Chip).

"As we sit right now," I said, "you guys inhabit two different universes." I began drawing a series of interconnected circles between the two "universes." "These circles represent all the different galaxies in between your two universes." Carl and his lawyer were fixated on the board as I spoke.

"Now typically, in a mediation or a negotiation like this, because you are in two different universes, you are stuck," I continued. "But each of you has your own starship, and each of you can set out toward the opposite universe. As you do, you will pass through various galaxies. If both of your starships enter the same galaxy, it's likely we can come to a settlement. But if neither of you starts your ship moving, you'll remain in separate universes and will miss the opportunity to enter the same galaxy, wherever on this spectrum that galaxy might be."

The lawyer, studying the board, wondered what would happen if the two sides were not simply in two different universes but in two different dimensions of time and space—or if the two sides were each heading in the opposite direction from his universe.

Carl piped up, "I'm not really into this *Star Trek* stuff," he said. "I'm seeing this as if Chip and I are on completely different golf courses playing by ourselves."

I noted that I was willing to switch metaphors but that, even so, Chip and Carl would need to get on the same golf course.

In the other room, I jettisoned my *Star Trek* theory and attempted to explain my brand-new Golf Theory of Mediation. Chip was unimpressed and said to tell Carl that he had ten minutes to decide whether to meet his demand. I wondered for a moment if maybe Chip would have preferred the *Star Trek* theory after all but abandoned any notion of further befuddlement. I didn't want to hasten the almost-certain downhill slide of this mediation.

A HOLE-IN-ONE SOLUTION

I noticed that Chip was holding a couple of golf balls in one hand, moving them around each other. It brought to mind two thoughts: one was of Captain Queeg in *The Caine Mutiny*; the other was of two guys caught on two little planets that were revolving around each other in a kind of perfect negative equilibrium—in close orbit but perpetually separated by mutual and unbreakable gravitational forces. After having these thoughts, I mentally kicked myself for having even started down the *Star Trek* and space physics road and decided to bring myself back to earth. If there were any hope for this mediation (the outlook was pretty slim), the answer would be *here*, on this day, on this planet.

"Do you always carry golf balls around with you?" I asked Chip.

He looked at the golf balls in his hand as if he'd just noticed them. "Yeah," he smiled. "They're like—I don't know, one of those talisman things. Closest thing to a golf course I've got on a day like this."

"Want to know what I think, Chip? I think you guys are wasting your time battling all this stuff out in a mediation or trial. I'm surprised you guys didn't just take this fight to the golf course in the first place." I was smiling. I was joking around. Sort of.

Chip's lawyer chuckled. Chip sat there juggling golf balls in his hand. I started for the door. I was planning on talking to the plaintiff and determining whether or not the mediation was over, considering Chip's ten-minute ultimatum.

"Wait a second," said Chip. "Why don't you ask about it?"

"About what?" I asked.

"About whether Carl might be willing to settle this on the golf course. You know, maybe just float it as a trial balloon, so to speak."

Back with the plaintiff, I said, "I've heard you talk a lot about golf today. Didn't you mention earlier this morning that you and Chip have played golf together before?"

Carl said that in fact the two had met on a golf course—out at Stone Terrace Country Club about five years ago—and that was where they came up with the idea of going into business together.

I stood and looked out the window. "Pretty day out there," I mused. "I'm guessing it would be more fun to be out there knocking the ball around than where we are."

Carl's attorney suggested that maybe golf would be a better choice than sitting around in the mediation because the mediation wasn't really working. I agreed, joking that the lawyers should have just sent Chip and Carl out to Stone Terrace to fight it out on the course. The lawyer laughed. I laughed.

Carl wasn't laughing. "You know, that's not such a crazy idea. I mean, considering that I want ten thousand from him, and he wants the same from me. . . . You think Chip might go for something like this?"

I shrugged. "I could check," I said.

The negotiations began. The game was afoot. For the last hour of the mediation, I put everyone together in the same room so that they could talk about details. The mediated agreement consisted of a determination of the "field of battle" (the golf course, which, not surprisingly, turned out to be Stone Terrace), an agreement on the handicaps, a "sudden death" play-off clause in case of a tie, and a specific but somewhat ambiguous clause that abated the litigation until after the date set for their match. The rest of the deal was a handshake agreement that the winner of the game would receive $10,000 and either partner had the option of instituting a dissolution of the partnership.

"It's like a duel," smiled Carl as he shook hands with Chip.

As they were leaving and we were shaking hands all around, I asked that they let me know how the golf "duel" turned out so that I could make a note in my file.

STILL TEEING OFF

It was a while before I finally received a call about the results of that golf game. Sometimes it's the case that once parties leave a mediation, the mediator fades from their minds even though we mediators like to imagine that they think of us constantly. Ten years after the mediation, I picked up the phone in my office and took a call.

"Mr. Cunningham, this is Chip Duffer. I'm in Houston now. Don't know if you remember me or not, but we once had a mediation with you that ended up in a golf game."

"I remember well, Chip. I've always been curious about that. What happened? Who won?"

It turned out, according to Chip, that by the time they got to the ninth hole, they decided to drop their lawsuits against each other. In fact, they came up with a new business venture idea that they decided to pursue together, and they sold the old business for a tidy profit.

Chip was calling, he said, about another problem—in the new business.

I sighed into the telephone. "Oh? That's a shame. . . ."

"No, no, I don't mean that Carl and I are crossways. We've been doing great all these years. Matter of fact, he and I have solved every problem we've had since then on the golf course. I think you came up with a better theory than that *Space Balls* thing you tried to pawn off on us."

"It was *Star Trek*," I said.

"Well, okay. Whatever. But the reason I'm calling is that we've got a big problem with an outside vendor, and both sides are threatening to sue, but we're thinking about maybe trying to mediate it first. . . ."

"Music to a mediator's ears," I said. "Tell me more."

Second Thoughts:

I have to say that this was the first and only time in more than twenty years of mediating that I've had a dispute that found its way to a golf course. It was a somewhat creative (and mutually agreeable) resolution and one of my favorite endings to a mediation, but very "mushy" through my lawyer eyes. I was never quite certain that it was in all respects exactly "kosher." However, it didn't surprise me in the least that it ultimately worked: I had the strong intuitive sense that, at bottom, Carl and Chip were solid friends who had backed themselves into respective bad corners, which had resulted in a game of "Quien es mas macho?" I had hoped that the resolution, such as it was, had presented to the parties the opportunity to save face and avoid the trial that, despite their slam dunk protestations to the contrary, neither side wanted.

Again, I'll mention the value of pre-mediation discussions with the attorneys representing Chip and Carl. These private conversations revealed some history of the parties. However, it is also a cautionary tale relating to pre-mediation communications and submissions: although both lawyers thought that the only solution was a business "divorce," the mediator should use such pre-mediation for gleaning information and not for formulating opinions. In fact, one of the things that mediators should avoid is ever deciding how a dispute *should* turn out. Mediators must always be open to results that are sometimes surprising; resolutions belong to the parties, not to the mediator or attorneys involved. And, often, the surprising party-driven resolutions are the most enduring, as in this case.

This mediation also suggests the (potentially) valuable use of humor in mediation, which can be a very good thing. However, humor is a tricky business and not always effective or appropriate. It was in this case. Each mediation is different, even mediations that are in similar categories. Each mediation needs to be evaluated on the dynamics of the situation, on the personalities involved in the mediation, and in light of the context of the dispute (the level of hostility, for example, between/among the parties or counsel for the parties, for that matter).

A mediator must always be listening not only to what is being said but also to what may be beneath what is being said. In this mediation, the lawyers were focused on the lawsuit; the parties were focused on a personal dispute that they had no way of escaping other than via all-out "war." The world gets small and myopic for people involved in disputes, and it is the task of a mediator to always be looking for opportunities to broaden perspectives. (And, I might add, golf courses are big places with lots of perspective and ways for people to channel their myopia from the tiny world of hitting a tiny ball to the more expansive world of the fairways and roughs and greens.)

Not all mediations lend themselves to, or require, creative solutions, but the mediator is remiss in not watching for such openings and noting them in the event that at some point they seem worth exploring.

A final note about creativity in mediations: It's always better to have the parties or their counsel come up with the creative ideas—even if the mediator is the one who might occasionally plant the seed.

7.
Unexpected Outcomes and Consequences

Lawrence M. Watson, Jr.

THE GENEROUS GIFT

An up-and-coming business firm built a multistory, high-end, "signature" office building in the downtown business district of its hometown to serve as its national headquarters. After occupying the building for a short time and enjoying substantial corporate growth, the company decided to relocate its offices to a larger metropolitan area. Rather than sell the office building, the company demonstrated its newly acquired prominence by generously donating the structure to a local college. The grateful school promptly put the building on the market. Due to its excellent location and superb construction quality and an expanding economy in the area, it was quickly sold for a considerable price. The selling school profited handsomely from the gift.

The new buyers immediately began plans to renovate the facility and started a marketing program aimed at attracting first-class tenants to their soon-to-be-restored upscale office space. Their leasing program went remarkably well. A major bank was secured as the prime tenant. Some of the biggest law firms in the state were attracted to sign extended leases. Before long, the building was almost completely leased.

A GOOD DEED NEVER GOES UNPUNISHED

Then disaster struck. In the midst of their renovation program, the new buyers discovered that the structural steel skeleton of the building was covered with a fireproofing material containing dangerous and highly toxic quantities of asbestos. Although quite legal at the time that the building was first built, current building codes flatly prohibited the use of the offending product. In order to secure permits to complete the renovation program and receive the appropriate final certificates of occupancy, therefore, all of the fireproofing material would have to be removed. This was no easy task. The entire building would have to be stripped down to the structural steel and the material removed in a protected "white suit" environment before being replaced with an acceptable substitute product. In addition to millions of dollars in unanticipated remediation costs, the buyers found themselves exposed to substantial business interruption claims from irate tenants expecting to move in on scheduled lease commencement dates. As might be expected, lawsuits were launched.

It was soon discovered that the original contractor and subcontractors involved in the installation of the material were out of business or otherwise financially unable to respond to any judgment that might be entered against them. To make matters worse, the insurance carriers who insured those trade contractors at the time were now aggressively asserting viable coverage defenses.

When it thus became apparent that the obvious defendants presented little in the way of available resources to meet their claims, the buyers used newly developed environmental laws to go up the chain of title and bring an action against the original owners. Albeit a bit of a stretch, a theory was developed to state a cause of action that survived summary judgment. Needless to say, that claim was not warmly received. Not only was there full compliance with all applicable laws at the time of construction and not only had the building been used for many years without any problems, but the original owners had charitably donated the building to a major university when they relocated. They had not realized a dime from the subsequent sale of the property, yet now they were being sued for several million dollars.

THE MEDIATION – FINDING SETTLEMENT IN UNEXPECTED PLACES

When the trial court pushed the case to mediation, the original owners appeared reluctantly, brimming with righteous indignation and animosity toward everyone connected with the lawsuit.

During a long and intense mediation process, settlements were reached with the insurance carriers involved with the old builders and the product manufacturer. As midnight approached, the case wound down to the one remaining claim between the buyers and the original owners. Even taking into account settlement proceeds generated to that point from the other players, the buyers were still several million dollars short of what they would need to meet the demands of the remediation program. Because of the dire financial consequences of canceling the existing lease arrangements, abandoning the project was not an option. The new buyers had to go through with the project at whatever cost; the original owners, however, were outraged, indignant, and steadfastly offering nothing. Tempers flared, threats were exchanged, impasse loomed.

Sometimes, though, we find settlements in unexpected places.

During a late private caucus with the original owners, the conversation shifted to the difficulties that the buyers would face to fund the remediation program if they did not get some relief from some source. Not only were their credit limits extended to the maximum, a recent jump in prevailing interest rates was making the cost of new money to complete the fix virtually prohibitive. Upon hearing of the difficulties that the buyers would be encountering in both securing a new loan and meeting its probable level of debt service, one of the original owners' representatives casually noted that their present financial status and banking relationships entitled them to borrow a significant amount of short-term money at roughly one-third the rate that the buyers would be facing. At that point, a "What if . . . ?" moment occurred.

A question was posed: "What if the original owners made a long-term loan to the buyers for the money they would need to complete the remediation program at the original owners' preferred short-term interest rates?" While the buyers would still be facing significant additional development costs, they would be reaping substantial savings on what they would have to spend to secure the new money. The original owners' loan could be protected by a secured position on the building, and all they would pay would be whatever their bank might charge to roll over the short-term loans as they became due. After some enthusiastic number crunching, the deal was struck. The original owners would lend the buyers the money required to remediate the building at their preferred short-term interest rates. The buyers would give the original owners a secured position on the building and the rents it would generate. Rather than pay money, the original owners would lend money. In essence, the defendants would be lending the plaintiffs the money to make the fixes. The deal was completed with an outcome that seemed to make everyone happy—for a little while, anyhow.

The Aftermath - Unexpected Consequences
Sometimes those settlements that we find in unexpected places lead to unexpected consequences.

Two weeks after the settlement was reached, I received a telephone call from the law firm representing the plaintiff buyers. It seems a dispute had broken out concerning the amount of the legal fees to be paid by the clients for the firm's work on the case. Under the terms of the contingency fee agreement signed by the buyers, the law firm was entitled to a percentage of not only the actual dollars recovered but also the value of any "other items" recovered as well. The law firm was strenuously arguing that the low-interest loan obtained for the buyers from the original owners of the building clearly fell into the category of "other items," something that had considerable value. The client buyers, however, were contending exactly the opposite: when the dust settled, they were *paying* money out in interest on the loan, albeit at a lower rate than otherwise commercially available. Why should they pay a fee based upon money going out as opposed to money recovered?

I then convened a new mediation session with the buyers and their lawyers. At my suggestion, each side appeared with a mortgage broker prepared to offer information on the commercial value of a long-term loan at the significantly reduced interest rate awarded to the buyers as part of their settlement. After some discussion, it was agreed that the low-rate loan actually had a value. It seems that there is a price to be paid for paying less, and paying less thus has a value. A mutually agreeable adjustment to the legal fee was reached. The case was finally settled in its entirety.

Second Thoughts:

A couple of lessons became obvious as this settlement unfolded. First, don't let the heat of the dispute distract the quest for a resolution. No matter how much anger and angst the parties may feel about the dispute they face, deep inside most will generally prefer striking a deal over staging a fight—all they need is a path to get them there without losing face. The outrage here was palatable, but this case demonstrated even the most intimidating animosity can be deflected with a firm and persistent focus on solutions.

The second lesson learned is a bit more complicated. Clearly, creativity in finding a path for settlement is important, and maintaining peripheral vision to anticipate the consequences of the deal, *and deal with those consequences*, is equally critical. In this case, something as strange and outside the box as the defendant lending money to the plaintiff ended up as the means for settlement, but the ensuing spat with plaintiff's counsel over legal fees caught everyone off guard. In retrospect, it might be said anticipating that particular consequence of the deal earlier could have saved time and expenses down the road. Dealing with that consequence at the time, however, might have been problematic. As it turned out, the parties needed information about the legal fee dispute that was not available at the first mediation, i.e., the actual commercial value of the low interest loan. Additionally, focusing on that problem at the time of the first mediation might have put the plaintiff's attorneys into the awkward position of jeopardizing their client's settlement over a dispute in their fees. While it is generally easier to deal with problems before they arise, sometimes it pays to let a problem take on more definition before addressing it.

PART III

The Principle of Unknowability

Whoever undertakes to set himself up as a judge of Truth and Knowledge is shipwrecked by the laughter of the gods.

Albert Einstein

8.
The Buzzard

Jeff Kichaven

THE "DESIGN" OF THE CASE

You never know what's going to happen when you ride up the elevator in the morning.

That day, it was an Americans with Disabilities Act (ADA) case. Jimmy, the plaintiff, was a paraplegic. He had been an electrician in a small Central California town who had saved for many years to buy a top-quality motorcycle. The day he finally bought one, it was a little rainy. He proudly put on his helmet to drive his new bike home. . . . You can guess how the story of that day ended.

The case involved architectural barriers to wheelchair access to a shopping center. I like these cases; they are fun. My dad was an architect, and when we were kids, my brother and I used to spend time with him designing and redesigning buildings. Mostly, they mixed the Streamline Moderne look of Los Angeles's iconic Pan Pacific Auditorium, which was a few blocks from where we lived, and the fantastic, futuristic/alien vertical skyscrapers that Carmine Infantino drew in the DC Comics of the 1960s. ADA cases can be like that—working hand in hand with lawyers, architects, engineers, and people with disabilities to design and redesign aspects of the built environment.

THE PLAYERS

The defense side was a remarkable group: lawyers and executives from a major regional developer and several national tenants, including supermarket, drugstore, and sandwich shop chains that we have all visited many times—in other words, a set of business cards that evidenced millions in marketing and brand consulting, with logos and colors that traversed the spectrum. No two of these people were from the same state.

One member of the defense side was the top executive of the developer, and the burden of any settlement was mainly going to fall on him: The Buzzard. That wasn't really his name, of course, but in my mind's eye, he earned that moniker instantly. His posture was tied up tighter than a new Scotch drum, to borrow from classic sportscaster Dick Lane.

The Buzzard was dressed to impress—well, actually, to intimidate: crisply pressed blue suit, powder blue shirt with white collar and cuffs, gold and diamond links, the de rigueur yellow power tie, loafers with tassels. The full Gordon Gekko look. I imagined him agonizing over whether to leave his Bentley with the Spanish-speaking valets who park cars underneath my building. As you can tell, my affections for him were limited, and I knew that I would have to watch myself carefully as I dealt with him to make sure that I kept him in the game.

Jimmy came to the mediation with his mom, who drove the family van a couple of hundred miles to my downtown Los Angeles office. With them were their counsel: two young, local civil rights lawyers whose names, according to Google, had never appeared in the press. They exuded humility and I liked them. Jimmy looked kind of scruffy. He had long, oily hair; an uneven beard; a flannel shirt; jeans; beat-up boots; and fingerless leather gloves to push his low-end wheelchair.

JIMMY PRESENTS HIS CASE

After some preliminary conversation with each side privately, an opening joint session seemed to be the thing to do, so we all sat down in my suite's largest conference room. Jimmy's lawyers introduced him to the group, and he told his story.

Jimmy had lived in this town and shopped at this center for many years. Before his accident, getting around the center was a snap. Now it was different. Parking spaces that could accommodate his van were far from the market—and downhill from it to boot. On days when nobody could drive him and he had to take the bus, getting from the bus stop to the market was arduous. Getting from store to store was not easy either due to the slope of the sidewalks and placement of the curb cuts. He had written many polite letters to the developer, the stores, and city government. The responses that he received were slow, bureaucratic, and noncommittal. Finally, he found these lawyers and sued.

Jimmy said that he wasn't really interested in a large monetary settlement but rather cared most about seeing the center reworked to give him greater access. My suspicion that he was an opportunist started to fade. His calm dignity reminded me of Sandy Koufax and the way Jane Leavy described the Dodgers' star in her great book, *A Lefty's Legacy*. But while Jimmy sounded sincere about his goals, with two contingent-fee lawyers sitting next to him, I said to myself, "We'll see. We'll see."

As Jimmy spoke, I occasionally glanced around the defense phalanx that took up most of the seats around the big conference table. Everyone was listening calmly and respectfully, either taking notes or nodding slowly with hands folded on the table. All except one, that is: The Buzzard, whose fingers were drumming, toes were tapping, and eyes were wandering to the ceiling.

GETTING NOWHERE

When the defense had its turn to speak, there were polite, basic statements of positions by the various lawyers. The Buzzard fidgeted with his arms folded throughout. When his lawyer finished, the Buzzard zeroed-in: "How come we all have to be here? Why does this have

95

to take all day? Why all the speech making? Why doesn't Jimmy just tell us what he wants, and we will either pay it or we won't? I am *not* happy to be here, and you have fifteen minutes to figure it all out, or I am leaving."

As calmly as I could, I explained to the Buzzard that while I wished it worked that way, it just didn't, and that his patience would pay off in the end. The plaintiff's ultimate position at the end of the day was likely to be far more palatable than any position the plaintiff's side might express right out of the box. When the Buzzard's repetitiveness seemed to annoy even his own lawyer, counsel asked him to step into the hallway. They came back in, the Buzzard grumbled, and his lawyer said that it was okay to go ahead with the mediation in the conventional way.

We did, for a few unproductive hours. I solicited a demand from Jimmy's side and conveyed it to the assembled defense. It was for a big seven-figure number and vague ideas about how to redesign wheelchair access. The defense responded with next to nothing and equally vague ideas about how little needed to be done. It went like this for a few hours, it got us nowhere, and it was boring.

AN UNEXPECTED REQUEST

About 3:00 p.m., with the defense side assembled, the Buzzard did something weird. He drummed his fingers on the table a few times, averted his gaze, and then, in his grumbliest tone of voice, asked whether he could speak privately with Jimmy. I asked him what he was thinking about saying because Jimmy's lawyers would surely ask me when I conveyed the request. None of my business, I was told.

As of this moment, the case was settled. Nobody knew it, though. Maybe not even the Buzzard.

The Buzzard's lawyer asked whether he could participate in this conversation. The Buzzard's answer? No. The Buzzard gave the same answer when his lawyer asked whether I could sit in on this.

Well, okay, I thought, I will convey this request, but I doubt that it will be received warmly. Sure enough, the Buzzard's initial request was rebuffed. Jimmy was kind of startled; his lawyers were amazed. Their answer was no. They wouldn't mind having the Buzzard talk to Jimmy if they were present, and they would prefer that I be present as well. But a one-on-one? No way. Back down the hall I walked.

After about thirty minutes of dickering back and forth, we agreed that Jimmy and both of his lawyers, the Buzzard and his lawyer, and I could meet. One of my conference rooms is set up with four large upholstered chairs and a coffee table. Before the mediation started, I removed the coffee table from the room and rearranged the chairs to make sure that there would be room for Jimmy's wheelchair to enter easily if the need arose. So in Jimmy wheeled, the rest of us followed on foot. The three lawyers and the Buzzard sat in the chairs. Lacking a chair myself, I was off to one side. I was quite curious to see what would happen and a bit anxious about my ability to intervene effectively if all hell broke loose.

A CHANGE OF HEART

It was silent and tense. Then the Buzzard began to speak. It's about a year now, but I still remember his words so clearly.

"Jimmy," he said. "I have given this a lot of thought. Before today, I never even tried to put myself in the shoes of a person in a wheelchair. I can't believe that I have been so oblivious to people in your situation. I will never look at a set of architectural plans the same way again. We're going to redesign this center so that you can use it. We want everybody in the community to be able to shop at our centers and use the stores there. That's what we are going to spend the rest of the day on. As for the money, just tell us your number. We're going to pay it. I'm sorry that we put you through all this."

He was slow and deliberate. He looked right into Jimmy's eyes every step of the way. He was as sincere as I have ever seen anyone be in a mediation. By the time he was done, his eyes were welling up with tears. So were Jimmy's. So were their lawyers'. And so were mine.

There wasn't much more to say. Jimmy's number was restrained— lowish six figures. He could have asked for ten times that much. Buzzy (for clearly, at this point, he was no longer the Buzzard) agreed and said that he would be responsible for figuring out how the defendants would divide this up among themselves.

Everybody gathered around the main table in the conference room with a set of blueprints and got to work. The idea of settlement had become beside the point in light of everything else that had happened. At sundown, the folks had more or less agreed on the architectural changes that needed to be made. I didn't have much of substance to add to the discussion, but Buzzy showed just how creative he could be when he set his mind to it. It was fun to watch.

Since the defendants had not gotten to the discussion of how they would divide the settlement amount to which they had all agreed, they decided to come back the next day to negotiate that. The mediation had been scheduled for only one day, but with so many out-of-towners gathered from various places, everybody booked hotel rooms and changed their flights. I had to change travel plans, too, and miss the first day of a two-day conference to stay with them. Okay by me—it goes with the territory.

AN ABOUT-FACE

The next day, Buzzy's elixir had worn off, and he was the Buzzard once again. It was a tortuous day. The defendants had already signed an agreement with Jimmy making them jointly and severally liable for the settlement amount, so the overall deal was never in jeopardy. But the negotiation was nasty, brutish, and long—especially so in light of the modest amount of dollars, all things considered, that Jimmy's side was to receive.

Once again at sundown, they made their deal. The Buzzard only grudgingly shook hands with his codefendants on the way out.

I still don't really understand what happened.

SECOND THOUGHTS:

It would never occur to me to say that I settled this case. Because I didn't.

In fact, no mediator has ever "settled a case." None of us has ever paid consideration or signed a release to settle any of the cases we mediate. "We" don't settle the cases that we mediate; "they" do. It's a healthy discipline to remember this and to recall what it is that we actually do. We create environments in which the parties and their counsel can do their best job of negotiating, and we facilitate those negotiations.

An anesthesiologist friend of mine once observed that what we do is similar to what he does. He keeps oxygen flowing through the system—keeps the patient alive—while the surgeons (or, in our mediations, the lawyers) do the glamour work and get the glory.

In this case, at the critical meeting in the room with the upholstered chairs, I said nothing. I gave them their space, and they did what needed to be done. I didn't have to say anything. I trusted them. And they came through. They almost always do.

Of course, this does not mean that I am, or that any other mediator is, a potted plant. Sometimes, I have to speak quite a lot. When I do, I am always asking myself whether it's really necessary and whether I have done enough to get them back on track and can be quiet again. Rarely, I do have to intervene with a lawyer who is SO wrong that I must take him aside and ask him to share whatever he has been smoking. The number of times when these "heavy artillery" interventions is necessary, though, is truly small.

This approach has been part of my practice since my very first training, with Jim Melamed, many years ago. He taught us to do only what was necessary, only when necessary. It still serves me well.

9.

Cookie Monster

Tracy Allen

HOW THE COOKIE CRUMBLES

It wasn't just that I wanted—really, really wanted—one of those cookies. (Although I did.) It was more the fact that someone had the nerve to take them all for himself. That completely unexpected—and decidedly rude—move was the final insult in a day of insults aimed at the whole mediation process, and it dissolved every remaining bit of neutrality that I possessed.

But let me start at the beginning.

A FATEFUL PHONE CALL

"Simon Tate is on the phone for you."

Simon Tate. Perhaps one of the most gifted negotiators and strategic advocates I had ever met. As I pushed the transfer button, I wondered why on earth he was calling me.

In his customarily understated tone, Simon engaged in the requisite niceties of conversation before getting to the purpose of the call. "I have a case for you. The plaintiff is Mr. Christopher Clark. He resides in Riverside. How soon can you run conflicts?"

I had been waiting for a call like this since 2001, the year when my name began appearing on all the short lists and I was getting big, difficult cases from all over the country, as well as some international work. Intellectually, I knew that I was competent to mediate a case for Simon's manufacturing company, DJC, but I questioned whether I was really up to his expected and deserved standards.

PAST ENCOUNTERS

I searched for the notes that I took on two different occasions when Simon took the podium and was quite relieved to find them in a file folder marked "Negotiation Strategies."

Sometime in the late 1990s, I attended the semiannual conference of my favorite alternative dispute resolution organization, the International Academy of Mediators. I was mesmerized as I sat in the audience and listened to Simon's carefully selected words. In a matter of fifty minutes, he went through a list of the seventy-two things that mediators do that irritate lawyers. I managed to get all seventy-two points onto my pad. Now, some four to five years later, as I attempted to decipher my handwriting, I laughed out loud. The points had far deeper meaning and held greater instructive insights for me than they did back then. I decided to keep the list in my notebook for this case.

The second presentation was at another national conference, mostly attended by advocates. Simon's topic: top tips for negotiating a livable settlement in mediation. As I reviewed my notes, I was reminded why I was appropriately nervous about mediating a case for Simon. In that speech, his skill was evident. His twenty-eight years as the associate general counsel of DJC came through in every carefully crafted word, emphasis, and piece of advice. Simon was the face of DJC in mediations worldwide. He designed and directed the early intervention, early resolution, and mediation programs that put DJC on the map more than twenty years ago as a leading force in business problem solving. In his years with DJC, Simon had attended over 1,200 mediations with a settlement success rate that would make any mediator or competent counsel drool.

Simon's style was firm yet gentle, trustworthy but strategic, open yet informed, willing but certain. I suspected that he had a unique negotiation plan for every dispute, contract, or situation that he encountered. Simon was gifted because he knew what twenty-eight years had taught him, but he also knew that there would be times when his certainty and instincts would be rightly challenged and need to be strategically adjusted.

AN UNEVENTFUL PRE-MEDIATION CONFERENCE CALL

A few days after Simon's phone call, my case manager managed to schedule a customary pre-mediation conference call with counsel. I decided that for this situation in particular, I would follow most of the fine advice that I delivered as a teacher, as opposed to what I might ordinarily do. "Do as I say, not as I do."

I knew that Simon expected to be included in the call even though DJC had local counsel appearing in the case. I also knew Simon would be not only the face of the company in the mediation but also the legal scholar and sole decision maker. Local counsel would be deferential.

The conference call was uneventful and lasted only fifteen minutes. Plaintiff's counsel, Sam Schuster of Foster and Schuster, was the older partner of the personal injury boutique firm. I had heard of the firm but was unfamiliar with its people, reputation, and success rate. Local defense counsel Joe Campen was a partner in a well-respected, small insurance defense firm known for its trial successes and reasonableness. Joe gave the stage to Simon during the call.

During the conference call, I would have described Sam's role in the process as nondescript. He was neither helpful nor obstreperous. He just wanted a date and some direction on the little effort he planned to exert to prepare a mediation summary. I made it clear that the exchange of "meaningful" summaries would be a forceful catalyst toward a resolution if done sufficiently in advance to be absorbed by the opponent and the mediator. Simon made it clear that he expected a joint session and, in fact, was a big fan of joint sessions. He also expected to meet Christopher Clark and to visibly inspect the extent of Mr. Clark's leg injury allegedly caused by DJC's faulty and/or defective equipment.

All in all, it was a good pre-mediation conference call. I felt that I held my ground, made my points, and began to build trust with all three attorneys.

CONTRASTING SUMMARIES

The summaries arrived in timely fashion. I read the plaintiff's summary first. It contained the usual factual and legal posturing that one would expect to read in a trial brief. Despite suggestions in a letter that I had sent to counsel after the pre-mediation conference call, the plaintiff's summary had no information about Mr. Clark, the plaintiff whose life was "irreparably ruined" as a consequence of the "crushing blow" to his leg and ankle when DJC's machinery negligently landed thereon more than two years ago. It contained no information about Mr. Clark's present or future physical limitations or potential future surgeries. It failed to address the existence of any medical liens or the amount of costs incurred for his care or to pursue the lawsuit. It had no description of how the injury had altered, if at all, his lifestyle, education, work performance, social life, etc. It was thus no surprise that the summary was void of any economic analysis of loss and lacked any suggestion of an opening demand to initiate settlement negotiations.

In sharp contrast, DJC's summary was clean, concise, and instructive. After reading it through twice, I felt that I might even be able to put the machinery together myself. According to DJC, Mr. Clark's injuries were entirely the result of his own negligence and failure to follow proper safety precautions, not the result of any mechanical failure of a safety clasp that would have kept the machinery from falling on Mr. Clark. In addition to the mechanical drawings, instructions, and expert's explanation, all in plain English, DJC set out its historical philosophy and intentions applicable to early mediation in similar cases. Perhaps what surprised me the most was, if read carefully, the words, without giving specifics, would clue Sam in on what economic zone of possible agreement DJC was willing to enter to settle the case. Defenses notwithstanding, it wasn't just a nominal sum.

MORE PHONE CALLS

Two days before the mediation, I placed my customary calls to counsel. I played phone tag with Sam but had a productive call with Joe. I was right—Simon would call the shots. Joe had represented DJC in prior cases in this venue, but he answered to Simon. Joe had no prior experience with Schuster and Foster, so he had no insights into Sam's approach to settlement negotiations. Joe found the plaintiff's summary helpful but not insightful. He figured that Simon would bridge that gap at the mediation.

HURRY UP AND WAIT

The mediation was scheduled to begin at 9:00 a.m. Simon flew in the night before and stayed at the Westin next door to my office. He had nowhere else to go, so Joe and Simon showed up at 8:00 a.m. The three of us chatted in a conference room over coffee and bagels.

At the stroke of nine, Mr. Clark arrived. He was seated as I entered the lobby to greet him. Mr. Clark was a young-looking twenty-six-year-old, lacking in eye contact and thin as a beanpole. He was respectfully dressed in slacks and a dress shirt, socks, and soft-soled shoes. No, he didn't want anything to drink. No, he didn't want to wait in a conference room; he would be just fine waiting in the lobby for his attorney.

I asked the receptionist to call me as soon as Sam arrived. By 9:30 a.m., with no word from Sam, Simon's patience was wearing thin. "Is this how outsiders are treated in this venue? Where is he, and why hasn't he at least given us the courtesy of a phone call to say he would be delayed?" asked Simon. Efforts by my case manager to locate Sam were unfruitful. His office didn't know where he was. He wasn't at home, and he didn't answer his cell phone. Mr. Clark remained waiting, virtually motionless, in the lobby. By 10:30 a.m., Simon had decided he would be leaving to catch the 12:30 p.m. flight back to Minnesota.

At 10:38 a.m., as I tried to concoct the next step for this case, the conference room phone rang. Attorney Thomas A. Foster was in the lobby for the mediation. I left and nearly ran to the lobby.

"Mr. Foster. How nice to meet you," I said. "We were worried. Simon Tate from DJC and his attorney, Joe Campen, were concerned that perhaps there had been a mix-up in the scheduling. Would you and Mr. Clark please follow me? I'd like us to spend a few minutes together before we meet with the other participants."

GIVE ME A NUMBER . . . OR ELSE

"Miss, I have no need to meet with you or with them," said Tom. "Do they have a number? If so, we can start there. If not, then we have nothing to discuss. I have to leave by noon, and any further delays on your part are only using up our negotiating time."

The curt message was clear, so I led them up the stairs to a conference room. On the way, I pointed out to Tom that during the pre-mediation conference call with Sam, it was agreed that there would be a joint session so that Simon Tate could meet him and his client and view the extent of his injuries. I also noted that the joint session would address not only items that weren't thoroughly developed in the summary but also legal questions.

"Were you not hearing me?" asked Tom. "I told you I am not doing a joint session. All I need is their number, and now it is 10:50 a.m. and you are wasting my time."

I made two more attempts to convince Tom that a joint session was necessary. Mr. Clark still said nothing.

I excused myself from the conference room and went down the hall to see Joe. I managed to pull him away from Simon and give him the lay of the land. I knew that to get to a joint session, Joe would have to confront Tom because obviously my pleas were being ignored.

After some heated debate between the two lawyers, Joe and Tom agreed that there would be a joint session but without any debate or advocacy. It would be swift, for the sole purpose of polite introductions and the chance for Simon to meet Mr. Clark and see his injury—and, by the way, so that DJC could give Tom its number.

JOINT SESSION ON A FAST TRACK

The fastest mediator's opening statement then ensued. By 11:05 a.m., Tom was in the spotlight, making no opening comments except to ask what the number was and to remind everyone that he was leaving at noon. He sat directly opposite Simon, six inches of files and papers in front of him, untouched, and no pen in hand. His client sat with his hands folded in his lap, again lacking eye contact with anyone in the room.

Joe made a brief introduction and politely turned the stage over to Simon, explaining that Simon was the person with the checkbook and would be making all the decisions on the settlement terms. Simon introduced himself and began to give some background on DJC and mediation.

Tom interrupted. "You are advocating. We agreed there would be no argument or advocacy. Do you have a number or not?"

"I'm sorry," said Simon. "I didn't think I was advocating, just merely explaining to your client how it is that I came to be here today and what DJC's philosophy is about our concerted efforts to work with possible claimants early after injuries because DJC and I believe that is clearly in the best interests of persons such as your client, Mr. Clark. But I'll move on. Mr. Clark, as your attorney knows, we at DJC take very seriously any allegations of wrongdoing. And, over the years, we have amassed substantial experience at evaluating . . ."

"I said no advocacy!" interrupted Tom. "It is 11:15 a.m., and I have to be leaving. What's your number? If you don't have a number, then just be honest about it, and we'll be out of here."

Simon responded simply that he needed to see Mr. Clark's leg and ankle. To my amazement, Tom did not object. After rotating his ankle for Simon, Mr. Clark, in response to Simon's question, said that he only had pain occasionally when he "overdid it." Mr. Clark said that he wasn't expecting to have any more surgeries and that his medical bills were covered by the insurance that his employer provided at the time of the accident. He was unmarried and had no children.

Simon thanked Mr. Clark, returned to his seat, and began again. "Mr. Clark, as I attempted to suggest earlier, at DJC we have a method for evaluating the nature and extent of injuries when a person such as yourself files a lawsuit against us claiming we have done something wrong. It doesn't happen very often, but in my twenty-eight years of experience as the face of DJC in discussions like the one we are having this morning, I have found it helpful to share with you some of our data so that when we begin to discuss the possibility of settlement, you have an understanding of how we work and think."

Now with a raised and excited voice, Tom nearly exploded. "Give us a number or we are leaving! You are advocating to my client, and I won't allow that!"

Up until this moment, I had allowed the interruptions, but I knew that I was losing control of the process. I confronted Tom before Simon had a chance to speak. I explained that the parties and counsel had been directed by the court to attend the mediation and that everyone had agreed on the process, a process that included the joint session that we were currently in, in which everyone has wide latitude and the opportunity to exchange information to assist them in making informed decisions. I added that the process helped me as the mediator to efficiently and neutrally handle the case by making inquiries and leading discussion on certain issues. I suggested that we stick with the agreement and continue what we started, knowing that Tom expected a swift and abbreviated joint discussion.

"I have no need for this stage of the process," said Tom. "Let's cut the bullshit and get down to the number. Do you have a number or not, Mr. Tate?"

Simon looked at his watch. It was 11:30 a.m.. Simon closed his notebook, looked at Tom, and firmly stated, "If you want a number, we will get you a number; but I suggest you make a demand because as far as I know, you haven't."

Tom's demand was $250,000 with a full release. Simon asked me to take him and Joe back to the conference room so that they could confer.

SUSTENANCE ARRIVES

As I opened the door, I nearly ran into the Rubbermaid cart containing the day's lunch fare: a large deli tray with all the sandwich makings including pickles, coleslaw, potato salad, chips, and soft drinks. On the second tier of the cart was what mattered most to me: a dozen four-inch-diameter chocolate chip, oatmeal, and peanut butter cookies still wrapped in plastic wrap on a large tray. I asked my case manager to set up the lunch on the buffet in the conference room that I had just exited so that Mr. Clark and his attorney could help themselves. Simon and Joe would return in a few minutes to do the same.

PLAYING THE ODDS

As Simon, Joe, and I walked down the hall, I was fuming. I felt entirely responsible for what had just happened and was wondering how I was going to regain my neutrality in order to close the case. My disdain for Tom's behavior was boiling beneath my calm exterior, and I debated how to apologize to Simon without losing any more control over the situation.

Once inside the conference room, I asked whether they wanted to speak alone or if I should stay for the discussion. Simon told me to join them. He was completely calm, which was only slightly infectious, and expressed no dismay at the behavior or rudeness he had just witnessed.

If Tom wanted a number, he'd give him a number. Simon started thinking out loud. Mr. Clark was obviously mostly healed. He wouldn't do well on the witness stand. He wouldn't make a compassionate witness whom a jury might be inclined to reward, even if one of his attorneys could do a makeover between now and the trial, more than six months away. This wasn't a $250,000 case: in fact, it wasn't a six-figure case; but like all plaintiff attorneys, Tom had to start somewhere.

Simon played around with the likelihood that Tom would accept $50,000 to settle; then he played around with the likelihood that Tom would accept $80,000. Simon decided that there was a 70 percent chance that Tom would accept $80,000 and a 95 percent chance that he'd take something in five figures.

"So here's what we are going to do," he said. "Let's open at $35,000 and see if he stays or goes." Simon asked me to pass along the message that he and Joe were there to settle and that Simon's flight didn't leave until 7:30 p.m., so he was prepared to engage in meaningful discussions if Mr. Clark and his attorney wanted to do so. Simon also said that he wanted a full release and dismissal with prejudice of the lawsuit. "I am purposefully not telling you how soon we can cut a check," Simon added, "so if he asks, you can be honest and say you don't know. Please don't offer any opinion on the topic."

I rose and exited the room. It was 11:45 a.m.

COOKIE CRUMBS

Needing time to collect my thoughts, I took the long route back to Tom and Mr. Clark.

What happened next will be forever imprinted on my brain. Never in a million years would I have expected what Tom had done—as if he hadn't done enough.

After I entered the conference room, I saw Mr. Clark shoveling potato salad into his mouth as if it was his last supper. His paper plate was overflowing with a large deli meat sandwich, four pickles, potato salad, and coleslaw. He was on his second Coke, the discarded can next to the napkin he hadn't used and a nearly empty bag of chips.

That vision paled as my eyes moved to Tom. Tom's pile of papers was still untouched—except for the plastic-wrapped tray of cookies on top, all still intact. He acted as if he had won a trophy as he proudly exclaimed, "This is great. I'm treat dad at my daughter's gymnastics today, and now I don't have to go to the grocery store."

My brain reverted to the fact that everything that I ever needed to know about life, I had learned in kindergarten—and to my grandmother's insistence on manners. My first reaction was one of amazement because Tom apparently didn't even offer a cookie to his own client! I quickly debated whether I would slap Tom's face, grab the cookies, or just start screaming at him. With great difficulty, I kept my mouth shut, flopping speechless into the chair next to Mr. Clark.

Tom blurted out, "What's their number?"

I decided to go with the pace and patience that Simon had exhibited in the joint session. I asked Mr. Clark if he needed anything else; he said no through the crunch of his chips. I apologized for talking business while he was eating but noted that Tom was on a tight schedule. Mr. Clark just nodded his head, jabbing his plastic fork into the coleslaw. Tom was standing, looking out the large picture window of the tenth floor office but saying nothing. I waited.

After what seemed like an eternity, Tom turned to face me and blandly asked, "Well?"

I looked at Tom and then turned back to Mr. Clark, asking him how he was doing, how the accident had impacted his work, and how much difficulty he had on a daily basis as a result of his injuries. Tom did not interrupt and began looking out the window again. It was a brief conversation in between the making of a second sandwich, but I gathered sufficient information to confirm what I suspected Simon already knew from his years of experience.

I looked at my watch. It was 11:55 a.m.

I then moved on to explain to Mr. Clark that it was customary in cases like this one for the parties to exchange numbers through many rounds before landing on a settlement figure that everyone could live with. I chattered on about how Tom, despite his time contraints, undoubtedly had Mr. Clark's best interests in mind; and how Simon and Joe had set aside the entire day to discuss settlement and how Simon had come to town for the sole purpose of meeting Mr. Clark and discussing a settlement.

Tom's patience expired, and, from across the room, he noted the time and said that he needed a number or he and Mr. Clark would be leaving as soon as Mr. Clark finished his lunch. The good news was that Mr. Clark's plate was still quite full.

THE COUNTEROFFER, COUNTER-COUNTEROFFER, ETC.

After delivering Simon's message and offer, Tom took no time to give a counteroffer of $190,000.

Simon and Joe came down to the conference room, filled their plates, and returned to their home station to discuss Tom's counterdemand and their response. Simon was pretty certain that his opening number was sufficient to peak Tom's interest, and he believed his response to the $190,000 would be pivotal to getting a deal done. If he went in too low, Tom might end the mediation; but Simon doubted that any number he delivered would be "too low" to keep going. The question was how low he could stay. Simon also believed that Mr. Clark wasn't the impetus behind any number, high or low, so his focus would be only on Tom for the time being.

Simon, Joe, and I discussed the probabilities of what Tom would accept. After some good dialogue and a private meeting with Joe, Simon told me to go back with $50,000.

It was 12:30 p.m., and to no one's surprise, Tom and Mr. Clark were still in their conference room. Tom was smelling victory, so his demeanor was more patient.

A few more rounds ensued, and ultimately the parties agreed on $74,500. The mediated settlement agreement was signed at 2:05 p.m., and Tom left with his client and the tray of cookies, still wrapped. I spent a few moments with Simon and Joe before calling a metro car for Simon. He would make the 5:00 p.m. flight, and, gaining an hour, he would be home in time for dinner with his wife.

HANKERING FOR A COOKIE

Both Simon and Joe were complimentary of my assistance and my role as mediator. Simon resolutely stated that he mediated cases with the Toms of the world on a frequent basis. He wasn't phased. Joe expressed no opinion other than to call Tom a few names that I wished I, too, could use. We all shook hands, and they headed down the elevator.

I returned to my office, stopping in the kitchen to grab a sandwich from the leftovers. While relieved that a deal had been reached, I was surprised at the anger that lingered in my stomach. I skipped the pickles and slopped a piece of pastrami on the Jewish rye while wondering where I was going to find a cookie.

I left the office early that day, before rush hour. I climbed into my car, noted the plane flying overhead, waved at what might be Simon, and put in a John Mellancamp CD. It would be forty-five minutes of decompression at eighty miles an hour across town. I wondered if it would be enough.

SECOND THOUGHTS:

I never told Simon or Joe about the cookies. Most who know me would say I am a very "slow boil." However, Tom's cookie move set me on fire. He had already been disrespectful of the process, of counsel, of his own client, and, least of all, of me. The purist in me wanted a process that mattered to Mr. Clark. I already knew that it mattered to Simon. Yet, Tom didn't honor or even try to work with anything that the others, including his own partner, had decided would be helpful to reaching an agreement. Further, I felt that he made it virtually impossible for me to add value to the mediation, and that really troubled me. I became almost resistant to anything that he said and, but for Mr. Clark, would have preferred to stay away from any caucus or further communication with Tom after the joint session. This made me less effective as a negotiation coach, and after the first round I realized my neutrality, such as it was, was totally blown. I would just have to endure the day and ignore Tom's shameful approach to mediation.

In hindsight, my bias probably didn't make any difference in outcome because Simon and Joe were sophisticated, seasoned attorneys, apparently nonplussed by Tom's approach to negotiation. The parties reached an agreement that each could accept. To this day, I have no idea whether the ultimate figure was close to anything that either party wanted it to be. I was just grateful that the parties left with a signed agreement. I never did another case for DJC; sadly, about a year after the case, Simon died. I have done other cases for Joe's clients but have never even heard mention of Tom or his firm again.

That wasn't the end of my "involvement" with this case, though. As Paul Harvey says, here's the rest of the story.

Eighteen months after this debacle, I was asked by my state bar to be the guinea pig in a coaching session with Ken Cloke. It was scheduled for my state's annual advanced negotiation and dispute resolution institute at which 180 attorneys attend. Blindly, I agreed "for the good of the cause." Ken told me in advance that he wanted me to share a story with him of a mediation in which I needed a coach. He was hoping that I could craft a situation so that he could demonstrate some of the benefits of co-mediation as well as self-reflection, introspection, and growth as a mediator.

Naturally, I thought of Tom and Simon. And so, from the stage in front of 179 of my clients and colleagues, I told the "cookie story." As Ken is so prone to do, he sat calmly and listened attentively while I relayed the saga. As I was telling of the events, I could hear the anger still in my voice. My impatience, my incredulousness, and my fear came through without any effort, which perhaps kept the audience's attention.

When I was finally done spewing my version of the mediation, Ken leaned forward in his chair, and the following dialogue ensued:

"You're still upset. In fact, I would go so far as to suggest you are still angry. "

"You bet."

"You felt he mistreated you in part because you are a woman, yes?"

"Yep."

"You were also embarrassed for Joe, your city, yourself, the process, and the International Academy of Mediators because here was a very gifted advocate being subjected to conduct that you found completely unacceptable, unprofessional, and downright rude. You felt responsible for the whole situation; and despite your gallant efforts, you were having no effect on changing the communication in a productive manner."

"Damn straight."

"Most of all, you felt Tom had no concern or respect for his client or his client's best interests. In fact, you probably decided in the first ten minutes with Tom that he was an idiot, undeserving of any kindness or money from Simon, and that, by all accounts, he was unprepared and just fishing for a settlement divisible by three. He saw the cookies as a bonus for his presence; and the rudeness of that maneuver pushed you to the edge, and you had to do some self-correction to stay the course."

"I'd say you have it all right."

In his usual manner, Ken sat back, reflected only briefly, and then softly asked me something that was almost as surprising as when Tom commandeered the cookie tray: "Did it ever occur to you that Tom didn't want to be there?"

"Excuse me?"

"Well, let's look at the objective information you have just shared. Sam didn't come as planned. No one could reach Sam or Tom before Tom showed up one and a half hours late. He never opened his papers, and he took no notes. He didn't engage in any meaningful conversation with Mr. Clark in your presence. He refused to have any substantive dialogue about the case facts, law, liability, or damages. The summary was void of anything you felt meaningful in addressing traditional aspects of risk analysis. He cut Simon off at every opportunity, and the only time he engaged in any part of the process was once the number negotiation began. Is it possible that something happened to Sam, and, at the last minute, Tom had to show up, in part because the opponent flew in from out of town? In other words, rather than adjourn the mediation, Tom came to negotiate numbers and had no clue about any facts of the case that would allow him to participate in a substantive dialogue. So, rather than admit the situation, he went on the offense."

Until that moment, it had never occurred to me that my first clue should have been the tardy arrival of a person I didn't expect. Tom's brash behavior, clearly escalated at the outset, through no contribution by anyone at the mediation, was the second clue. Although I didn't take the bull head-on, I took the bait. In my effort to deliver a process, I lost sight of Tom as a person, who was clearly in an agitated state. Rather than address that situation, I tried to ram my process at him and his client and met resistance from the outset. Clearly I was more concerned with "me" than anyone or anything else in the process.

How many times have we said that resistance is evidence of an unmet need? I know better now and I certainly knew better then; however, "thinking it's all about me," kept me from what mediators do best—suspend judgment and work with what you have. If we identify the source of the problem, we can often find the solution. Sometimes even the best of us become too focused on where we want to take the participants in mediation because we think we know better than they, about what's best for them. Instead, we should be more mindful of the art of Tai Chi and help them move in the directions they feel comfortable going.

Those moments with Ken were rude awakenings of some of my own weaknesses as a neutral negotiation coach and teacher. From that session, I learned that in every mediation "you don't know what you don't know." I also have a permanent reminder of something a longtime mentor shared with me in my first years as a mediator: "It's not my problem." In other words, when we take ownership or assume responsibility for every aspect of a mediation process and outcome, we do more harm than just bringing into question our neutrality. We lose our objective perch, and we begin to erode the participants' right to self-determination and self-empowerment. As long as we believe that these are two hallmarks of the process and that they are, at their core, immeasurable benefits of the mediation experience, we can lighten our load and loosen our grasp on process and outcome. We don't need to own the process or the result; we only need to steer it in a proper direction and keep it fueled—perhaps with cookies.

So, the next time I sense my own anger or realize I am falling prey to bias, the cookie monster will remind me to listen constantly, to listen for what's not being said, to act in the moment, and to follow up on cues that participants send. Ironically, I will remember, with gratitude, the cookie monster.

10.

Something Is Happening Here and You Don't Know What It Is

Lela P. Love

Every once in a while in mediation—and often in thinking about mediation—I am reminded of the lyrics from Bob Dylan's "Ballad of A Thin Man": *Something is Happening Here. But You Don't Know What It Is. Do You, Mr. Jones?* Dylan sings the line with an emphasis suggesting to me the absurdity of Mr. Jones (or, for me, anyone) thinking that he does know what's happening. Here's a story that keeps Dylan's lyrics reverberating in my mediator's world view ...

HIGH-RISE MEDIATION

One evening in a New York City skyscraper, I mediated a case that began at 5:00 p.m. That was the earliest time everyone was free, and we expected to take three, at the most four, hours. We were up on a high floor in the building, and it didn't occur to me at first to worry that we might get locked in if we went too late. Nearly seven hours later, with absolutely no progress made, we were still around the conference table; and I remembered that the building might close and the elevators might get shut down at midnight.

REMNANTS OF A ROMANCE

The case involved two parties, Cecelia and Jim, who wanted to end a partnership concerning the shared ownership of some property in New Jersey. The relationship between Jim and Cecelia had started as a romance, but the romance ended after a year, leaving them with a property owned jointly. They had held the property together for five years by renting it out for income. In addition to the other tenants, Jim lived in it.

Each partner raised many issues. There were at least ten issues on the table that pertained to the real estate aspect of the partnership. In addition, a host of concerns about incivility and slights over the five-year partnership kept arising.

PROPERTY AND PROPERTY-RELATED ISSUES

There were numerous property and property-related issues.

One of the issues concerned the buyout value of the property (land and building) if the partnership broke up, which was the hoped-for conclusion of the mediation, I had been told. Jim and Cecelia could agree on neither an amount nor a method of setting a value. In broad strokes, Cecelia wanted the current value as determined by an appraiser of her choice without any discount for a broker's fee; Jim wanted significant discounts for being the finder and developer of the property if the property went to him or, on the other hand, significant payback for his efforts if he were bought out. He wanted an appraiser of his choice, and he wanted a discount from the appraised value if no broker were used.

In addition to the property itself, there were numerous items that went with the property that neither Jim nor Cecelia wanted if selling his/her interest: vacuum cleaners, mowers, a tractor, furniture, and so on. These had to be valued for purchase by whoever kept the house as they were needed for the property's operation. Complete deadlock on how to value the items and disagreement about whether Jim should be taxed for his use of these things during his tenancy on the premises ensued.

Now, you, the reader, may be thinking that there is nothing particularly difficult about any of these issues, that issues like these have multiple possible procedural resolutions even if the parties themselves cannot agree on a substantive resolution. I don't disagree. That's why it seemed so remarkable that we got zero movement in seven hours despite working very hard. In fact, addressing any one issue was like opening a can of worms: myriad problems slithered out.

Another issue was which partner would have the opportunity to buy out the other. It was presumed that Jim would buy out Cecelia because the property was Jim's home. But Cecelia seemed to be open to becoming the full owner, too, in lieu of accepting a suboptimal price. Simply selling the property and splitting the proceeds was another direction, but that idea got no traction either. And no, flipping a coin or having the parties each make simultaneous "bids" and going with the highest would not work to resolve this question, nor would a variety of other proposals that each party made.

Various purchases and transactions over the years that had resulted in controversy were also the subject of much unproductive conversation. For example, Jim had purchased a new stove for their tenants without Cecelia's approval. Cecelia refused, consequently, to share the cost. Her position was that the old stove was repairable. Deadlock.

Heating expenses were an issue because Jim set the thermostat (common to both his apartment and the tenants' apartments) higher than Cecelia thought was appropriate. Consequently, since heat was a cost that was netted out of what Cecelia realized from the property rental, she wanted to be compensated for that loss.

The value of Jim's labor on the premises was addressed at great length. Jim mowed the extensive grounds in the summer and shoveled the snow in the winter. He repaired various items—doors, locks, storm windows, appliances, Internet connections—when those things broke. He painted rooms, fixed the plumbing, and troubleshot with respect to mice and cockroaches in tenants' apartments. He wanted monetary recognition of those efforts, at least as an offset to the rent that was imputed for his use of the apartment in their building. Since many years were at issue when these controversies festered, the amount of money involved was considerable. Cecelia wanted to give him nothing for his labor and, furthermore, wanted the full rental value of Jim's apartment to be factored into any deal that was made since they could have rented it to others if he were out. She felt that the types of things that Jim did were simply what anyone would do when living somewhere. Jim felt that his presence on the premises saved them both from innumerable headaches and costs and that at least the cost of gasoline, cleaning expenses on several occasions, and other out-of-pocket expenses that benefited the entire property should be shared. Cecelia refused to pay these expenses, much less pay for Jim's labor.

Collectively, these expenses added up to significant sums. Each issue had its own backstory and generated a lot of heat. And each side had a position, and no one would budge.

INTERPERSONAL ISSUES

The interpersonal issues also seemed very pressing to the parties even though they had broken up as a couple and wanted to break up as business partners.

For example, a pattern of frustrating communications had angered both of them. Jim was an avid and punctual emailer who very much liked timely responses. Cecelia didn't like email, could take a very long time to respond (or wouldn't respond at all if she felt that she had already made her position clear), and also wasn't particularly eager to return phone calls because Jim was always (in her words) making unreasonable demands in an unpleasant tone. Jim felt, despite the admittedly poor relationship, that partners needed to be responsive about issues pertaining to their common interests. Cecelia felt that she had made her positions and policies clear.

Incidents of name-calling and insults had made conversation toxic. Jim had called Cecelia an "uptight bitch" (probably the worst insult), and Cecelia had responded in kind. In the mediation, the parties tended to vilify each other at every opportunity despite efforts to negotiate about standards of civility.

Past hurts connected with the breakup of what had started, many years earlier, as a romantic relationship underlay the discussions. The romance had ended several years previous when Cecelia moved out of the apartment (now occupied by Jim) in their house.

Were any apologies made? Were any acknowledgments given by the parties? No and no.

NONEXISTENT PROGRESS

What was remarkable about the mediation was that by 11:30 p.m., NOTHING—not one small issue—had been successfully resolved. It seemed as if every topic became simply another opening for the parties to put each other down and become intractable. As mediator, I could not hit on any approach that seemed to allow the parties to see each other's point of view. Calling for them to see a question standing in the shoes of the other, asking whether they wanted to have a free-flowing talk to air their grievances or make an effort to put the conflict behind them and move on—nothing helped to shift the conversation in the direction of allowing closure.

So, at 11:30 p.m., knowing that the building closed at midnight and not wanting to get locked in for the night—or, for that matter, continue what appeared to be an unproductive conversation—I announced a close of the mediation, reciting that I was sorry that I had been unable to help put the matter behind them that night. Though I offered to meet again with Cecelia and Jim, I was not very hopeful about such a meeting because the lack of any progress at all and of any softening

121

toward one another in terms of openness to the other or flexibility or willingness to figure out options seemed so extreme.

WORKING WELL WITH A DEADLINE

What happened next is the point of this story. Both parties, understanding the imminent end of the mediation, came up—together—with a plan to end the whole dispute and to settle all of the many issues that I had noted. All of them! And it all happened in the ten minutes that I was willing to work, given that I was afraid of us all being victims of an elevator lockdown. I was simply astounded. No sign of any movement had been visible. No lessening of tension had shifted the exchanges. No vulnerabilities were shown. And, suddenly, with my announcement of a deadline (that we had to be out before midnight), everything was resolved. In fact, everything was not only resolved, but both Jim and Cecelia seemed okay with the resolution—*happy* would be too strong a description of how they felt, but they seemed at peace with the resolution and with each other.

We quickly captured the points of agreement and got out of the building before midnight. Walking out together, everyone was cordial and grateful.

SECOND THOUGHTS:

This case, probably the most dramatic 180-degree turnaround that I have witnessed, highlights two doctrines that I have come to embrace.

THE POWER OF DEADLINES

In this case, I expect it was the announcement of an imminent deadline that catapulted the parties into a recognition that they were about to lose a chance to get out of an unpleasant situation. Perhaps they also wanted to recognize the truth or validity of aspects of what the other person was saying, and the deadline provided a last-chance opportunity to do that. The fact that it remained as unpleasant as ever from 5:00 p.m. to 11:30 p.m. would have to be a catalyst for most people to seek a door out. Both parties had been listening to the other (appearances to the contrary notwithstanding), and both had generated a plan for ending their partnership that was likely to be acceptable to the other. Eureka! When I said we had to close, the plans were displayed. So, you never know what is having a positive impact, and you never know how close you are to helping parties find release. In one way, I believe the phenomenon is related to loss aversion. Suddenly, parties to a mediation realize that they are about to lose their chance of moving on in a positive way; and, at that point, closure emerges.

THE PRINCIPLE OF UNKNOWABILITY

As a witness to negotiations, it is not possible to know when parties have been moved by what is happening. "Saving face" can result in unreadable demeanors. You may as well assume that interventions that have no visible impact are having an invisible impact. Any third party should be utterly humble about his take on the situation. This principle of unknowability has always helped me stay impartial. It's true that I don't enjoy some behaviors that parties display, but, in the back of my mind, I'm thinking, "They may have good cause for this behavior. I don't know."

Occasionally, I sit as an arbitrator, and, as I write down my award, I am haunted by the principle of unknowability. What I know best is that I might be wrong. This is one of the reasons I like mediation so much: the people who know the most make the decisions.

Hence, the title of this piece: Something is happening, and you don't know what it is. Furthermore, the mediator doesn't need to know: it's all about giving the parties every opening to find the best route out of their dilemma. If anyone knows what's happening, it's most likely to be the parties.

PART IV

Listening for the Undercurrents and Finding Missing Pieces

If we could read the secret history of our enemies, we would find sorrow and suffering enough to dispel all hostility.

Henry Wadsworth Longfellow

11.

The Problem of Sharing Space

Jeff Jury

RUNNING LATE

Some people just aren't supposed to live next to each other, I thought as I sank into my chair.

It was now 7:25 p.m., forty minutes after the start of Sarah's volleyball game, which I had promised not to miss, and one hundred thirty minutes after the time that my clients insisted everyone had to be out the door—the basis of my promise not to miss the game. Darren needed help with his math homework. A red message light blinked rhythmically at me from my desk phone. My cell phone, silenced two hours ago, ticked up the new voice mail message counter from three to four as I exhaled. My thoughts wandered back to how this thing had started. . . .

GOOD FENCES MAKE GOOD NEIGHBORS

Forty-two years earlier, A.W. Kemp bought a parcel of land at what was then beyond the edge of town, just outside the city limits. Mr. Kemp enjoyed the outdoors; woodworking; and walking the "back half" of the property, which was thickly wooded with an ample creek running through it. The ranch-style house he built, mostly by himself, had a large covered patio, where he spent many evenings listening to the life cycle of the seasons. Two years later, Mr. Kemp married Phyllis; and three years after that, Ronnie was born. One set of roles was now cast.

When Ronnie was four, now thirty-three years ago, Lt. Col. Arthur Symington, United States Air Force (Ret.), bought the old Murphy place next door, to the right of the Kemps. Col. Symington, "Sy" to his friends, and his second bride (the Air Force was his first wife) of twenty-five years, Patricia, built a two-story house with a second-floor deck that gave them a grand view of the creek-fed woods. Casting this phase of the drama was now complete.

The Kemp and Symington families were friendly but not close. Both A.W. and Sy believed the words of Robert Frost that "good fences make good neighbors," so they agreed to split the cost of a simple wooden fence that ran the length of the property line from the front road to a spot seventy-five feet from the creek. They worked together to build the fence on successive gray Saturdays in October. Phyllis and Patricia alternated making dinner on those Saturday evenings, with the sound of the Lawrence Welk Show playing at the Symington house and the sound of Ronnie being a kid or misbehaving, depending on one's point of view, at the Kemp house.

Those Saturday post-construction dinners were about the deepest level of socializing that the families shared together. A.W. worked long hours at the store, and Sy traveled frequently for his retirement job. Besides, Sy was annoyed by Ronnie. He thought that the Kemps spoiled their son and that Ronnie lacked manners and respect for others.

The ensuing years brought many changes. More houses sprang vertically in the area. Mr. and Mrs. Dobbins built a house to the right of the Symingtons. Being of like mind about parameters, Mr. Dobbins (no one seemed to know his first name) and Sy built a wooden fence that matched the Kemp-Symington fence. Helen Dobbins seemed to have an antique shop or some kind of ongoing basement sale going on at their house. Sy thought that this brought too much traffic into the area, and potentially some "undesirables"; but because it was hidden from his view, he let it go.

Larry and Rhonda McCoy, with their four kids, moved in across the road. He drove a bread truck route, so he was up and out the door by 4:30 a.m. every day. A.W. and Sy respected how hard Larry worked—he was always working on a car or something around his house—and Mary kept the kids in line. The kids said "Yes, sir" and "No, sir," so the Symingtons made special Halloween bags for them every year.

THE CHAFING SORE
During these years, Ronnie became a source of increasing irritation to Sy. Ronnie and his buddies "left their damn beer cans and cigarette butts" down by the creek, although on the Kemp side of the fence. Ronnie always seemed to pour on the gas and peel out loudly in front of the Symington house after the Kemps spoiled him with a car on his sixteenth birthday. Sy swore that he saw Ronnie and "the other longhairs" urinating in his yard during one of their summertime gatherings by the creek.

Sy's displeasure transferred in two directions. The first victim was Patricia, quiet and nervous by nature, who felt relaxed during the time that Ronnie was away at college but started fretting in advance of his return from breaks, which were carefully calendared by Sy. The other victim was the fence, which endured the normal life cycle of wooden fences but became an emblem of the growing enmity that Sy felt toward his neighbors. A.W. and Sy kept up the fence, but they usually didn't work on it together, and there were no post-construction dinners.

ALLIANCES
Finally, about twenty years ago, the families proved that common enemies can create new alliances. An out-of-town, big-city developer bought the Redding Ranch, some 800 acres on the other side of the

creek, and built a "community" of deed-restricted homes. The city borders had crept, killer fog–like, around Redding Ranch and some of the surrounding area, leaving the area where these families lived an island surrounded by the sea of the city. For a time, the four families were united like the Bremen Town musicians in their goal of preserving the way of life that they enjoyed; and, for some reason, they managed to avoid being regulated by the encroaching city or overrun by the new development.

TRANSITIONS
Patricia Symington was the first to leave the old neighborhood. Sy woke at his usual hour one morning, made the coffee, and faithfully brought Patricia her cup with a splash of cream. She didn't wake up that morning. Her funeral was sparsely attended in general but unanimously attended by the neighborhood, even Ronnie, who by then had become an accountant and financial planner in one of the big cities.

Mr. Dobbins's cancer caught up with him next. A.W. had a heart attack at the store and was gone before he hit the floor. Phyllis had a stroke four months later.

Then, three years before the current mediation, Ronnie moved back to the home where he was raised.

BREAKING THE CAMEL'S BACK
One of the first things that Ronnie noticed was that the fence had fallen into disrepair. It had withered and aged on a parallel track with the founders of the neighborhood. Ronnie wondered if the fence was really necessary. Sy was scarcely seen about and didn't answer Ronnie's knocks at his door to discuss the fence. The fence was an eyesore, and the Kemp house needed to be updated.

Ronnie paid visits to Mrs. Dobbins and Larry McCoy to say hello and tell them that he was planning on doing some landscaping and "sprucing up" of the house. Ronnie looked and talked like a responsible adult, and neither Mrs. Dobbins nor Larry objected to the neighborhood being improved. Ronnie made two unsuccessful visits to Sy's front door and taped to the door a typed note, with a business card stapled to it, on his third attempt: "Dear Col. Symington: I am going to have a crew doing some work around the yard. They will be using power equipment. Once they get going, I'm going to make a decision about whether to keep the fence. Please let me know if you object to me tearing down the fence. I hope you are doing well—Ronnie Kemp."

Sy carefully peered out the curtains of Patricia's room at the crew working down by the creek. He quickly became an unhappy neighbor. The first crew jabbered all day long in another language and played loud music throughout the day, except when Ronnie was home. They excavated around the creek with a backhoe, stirring up silt and widening the creek.

If that wasn't bad enough, it looked like Ronnie had hired a couple of homeless men to run a bulldozer that scraped part of the property bare. Then they brought in some giant boulders and dropped them, helter-skelter, near the creek. What in the world was Ronnie doing? Sy wondered.

The last crew worked day and night by the creek. Sy went to the hardware store and bought a portable light stand affixed with bright halogen lights. He set one of his light timers to come on around nightfall to keep the creek area on the Kemp side illuminated. Who knew what these people were up to and whether they spoke English. Had the activity gone from beer and cigarettes to worse? Sy kept meticulous notes and continued not to answer the knocks at the door.

One Tuesday morning, after Ronnie left the house, Sy walked across to the decaying fence for the first time since Ronnie moved in and was shocked by what he saw: Ronnie had a pond installed at the widest part of the creek! What the hell was he doing? Sy then moved as quickly as he could to the creek's edge, slipping and falling once on the uneven ground, and saw that the creek had widened and was moving slowly. "That Goddamn pond!" Sy exclaimed aloud. Then he noticed that his knee was bleeding from where he had fallen. "Sonofabitch! Little rat bastard!" Sy grumbled as he limped back inside.

Sy may not have slept at all over the next two days, as he later remembered them in our introductory meeting. Relying on the military training that served him well for years, he assembled his documentation of the construction events and the long-ago events involving Ronnie and compiled a list of objections regarding the construction.

At 8:45 a.m. on the second day of working on his case against Ronnie, Sy heard a pounding. Carefully parting the living room curtains, he saw another crew at work tearing down the fence. He stood silently for a moment, and a tear rolled down one cheek as he remembered his friend A.W. Kemp and the good times they had building that fence. Sy knew that if A.W. was alive, he would give Ronnie the whipping he had always had coming to him. Then Sy grabbed his Polaroid.

The final insult came just two days later. Sy heard a commotion in Ronnie's backyard. He retrieved his binoculars out of his footlocker, which he pulled out from the back of his closet. He could not believe what he saw: a woman in a wedding dress was posing for pictures by the creek. It looked like a full Hollywood camera crew at work, snapping pictures of the bride, and later the bride and groom, in Ronnie's backyard.

Enough was enough. "This will fix their chickens," Sy muttered as he went downstairs to the dormant light timer to fire up the only weapon available to him: halogen lights.

No lawsuit had been filed, but both sides had hired lawyers and exchanged "Surrender, Dorothy" letters.

A MIXED BAG OF DEMANDS

In my pre-mediation meeting with Col. Symington, his counsel (a repeat mediation client), and his niece, who drove him to the mediation, I was handed a "bill of particulars" detailing the grievances against Ronnie. They were bulleted as follows:

- Ronnie Kemp committed trespass, beginning on 4 October, by commencing demolition and destruction on his side of the property, which disturbed the quiet enjoyment of property by Lt. Col. A. Symington (Ret.);

- Ronnie Kemp violated United States and local law by hiring and employing persons of questionable character and immigration status, creating potential for criminal harm;
- Ronnie Kemp permanently altered the contour and extent of said A. Symington's usable land by changing the dimensions and depth of the creek;
- Ronnie Kemp permanently altered the natural flow of water across said A. Symington's property, in violation of state natural resource laws;
- Ronnie Kemp created and/or facilitated further trespass by construction noise, loud talking by workers, and the playing of loud, undesirable music;
- Ronnie Kemp violated environmental protection laws by causing the denuding of the land, removal of natural vegetation, and creation of silt runoff into the creek; and
- Ronnie Kemp violated city ordinances by running a service business out of his home.

Col. Symington, while deferring to legal counsel, had looked into the law. He knew the city ordinance didn't technically apply to the neighborhood, but he was sure that there was a way to get it to apply in this unique situation. Again, prefacing by saying that he would defer to counsel, he was nevertheless firmly convinced that he could recover personal injury damages for his fall and treble damages and attorney fees under the natural resources law and obtain an injunction forcing Ronnie to restore the property to its original condition and to pay for the reinstallation of the fence.

After listening to Sy's presentation, I pulled the first tool I could reach. "Col. Symington, what do you want to happen at the end of the day?"

"I want him out, but I know that probably won't happen" was the first response. "If I can't have that, I just want things back to the way they were when his parents lived there. And I want Ronnie to build the fence back to my specifications, at his cost." Before I could speak to his counsel, Sy added one more item for the list: "And another thing—he used my water for his damn pond, so I want 50 percent of the profits from his photography business."

At this point, Sy's counsel spoke up, asking about a general session. I took this as a cue that he thought a general session was appropriate, so I made some concluding remarks about how the general session would be conducted: everyone would have the chance to speak without interruption and everyone would listen so that a safe environment in which to discuss the issues in a respectful, businesslike manner would be created. I hoped that this would appeal to the rule-following region of Sy's brain.

I packed Sy's mixed bag of demands and carried it down the hall.

THE FLIP SIDE OF THE PANCAKE

Ronnie and his lawyer, both of whom I was meeting for the first time and both of whom were attending their first mediation, looked like strangers in a strange land. Ronnie's lawyer was a service club acquaintance whose practice was primarily in estate planning. Ronnie belonged to a tort reform organization, believed that lawsuits were a long-term threat to the economic viability of the U.S. economy, and followed his handshake and hello with "Can you get this crazy old geezer off my back?"

The flipped pancake of this dispute looked very different in Ronnie's room. "I don't want a dispute with anyone, especially my neighbor," intoned Ronnie very seriously.

"The colonel has always had it in for me," continued Ronnie. "I was scared of him when I was a kid. My parents warned me never to go onto his property. I went into his yard to get a ball once when I was nine years old, and he went nuts. I thought he was going to call in an air strike." I asked if he was sure that he was nine years old at the time, which Ronnie strongly confirmed. Ronnie then extensively shared stories of Sy functioning as a one-man neighborhood watch association. He told how his father dreaded getting the call from Sy when it was time for the annual "fence detail" and how Sy glared at him at Patricia's funeral. "You can't reach out to the guy," said Ronnie.

After a level of venting symmetrical to the events down the hall, we discussed whether to have a general session and the balance between making matters worse and the need to break eggs as a necessary step in the process of making a cake. I explained the same customs and rules that were given in the other room, and they sounded encouraged. But before we moved to the general session, I shared Sy's list with Ronnie and his counsel.

Thirty extra minutes later, having pried Ronnie from the ceiling, we made our way to the general session. We discussed whether the mediation should go forward at all, how the journey of a thousand miles begins with a single step, and some of the other metaphors that we mediators use at such times. Ronnie replied, directly but not sternly, "Look, I'm not interested in analogies and stories, sir. I'm a businessman, and I want to settle this thing in a businesslike way. If it can't be done, I don't want to waste anyone's time today. Let's get this done or not and move to the next process if we have to." He mentioned the name of an expensive, guns-and-knives-style litigator friend who was "salivating" at the opportunity to take his case going forward. I wondered, but did not ask, why that person was not there that day.

THE GENERAL SESSION: MEETING WITHOUT A FENCE

The general session was not as bad as you might expect, but still not easy. Sy greeted the group with "What took you so long?" when we entered the room. Ronnie shook his head and rolled his eyes during the presentation by Sy's counsel. Ronnie's counsel was interrupted four times by Sy, who corrected him on "factual misrepresentations" despite requests not to interrupt.

At the conclusion of the presentations, not wishing to open the floor to further discussion, I suggested that Ronnie and his lawyer excuse themselves to their room. Before they left, Sy spoke up. "I just have one thing to say to you, Ronnie. Your father was a decent man, and he and I could have worked something like this out. I know he's ashamed at you and what you're doing. Dismiss—uh, that's all." Ronnie looked back at Sy for a moment with narrowed eyes and then strode out of the room.

I stayed in Sy's room for an appropriate amount of time, both to let Ronnie cool a moment and to see if more airtime would help in Sy's room. Sy's lawyer gave a coded message: "At some point, I want your viewpoint on what the range of outcomes might be in a case like this, understanding that this is all confidential and that no one can really predict what a judge or jury can do." The niece spoke for the first time, adding, "Yes, I told Uncle Sy that he really needs to hear that opinion from someone who isn't involved in this fight. Isn't that one of the benefits of mediation?"

Like other experienced mediators, I have a series of disclaimers that precede the offering of any opinion: I'm neutral, I've spent the least amount of time with this dispute, no one has a crystal ball, my opinion is just one opinion that will probably make everybody mad . . . But the nonverbal cues from Sy's lawyer and his niece told me that they wanted some help. I started by drawing the largest in a series of shrinking concentric circles around the problems I saw.

Then it was time for another walk down the hall. Both Ronnie and his lawyer were standing with bags packed and coats on, ready to leave. "That old bastard didn't know my father," said Ronnie indignantly. "How dare he sit there and tell me what my father would feel or say. I'll tell you what he would have done. He would have kicked that old man's ass, like I'm going to in court!"

So it began. After asking Ronnie and his lawyer to give me twenty minutes before leaving, I started a teaching discussion of reactive devaluation, anchoring bias, and the benefit of using the mediation process to damper down feelings and get to a livable solution. They were unmoved and prepared to invest in a lawsuit.

But then I found the idea that caught Ronnie's interest. "It sounds like going to litigation will give the colonel an awful lot of power over your life," I said.

"How is that?" Ronnie asked, seeming at least curious.

I asked for a detailing of attorney fees and expenses that would be incurred, which Ronnie did not find compelling and which could probably not be predicted accurately by his counsel. I then moved to a list of the nonrefundable costs of litigation, including time away from his business, peace-of-mind costs, and a presentation to a court or jury that would have limited time to process this information. "Despite everyone's best efforts," I noted, "if Sy comes off as crazy as Ronnie thinks he is, could some stranger conclude that this now elderly man was ill-used by a bright, young, business-savvy man who had the power to change the flow of a creek, the brass to tear down a long-standing fence, and the resources to hire a big-time litigator?"

A different set of gears now seemed to be turning in Ronnie's head. "You might have something there" Ronnie said, "but for this." He pulled out a letter with a certified mail return card that looked to be signed by Sy, which outlined what he planned to do with the property in deep specifics, including creating a site that would be attractive for photography. It included an offer to update the fence to make it more attractive and affirming that if the creek backed up on Sy's property, Ronnie would pay for an appraiser of Sy's choice to calculate the diminution in the value of property and the appropriate payment.

"Bet the colonel and his lawyer didn't mention any of that," said Ronnie. Answering so as not to unseal any confidences, I asked if I could discuss the specifics of the letter and prepared for a sortie down the hall. As if on cue, Ronnie mentioned one last thing before my hand reached the door handle. "By the way, if he is so against the concept of me running a business on my property, ask him why he hasn't bitched about Larry McCoy's bread truck parked in his driveway every night or Mrs. Dobbins's perpetual garage sale." I assured him that I would think of a mediator-like way to include that in the discussion and made my way out.

The letter was news in the colonel's room. Sy questioned the signature and said he didn't remember getting any letter.

After about twenty minutes, the niece asked if there was a place she could go to smoke; she had that look that whispered, "I want to speak with you privately." Out of the view of anyone else involved, the niece, wiping away tears, told me that she was afraid for Uncle Sy. She said that he was very forgetful, that in fact the signature on the certified

137

mail was his and he probably threw it away, and that all he did was talk about declaring war on Ronnie Kemp. She told me that her husband had removed the light tree, and Sy didn't notice. "How can we get this over with?" was her last question to me during that visit.

SHARING THE ROCK

Over course of the day, stretching beyond the allotted time, offers were made that probably exceeded the relief that Sy could expect from any judge or jury. Difficult discussions occurred about things unrelated to Ronnie Kemp or any lawsuit; two lawyer-only meetings occurred; and a private meeting between Ronnie and the niece took place, after which both of them emerged with moistened eyes.

All I can tell you is that they got close—so close that I missed the start of the volleyball game, for which I would have amends to pay—but the case did not settle that day. Maybe more work needed to be done on another day. Maybe a night or two of sleep would help everyone see the dispute differently. Maybe this process would make a difference in the decision path. I hoped so.

We are all fellow human beings on a large rock that is tumbling through space. I could think of many reasons why we should take better care of this rock and why we should cheerfully share the space we have on this rock with those around us, regardless of how different they are. But at that moment, I had a call to make—and another bill to pay, for which no one can print paper currency.

SECOND THOUGHTS:

All disputes are stew. A stew is a mixture of different ingredients that, in different combinations, produce very different flavors. In this recipe, I've tried to present those ingredients that often emerge in cases involving the flavor of property we call *home*.

Home means some combination of family, security, respite, memories, legacy, and many other ingredients that will emerge in different combinations and intensity as the dispute works through the process. The subject matter of a dispute will probably be emblematic of many other things. While a dispute may look like a smooth sphere or a perfect cube, it will almost always be heavy, bumpy, and uneven and have a gooey center when you break it apart. Put another way, the matters at dispute may become vessels into which the parties pour a concoction of feelings and history—shaken, stirred, or both.

Memory is a lens with interchangeable emotional filters and backlighting. Often, I wonder if the good times were, objectively, as good as they are now recalled, or the bad times as bad as they now seem. I once heard a brilliant lawyer respond after a rigorous discussion of the law, "I no longer think I am as right as I was before this discussion started, but I also don't think I am as wrong as you say I am."

Mediation is a dynamic process. Things morph, change and distort as the process evolves. A skilled mediator develops a set of instruments to measure, weigh, or dissect—as the situation dictates—the problem to resolution (or as close to it as possible).

Mediators invest energy, make sacrifices and accommodations, ask those around us to make sacrifices, and experience a unique sense of loneliness during and after every mediation (even one that ends in settlement), which is hard to understand unless you've been there. It isn't as easy as it looks.

Mediation is especially difficult when it involves homes. Places are critically important to people. Perceived invasions or insults to the place we call home provoke strong, visceral reactions. Psychologists could give us explanations from the hierarchy of needs to the socialization of our species to the reptilian part of our brain, all of which make sense. But the lesson here is what I'll call the Dorothy Rule: There really is no place like home.

12.

The Whistle-Blower: Mediating an Employment Termination Dispute

David A. Hoffman

THE BOOT

Sam Hartnett was not entirely surprised when he was fired from his job as a mid-level manager in the national financial services company where he had worked for six years. A former army sergeant who had retired from military service after twenty years, he had been skirmishing with the upper management of the company for the last several years. Even so, he did not think that they would go so far as to actually give him the boot. He was furious and hired a lawyer to sue the company for wrongful termination.

A Firm Handshake

By the time the case came to me for mediation, the preliminary rounds of litigation had been completed: depositions had been taken, various motions had been filed, and the case was scheduled for trial. Counsel on both sides were well known for their trial work and were looking forward to trying the case.

"I think you'll like Sam," his lawyer said to me privately as we waited for her client and the other parties and counsel to arrive. "I *know* the jury is going to like him."

Sam was the next to arrive, and it was immediately obvious why his lawyer thought he would play well to a jury. Tall, with piercing blue eyes and a lean physique, he looked like a Marlboro man, straight from Central Casting, except for a scar that ran from the side of his right eye to the top of a high cheekbone. When I shook his hand, I tried not to wince: he was evidently one of those people who judges a person by the firmness of his handshake. Belying his crushing grip, however, was a shyness in his smile—a hint of discomfort with social situations.

"I'm Sam Hartnett," he said quietly. "I hope you can help us out today."

"I'll do my best," I said. What a likable guy, I thought to myself, while at the same time trying to hold back a little. I reflected fleetingly on the times that I had been totally taken with one party or another in a mediation only to feel disillusioned when I saw their less appealing sides. "We'll get started as soon as the others arrive."

I showed them to a conference room and returned to my own office to look at the file one more time.

Whistle-Blower Claim

The basis for Sam's claim against the company was his contention that he was a whistle-blower who had been fired unlawfully for complaining about unethical and illegal business practices. For example, in the company's overseas operations, company officials routinely took potential business partners on expensive junkets, which included nightclubs and risqué entertainment. Sam considered such expenditures bribes and was not shy about his accusations.

Sam had been sending blistering emails and memos to his superiors about these practices, and each time his superiors passed the complaints along to the officers of the company. On two occasions, the board of directors had convened an ethics committee to review the assertions of unethical behavior by the company, and each time the company concluded that its practices were sound, both legally and ethically.

Despite these conclusions by people at the highest levels within the company, Sam continued to complain. He was convinced that he was right, they were wrong, and the company could get in trouble if it continued to do business as it was then doing. Sam's seemingly unending stream of memos continued, and so the company put Sam on notice that if he did not stop, he would be fired. Sam strenuously objected; sent another round of emails, this time alleging that the company's efforts to keep him quiet amounted to an illegal scheme to cover up past misdeeds; and was terminated.

SETTLEMENT PROPOSALS

In the mediation, it became clear that Sam was not going to be rehired, nor was he interested in returning to the company. Therefore, the primary issue was what amount the company would pay to settle the claim. The gap between Sam's proposed settlement and the company's was substantial, and both sides appeared to be rather dug in.

I confess that I was feeling frustrated with both sides' intransigence—and, in particular, Sam's. Having mediated and served as counsel in a number of employment cases, it seemed to me that the company's proposals were in a reasonable range based on the facts and circumstances of the case and the magnitude of the alleged damages. Sam had been out of work for about six months but had been receiving unemployment insurance. He was not alleging emotional distress damages; the firing had not led him to see a psychotherapist. When I brought up the subject of therapy in a caucus session, he said that he had not needed to see a therapist because he wasn't depressed; he was merely angry.

Sam's settlement proposal, on the other hand, was—based on my experience—at the very far end of the bell curve of reasonableness. Sam did not seem to care that his proposals were on the high side, and I noticed a judgment welling up inside me. My inner voice was saying: Sam's going to be trouble – he marches to the beat of his own drummer.

Meanwhile, the company was getting fed up with Sam's intransigence about settlement. Two of the company's representatives had flown in from out-of-town offices and felt like the mediation was becoming a gigantic waste of their time. "This is simply *not* a six-figure case," the company's lawyer proclaimed. "Even if a jury agrees with Sam, which I sincerely doubt, there are virtually no damages. Besides, it could be years before he ever sees a dime from a trial, even if he wins, because the appeals court has a huge backlog."

SETTLEMENT CHANCES: NEAR ZERO

In the initial joint session with all parties and counsel present, clenched jaws and fidgety body language told me from the outset that both sides were quite fed up with each other. After two rounds of caucus sessions with each side, in which the parties' proposals barely moved at all, I asked to meet with just counsel in my office.

"Is there any chance we're going to get this case settled?" I asked both lawyers.

Sam's lawyer was the first to respond. She noted that for Sam, the case was personal. She said that Sam was very committed to trying the case because he felt wronged and wanted his day in court. She added that Sam felt that even if he lost, his case would send a message to the company and maybe to people outside the company.

When I asked why they were willing to mediate, the lawyer said that it was because the judge told them to give mediation a try before impaneling a jury and that she had told Sam they had nothing to lose because the company agreed to pay the mediation fee. She looked over at the company's lawyer and nodded with a smile. "This is your nickel. Do you think the case can settle?"

The company's lawyer agreed that there was little likelihood that the case would settle. He noted that Sam gave the company no reason to think that he would be reasonable. And, he added, the company was even angrier about his sky-high settlement proposals than they were about his flaming emails.

I wondered about other possibilities to improve the chances of settlement, such as an apology from either or both sides, a letter of recommendation, or anything else besides an exchange of money.

Both lawyers looked skeptical. Both agreed that no apology would be forthcoming from their client. And Sam's lawyer said that Sam wasn't interested in a letter of recommendation from *that* company.

"Okay," I said. "Let's focus on the money. I want to talk further with each side to see if there might be a bit more flexibility."

GETTING TO KNOW SAM

In a caucus session with Sam and his counsel, we talked about the usual issues. How long would it take to complete the trial? How long if there was an appeal? What would the out-of-pocket costs be for Sam? Would there be expert witnesses on the business ethics issues? Which arguments on each side seemed like the most compelling? Were there any legal precedents that might swing the outcome in one direction or another? Were there other options for settlement besides an exchange of money? None of these questions seemed to move us in a promising direction.

Then I looked over Sam's résumé, which was one of the exhibits in the case. I wondered about his twenty years of military service prior to his employment at the company.

I asked if he'd been in combat. Sam said that his unit saw a lot of combat. He described his service in the Army with intensity. He had served in Vietnam. He had made friends and lost friends there.

"I left Vietnam," he said, "with a lot of scars, both inside and out. But the thing I liked about the Army is that everybody turns square corners. You can count on your buddies to watch your back. You know what the rules are, and people obey them because your life depends on it."

Then he compared the army to his former employer, his only job since leaving the Army. He noted that when he retired from the Army, he immediately went into the private sector and felt like he was entering a foreign territory. "There was no code to follow. It seemed to me like 'anything goes.' You know—whatever you can get away with. It's just wrong."

Sam got more animated as he spoke and then became calmer. I could see the proverbial light bulb switching on over his head. "I think I wound up in the wrong place," he said. "I should have stuck with the Army." I asked Sam if he was thinking about going back to the Army. He said that he probably wouldn't do that but that he needed a job more like the military—"working with people who care about rules and believe in following them."

An Unexpected Offer

We turned to the subject of settlement offers. I stood at the whiteboard in the conference room and jotted down the offers and counteroffers that had been made that day.

Sam proposed moderating his demand by a considerable margin, and his lawyer agreed. I was astonished, while trying hard not to show it. I looked over at the lawyer. "This is Sam's call," his lawyer said. They authorized me to communicate their offer, which I was confident would be viewed as reasonable by the other side.

I walked down the hall to the conference room in which the company's representatives and counsel sat. "What took you so long in there?" the company's lawyer asked. "We thought you might have given up on this case."

"No settlement before it's time," I said, but there was not much appetite for humor in the room.

I gave them Sam's proposal and noticed the surprised looks on faces trying hard to be inscrutable. They glanced at each other, not sure how to respond. The company's lawyer wondered what I had done and why Sam was being so reasonable all of a sudden.

I reminded them that my conversations with each side are confidential, but I did say that Sam thought it over carefully and just wanted to move on.

The company's lawyer asked me to step out of the room for a few minutes so that he and his clients could digest this sudden progress in private. When they invited me back in, they explained their counteroffer.

"We're willing to pay him 90 percent of his proposed settlement, but it will come out the same after taxes because we will pay a third of the settlement directly to his lawyer for attorney fees. That way, Sam won't have to pay taxes on that portion. We've done this in other cases. The math works. He'll be getting the same amount either way, but this way the company can save a few bucks.

When I returned to meet separately with Sam and his lawyer, they quickly agreed with the company's approach.

READY TO MOVE ON

Ordinarily, I would reconvene all of the parties and their lawyers to discuss the settlement, congratulate the parties, and help them reach genuine closure. But Sam did not want to see the other side. "I'm ready to move on," he said. "This money will help me transition, but I really do *not* want to see those guys."

I asked the lawyers from both sides to meet with me again in my office. We hammered out a brief terms sheet on my laptop, and I printed it out. The company's lawyer agreed to write up the formal settlement agreement within a week. I waited in my office while the lawyers showed a copy of the terms sheet to their respective clients. We then exchanged signed copies, one for each side and one for me.

The company agreed that a final joint session was unnecessary. They were already packing up their briefcases when I walked in to meet with them separately. I thanked them for their hard work and patience and wished them a safe journey home.

"I'm not sure how you got Sam to see reason," the company's lawyer commented. "But whatever you did in there, we're grateful."

"Sometimes," I said to them, "the logic of a situation just unfolds in its own way. Both sides needed to be reasonable in order to get the job done."

I returned to meet with Sam and his lawyer. I told him that I was glad that he and the company were able to resolve the situation.

Sam was glad, too. He said that the whole situation had been eating him up and that it was all he'd thought about for many months. He added that it had been hard on his wife, too; she'd been worried about the way that the case had consumed him. He told me how much he appreciated what I had done.

Then he reached out his hand. This time I was prepared. "You know, Sam," I said as we parted, "you've got a really firm handshake. I like that about a guy."

He looked at me sheepishly. "Thank you," he said.

Second Thoughts:

My impression is that Sam acquired insight about himself in the caucus session when his strongly held ideas were considered from different angles, especially the angle of comparing his private-sector employer to the Army. He left the mediation with a settlement agreement under which he received a payment of his legal fees and a portion of back wages. More importantly, he left with a greater understanding about what went wrong when his expectations about how the company should act collided with the norms that twenty years of military service had instilled in him. As we wrapped up the paperwork from the mediation, he said to me, "I am much clearer now about the kind of job I'm going to look for."

Mediations do not always result in such satisfying settlements. Sam's case has stuck with me over the years for four reasons.

First, I learned something about the value of caucusing. I don't think Sam and I could have done the personal exploration of his military service in a joint session setting. Caucuses create opportunities for personal engagement that are often absent in joint sessions. Sam and I, with his lawyer participating at times, got up close and personal in a way that the glare of joint sessions makes far more challenging. If commercial and employment mediations took place over the course of several days or if the parties were collectively comfortable with deeply personal discussions, perhaps caucuses would not be needed in order to have the conversation that led to Sam's settlement. But the legal marketplace typically allocates a day for cases like Sam's, and achieving comfort with personal disclosures in joint sessions, as opposed to caucus sessions, rarely happens in such a limited span of time.

Second, I rediscovered the value of simple curiosity. I am not sure what led me to inquire about Sam's military service. Perhaps I was feeling stuck and was simply fishing for something to talk about. I do recall feeling genuinely curious about Sam's life experiences and perspectives. And there is certainly a voyeuristic element in mediation: mediators get to see in a more intimate way what makes the world work and what makes people tick. Mediation often opens a door into personal material that is available to no one else but therapists, clergy, spouses, and the closest of friends—and sometimes not even *they* are invited in.

Third, I learned a lesson taught in Viktor Frankl's book *Man's Search for Meaning*—namely, that people sometimes act in ways that are contrary to their material interest because of a belief in some higher value or meaning. For Sam, adherence to ethical principles was more important than keeping his job. It was not my place to judge whether he or the company was right about those principles. Indeed, any judgment that I might make in that regard would have impaired my effectiveness as a mediator. It was my place, however, to listen respectfully to Sam's perspective and, in doing so, to honor his commitment to principle.

Finally, I was reminded of the power of mediation to change people. Even when a settlement does not result in a "kumbaya" moment involving tears, forgiveness, hugs, and heartfelt reconciliation, mediation can be personally transformative as each participant—including the mediator—engages in some valuable learning and personal growth. One of my mediation colleagues, psychologist and mediator Richard Wolman, often says that mediation is not therapy but that it can be therapeutic. Sam and I helped each other in this mediation. In my private conversation with Sam and his lawyer, Sam found his way to a new understanding of his values, how important they are to him, and how they can also get him into trouble at times. His tenacity and commitment to principle gave me a new appreciation of how complex and idealistic we human beings can be and what a rare privilege it is to be invited into a conversation with people each day about what matters most to them—and to us.

13.
The Bad Boy Who Almost Got Away

Jan Frankel Schau

AN UNWARRANTED SHOOTING

Josh came to the mediation in baggy blue jeans and a borrowed button-down shirt. His head was shaven, but his most visible tattoos were covered. He was a nervous mess, and he avoided eye contact for the entire hearing.

Here was the story his lawyer told: The police were lying about the circumstances of the shooting. Josh was not, as they alleged, resisting arrest, but in flight when the policeman shot him in the leg. This was a violation of Josh's civil rights, and even though a convicted felon for the theft of a car on the day in question, the city police had no right to shoot a man who was not an immediate threat to their own safety.

THE PLAINTIFF'S STORY

Josh's lawyer, Guido, was a small Hispanic man with a gold cap on his front tooth and a mismatched suit. He spoke with an accent that was more akin to street slang in Los Angeles than the usual courtroom vocabulary heard in the halls of my offices. Guido had been brought into the case by Josh's main counsel, a very well-known and respected civil rights advocate, after the deposition.

Guido presented Josh's case somewhat compellingly. His client had committed a crime by hot-wiring and taking a car. When the police approached him, Josh, at age twenty-two, got scared, exited the vehicle, and took off over a brick wall to hide from arrest. The police called after him, but he refused to turn around. Although it is true that when he exited the vehicle, he had in his hand the metal tool that he used to start the car, he had to drop it on the grass of the home before he attempted to scale the wall. The police tried to catch him but were unable to do so. Thus, one of them shot him in the leg. Once he was on the ground, they punched him repeatedly; demanded that he roll over onto the ground; and then, before calling an ambulance, wrote a report alleging that he was charging at them with this metal object, which they took to be a deadly weapon.

Josh did not exactly cut a sympathetic figure. He was clean-shaven but a little rough-looking. He was baby-faced, but there was a distance in his eyes and he never smiled. He had dropped out of high school and had never really held a job. He had fathered two children but wasn't living with their mother and had not yet married. His last job was part-time at a fast-food chain at minimum wage. In fact, he had never earned more than $15,000 in a year and did not financially support his children. It wasn't clear how he supported himself. Still, he had no criminal record before this car theft, nor was there any evidence of substance abuse or domestic violence. The young man just seemed lost.

THE DEFENSE STORY

In the other caucus room was Mr. Walker, a very tall, thin Caucasian lawyer who was extremely smooth and confident, together with a claims adjuster who had flown out to Los Angeles from the Midwest to try to "adjust this claim." They were very stern and very clear.

The dynamic between the defense attorney and the adjuster was particularly interesting. The adjuster's company had flown the adjuster to Los Angeles in time to meet the lawyer for dinner the night before the hearing. The adjuster had, of course, discussed the case with his own supervisors as well as outside counsel and had carefully analyzed the prospects for a defense verdict, the likely costs of handling the case for four more months before the trial, and the adverse verdict range potential. After traveling for a full day, checking into his hotel, and renting a car with a navigation system that would be adequate to make his way to downtown Los Angeles and then the next day to Century City, the adjuster cared more about a cocktail than the details of the evidence or the strategies for settling the case at the hearing. Nonetheless, the two men did discuss the case and didn't disagree with one another's financial analysis on the eve of the mediation.

The defense team felt that the facts were on its side: There were three police officers who investigated and reported this incident involving Josh. All of them had not only previously testified but had withstood internal investigations. All of them concurred that this young man, now a convicted felon, had been resisting arrest and came at them with a potentially deadly weapon. The shooting was absolutely justified; there were no medical bills (he had the surgery while incarcerated and recovered while serving time for the crime).

Here's what they were thinking: The jury was extremely unlikely to believe a convicted felon when three sworn officers would contradict his testimony. Although the plaintiff's main counsel had an incredibly good record for obtaining large verdicts in civil rights cases, he had shown little interest in this case and was unlikely to push for a sensationalized trial.

The prospects for a defense verdict, according to the defense team's analysis, were better than 80 percent. On the other hand, outside counsel would have to spend some time preparing the three witnesses and taking the deposition of the plaintiff and spend some money retaining probably two high-end experts to testify about the ballistics and the medical treatment and recovery. The cost of taking this case to trial would be at least $30,000, and there was no prospect for recovering any of it even if the city got a defense verdict.

As to the adverse verdict range, that would be harder to assess. The plaintiff had no special damages as his treatment was all paid for by the state during his incarceration. He had no lost wages since he was serving time during the two years since the incident. He did have a small scar where the bullet had entered and (on the opposite side of his lower leg) exited. But he also had tattoos covering much of his lower limbs, so the scarring could hardly be a justification for a large damage verdict. According to this analysis, the defendants couldn't imagine this case getting a verdict over $100,000 for the plaintiff.

Armed with this thorough analysis, and after the first rounds of scotch and soda, the adjuster told Mr. Walker that they had put a cap for settlement purposes on this matter at $50,000, but he urged the attorney to "bring it in" at about $35,000. In other words, no offers beyond a minimal nuisance value would be forthcoming.

BALLISTICS EVIDENCE

Back in the plaintiff's room, I asked about the physical evidence of the gunshot wound. Apparently, nobody had investigated the case enough to get full medical records. What they did have was the operative report. It showed that the bullet went through Josh's leg at an angle, likely entering at the back of his leg and angling upward, exiting the front of his leg just below the knee.

Guido tried to persuade me that the only way this made sense is if Josh was midway up the wall when the shot was fired. Otherwise, the policeman would have had to take a shot while he was on his knees in order to strike the young man's lower leg at such an angle. He stood up and demonstrated as though he were shooting me. The physics made sense to me.

I went to the defense counsel and demonstrated what I'd just seen: I asked Mr. Walker to stand. Then I posed as though I had a gun in my hand, put two hands on the gun, and aimed at the defense counsel. I was at least eight inches shorter than the defense counsel, so it was easier for me to shoot him in the lower leg; still, it was pretty evident that the trajectory of the bullet would not have pierced his lower leg if I were in a standing position. Nonetheless, the police department had fully investigated these officers, as they were required to do in any shooting case, and had exonerated them from any wrongdoing. Maybe the gun slipped; maybe he was jumping up; or maybe he fell onto the ground and then scurried to get back up, metal object in hand. Certainly, the evidence from the investigative hearing was compelling.

Officer Abel had testified that he and his partner, Officer Bay, had responded to a call regarding a stolen vehicle at 0300 that Tuesday morning. They cruised around the area; and just as they were about to go on a break, they saw the vehicle parked in a residential cul-de-sac with lights off. They carefully approached the vehicle and were surprised that the alleged car thief was inside. Quickly, the young man exited the car and fled by foot. Officer Bay took off to chase him while Officer Abel called for backup. By the time the officers confronted Josh in the backyard of one of the residences, Officer Carroll had joined them on the scene. All three of the officers shouted to the young car thief, "Stop! Police! Get down on the ground!" Josh not only resisted but also, according to their sworn testimony and statements as well as the police report, came at them with a sharp metal object and refused to comply with their orders. It was then that they shot him in the lower leg and completed the arrest.

Back in the plaintiff's room, Guido showed me photos of the outside of the residence where the arrest was made and where the shooting happened. For the first time, the young man spoke up. He described the events of that night: He was scared. He'd never been arrested before and didn't know what to do. He tried to run. He found himself cornered by three policemen in a residential cul-de-sac. He tried desperately to climb over a brick wall and continue to run. He heard the gunshot before realizing it was his own leg that had been shot. He fell to the ground and cried out, "I got shot! I got shot!" The police officers screamed at him to turn over and face the ground. He couldn't move and cried out to them, "I can't move! I'm shot! I'm shot!"

The policemen presented none of this evidence when they were interviewed or investigated by Internal Affairs. Instead, all three officers presented a consistent story suggesting that Josh fell down from the wall he was attempting to scale, scurried toward the officers with the metal tool he'd used to start the car, and was shot by the officers as they were defending themselves against great bodily harm.

There was also the police report, which was completely consistent with the officers' testimony at the Internal Affairs hearing: Josh fell off the wall and then came at the officers with a sharp metal object. The shooting was both necessary and justifiable.

THE NEGOTIATION DANCE

After several hours, the defense side asked for a concrete demand to settle the case, still intending to offer only nuisance value. The initial demand was $450,000. The initial offer in response was $15,000.

As the day wore on, Josh became both agitated and removed. There was something about him that seemed disinterested in this case. He explained to me that he had two young children, ages three and one, he was unmarried, and he was looking for work but was uneducated and unemployed. I felt that he wasn't entirely forthcoming. By midday, I had the strong impression that the young man would have taken any offer adequate to pay his lawyer and costs in order to avoid having to go back into a courtroom in the city in which he was arrested. Josh was concerned that the local police would retaliate against him if he won this trial and sensationalized both the violent act and cover-up of evidence that he was shot while fleeing the scene of the crime. By age twenty-two, he had been shot, had surgery, been convicted of a felony, served prison time, and faced a completely uncertain future. In short, he genuinely feared the force that was designed to protect its citizens.

The next demand came from the defendants. The officers were not present, but their lawyer was hired to preserve and protect their professional reputation, not just the city coffers, in a settlement. He was righteously indignant about the officers having been individually named. They had already overcome a full investigation and their names had been exonerated. They would offer something more than $15,000—

they didn't specify what—if and only if the plaintiff would agree that at the end of the day if a settlement were achieved, he would dismiss his claims against the individual officers with prejudice and all settlement money would be paid on behalf of the city alone. Not surprisingly, the plaintiff agreed.

Still, the plaintiff's attorney was conservative with his negotiation moves, fearing that this was but a ruse by the defendants to get a cheap deal struck. Next demand: $425,000.

At this point, the plaintiff's attorney reminded me that there was a timely irony that the defendants hadn't taken into consideration yet. Recently, a certain city had been all over the news for corruption of its city political leaders. Although not the same city as the city in which this case was taking place, the name of the other city and its geographical location were strikingly similar. If the jury became confused, this could end up being a runaway verdict in the high six figures.

I returned to the defense caucus room with the reduced (but still very inflated) demand of $425,000 and the suggestion that the recent corruption in the similarly named city might cause confusion in a local jury. The defendants began to see that this matter had the potential of being problematic to their municipality. The plaintiff, if believed, could indeed garner a verdict higher than they had assessed. Offer: $25,000.

It appeared that the matter was not going to be easily resolved by distributive bargaining. It was getting late in the day in the Midwest, which was two hours later than the West Coast, where the mediation was taking place, so I asked Mr. Walker to confer with his principal about reevaluating their reserves and being conferred a much higher level of authority to bargain.

BRACKET BOUNDARIES

As I do in many cases where the parties are too far apart to get to a midpoint by a back-and-forth negotiation, I asked each side to consider the confines of a comfortable bracket. The defense side, which had initially evaluated the case with a value of $35,000 to $50,000, proposed a bracket of $35,000 to $100,000. The plaintiff's lawyer, who insisted that he would get a verdict of at least six figures even with a convicted felon as his client, asked for a bracket of $250,000 to $400,000.

It was time for some creative moves. One of the ways to do this is to change the dynamic of the negotiation. I was obviously not getting through to Mr. Walker as effectively as I thought Guido might. Mr. Walker and Guido had not met yet. Once together, I asked the two lawyers to communicate outside of their clients' presence about the range that they would feel comfortable recommending to their clients so that we could at least get into a bracket and begin negotiating in earnest. I never know how these private joint sessions are going to go, but in this instance I thought that the plaintiff's lawyer was slightly intimidated by the defense lawyer. He had tears in his eyes when he pleaded with Mr. Walker to "take care of this kid." There was something genuine and raw about his emotions in that room.

Mr. Walker calmly explained that there was no possibility that his client would ever pay more than $100,000 on this case, but Guido wasn't willing to accept that he could never get this case settled at a fair range in the six figures. At the end, they both agreed to discuss with their respective clients a range that would be $50,000 to $250,000. Progress.

BENDING THE CURVE

In the predictable arc of negotiation, this case should have settled a couple of hours later for about $150,000. But this was not the case. The defendants had several bankers' boxes full of evidence exonerating the police from misconduct. The plaintiff was a convicted felon. The case threatened to impasse at the very next move.

After the negotiation of the bracket, the plaintiff's side made a demand of $245,000. The defendants authorized me to take back an offer of $60,000 with the message that this was already well beyond their initial evaluation and perilously close to their ultimate stopping point. Although the midpoint again pointed to a settlement in the midhundreds, Mr. Walker remained adamant that he would not be able to get a settlement approved by the city counsel unless it was under $100,000.

The response, after a lot of prodding, was that if the defendants would get into the $100,000 to $200,000 range, the plaintiff's side would continue to negotiate. The plaintiff moved to $225,000 but authorized me to communicate that any offer above $100,000 would get a response under $200,000. Otherwise, the plaintiff was prepared to try the case. By this time, Guido had told me that he had calculated that he would likely have to dip below $200,000, but under no circumstances would he agree to go below $195,000. The case had real value before a jury, and "the kid" deserved better, he said.

After about an hour on the phone and conducting a roundtable, the defense team could not wrap its arms around a settlement of this case over $100,000. Instead, the team offered $75,000 and asked me to let the plaintiff know that the defense had only one more move and then would have to resume litigation. The initial evaluation had put a $50,000 lid on this case. The defense team would only move again if it knew that the plaintiff would accept $80,000.

In an effort to get to that very highest offer, the plaintiff's side responded to the $75,000 offer with a demand of $195,000. The defendants countered with $85,000 and started packing up for the day. The case truly did appear to be headed toward an impasse.

At that point, I spoke with Mr. Walker again privately. For the first time that day (by now it was evening), he confided in me that the version of the incident that the plaintiff had presented that morning made sense to him and that he feared there was not only a potential for a plaintiff verdict but a real possibility that if he didn't succeed in settling the case, the city could get a verdict against it that included punitive damages, the first in its history. What's more, Mr. Walker's law partner was the city attorney; and if his firm represented the defense and lost this case, it could reflect terribly on the all defense players involved for all the wrong reasons. Still, Mr. Walker's hands were tied as he now had succeeded in getting the client to more than double the hoped-for outcome.

The kernel of possibility that I heard in this conversation was that anything that was agreed upon as a settlement would need to be approved by the city council and that the city would likely reject anything over $100,000. Still, this gave me hope.

After explaining this procedural dilemma (without revealing the lawyer's own analysis, of course), Guido and Josh finally agreed to reduce their demand to $150,000. They asked me to urge Mr. Walker to recommend that as a settlement to the city council rather than a lower figure.

In a couple more moves, the defendants did agree to recommend $125,000 and told me that would be their final offer, and it was uncertain whether they would get that authority as they only had authority for $85,000 on the day of the hearing. At that time, the plaintiff was at a firm $150,000. When I believed that they meant it, I turned to Josh and helped him to understand what $125,000 could buy for him and his young family: a chance for Josh to go back to school without having to work for two years, babysitting twice a week during that time, and nursery school for the kids when they were ready. A chance to start over.

For the first time all day, Josh looked me in the eye and said, "Could you see if you can get $130,000?"

POSTSCRIPT

The case did settle for $130,000. As Josh got up to leave and I shook his hand, I couldn't resist the chance to express the fact that I hoped he would never need to come back—that he would never find himself in another entanglement with police based upon his own conduct or theirs.

As I congratulated Guido and shook his hand as well, I noticed that each of his knuckles had a tattoo on it. I must have looked quizzical because he chuckled and explained to me that those tattoos were the story behind why he took this case and felt so passionately about Josh's rights.

Guido then proceeded to tell me his own life story. He began by laughing in a self-deprecating way, saying: "I been in a lot more trouble than him by the time I was his age." Guido was a juvenile offender and was sent off to juvenile detention camps as a very young teen. He was a member of the street gang in Los Angeles whose symbols were tattooed on his knuckles.

But instead of letting him get away, the federal government singled him out as a part of a social experiment that took place in the 1980s. His IQ was tested, along with every other juvenile in detention across the country. It turned out that Guido placed among the top 5 percent, so he was offered a challenge and an opportunity.

The government agreed to assign mentors to such convicted criminals to encourage them to pursue an education with the hope that they could overcome their criminal pasts. Guido was required to meet with a small group of about thirty other juveniles and their mentors monthly until he received his GED. Then he was given a full scholarship to a state university, where he was required to maintain a certain grade point average and to meet with his own mentor monthly throughout his four years of college. Guido graduated with honors from the California state system, with two bachelor's degrees in four years. He applied to law school in his senior year and was admitted to the bar three years later.

Guido, like his young client, was a bad boy who almost got away. Thankfully for both Guido and Josh, the federal government had the foresight to look deeper into the facts and circumstances and not give up hope for a better future.

SECOND THOUGHTS:

Oftentimes, we don't know what motivates a particular person to react to a particular set of events by choosing to seek a lawyer and then sue. In the same auto accident, one victim may choose to get medical treatment, one may seek out legal help, and another may go to church that weekend and thank God that he wasn't killed. Most of us manage to get through life without ever being involved in a lawsuit. Whether it's the messy entanglement of business, professional dealings, marriages, or even traffic on the highways, in most interpersonal encounters, people are able to communicate and either get what they want or agree to give up on getting full satisfaction in every encounter. Those that become involved in lawsuits are a special segment of the population who are unable to resolve their conflicts at the interpersonal level.

Most attorneys who are engaged to help their clients get what they believe to be theirs (or keep what someone else wants from them) make an initial attempt to resolve the dispute before it escalates to litigation. And once a lawsuit is filed, most modern courts encourage or demand that the attorneys try again to resolve the dispute that neither they nor their clients could settle before that time.

Naturally, this brings us to mediation. For those who are unable to get the relief they demand and unwilling to let the dispute go, there are mediators. The disputes that we mediators hear share two challenging qualities: the parties themselves have been unable to persuasively articulate their grievances and the lawyers whom they engaged to represent them disagree upon the facts, law, or value of damages (or all three).

With these thoughts in mind, it's fascinating to examine the various participants in mediation to try to discern what drives each of them toward settlement or perpetuation of the conflict. In this case, it wasn't until the end of the mediation that I learned of Guido's personal history, which was clearly a most dramatic motivator for representing Josh in this dispute. On the other side, the defense lawyer had his own strong motivations for getting the case settled in order to preserve his partner's position as city attorney, a position that technically gave him the responsibility for assuring that the Internal Affairs investigation was conducted thoroughly and the outcome was reached with integrity. The adjuster, on the other hand, was not as interested or motivated to settle the case as he was to please his supervisor by sticking to the initial evaluation. He had limited authority in every sense of the word and simply couldn't exceed it under any circumstances. Josh, the plaintiff, was not the driving force in this matter. He was, to use a metaphor, already "shot down." Whether he got a settlement of $15,000 or $150,000 that day would not have changed the fact that he had a felony conviction, had served time, had suffered a gunshot wound to his leg, and had no means of supporting himself or his two children.

One of the keys to resolving this dispute was gaining the trust of both sides. Some of this trust was gained early on, which enabled me to get small concessions (such as an early agreement not to pursue the individual officers for money if the case was settled). Those small concessions were celebrated as gestures of cooperation and goodwill.

The other key to resolving this dispute was finding a way to communicate that I had genuine respect for each participant's unique perspective. Sometimes it's difficult to find a reason for showing respect—for example, in situations when a person has committed evil acts that resulted in the mediation—but I find that if I dig deep enough, there is almost always some basic good in everybody. For example, I have found myself talking about geographic landmarks with a convicted pedophile who was being sued for violating a restraining order in the neighborhood where I went to high school. I have found myself conducting a mediation in Spanish for the benefit of six illegal aliens facing deportment after giving their "notario" over $20,000 on the pretense that he could get them citizenship. And I have found myself asking to see photos of the baby that was born to a receptionist who, after ten months' leave of absence and then being terminated from her job, was seeking damages that were four times what I made annually as a new lawyer (at the same age with a baby at home!).

Communicating genuine respect for other's perspectives involves going back to the seeds of the conflict and trying to assess what went wrong. What was or was not communicated that would have made the other party understand the needs or hurts of the other? What does each party need to feel whole and valued and respected? What and who are driving the conflict, and who is standing in the way of letting it go? How does this get resolved while preserving the dignity of all parties in a way that the courthouse can't?

Ultimately, both the delight and the dilemma of the business of mediation is that everybody has a unique story. Once you've gained the trust of the participants, they are usually glad to share their stories. And once you've heard those stories, there is usually something that reveals not only the reasons that they were unable to fully communicate their issues, which led them into the dispute in the first place, but also the ways in which they can improve their communication and thus achieve a satisfying resolution.

14.
Random Conversation

Margaret Shaw

THE ASKING PRICE

We started the mediation promptly at 9:00 a.m.
George claimed that he was a victim of his company's downsizing because of a complaint of discrimination he had lodged earlier with Human Resources. He was in a bad spot. He found himself out of a job in a tough economy. A tall, lanky man, he had a wife and child. And he was angry about the situation in which he found himself.

To compensate for what he had decided could only constitute retaliation, he demanded many years of annual compensation and benefits totaling about $375,000. The company, for its part, adamant that they had not singled out George, was willing to pay only a few months of compensation and some outplacement, totaling roughly $25,000.

A FEW WORDS WITH GEORGE

At one point in the early afternoon, as the company representatives were conferring at length amongst themselves, I was walking the halls and ran into George sitting on a bench outside the room to which he had been assigned. I sat down with him and began to chat, asking him more about his family, where he lived, and what he liked to do when he wasn't working. Among other things, George told me that he liked fixing up his house and that he had a pretty large mortgage on his house—about $140,000. He then he went on to tell me about his two daughters.

NOT ONE MORE CENT

The company representatives called me back in, and the mediation progressed, steadily but painfully. By mid to late afternoon frustrations were running high on both sides of the table. On the one hand, the company representatives had been pushed to a dollar amount that was higher than the amount they had initially been authorized to offer. And, on the other hand, the employee felt chiseled by the company to which he had devoted a number of years of service. The hour was getting late.

The company representatives finally agreed to put $145,000 on the table but told me in no uncertain terms that they were done. They would not pay a penny more.

When I reported this to George, he was very upset. He had dropped during the day from $375,000 to $175,000! Now he was being asked to drop even further? He was feeling very uncomfortably squeezed.

A NEW PERSPECTIVE

Suddenly lightning struck! I remembered my previous conversation with George that morning about his child, his house and his mortgage. "You know George," I said, "if you accept the company's offer, you know what that will mean? That will mean that you can pay off your mortgage!" George perked up a bit, thought about the offer for a while, and ultimately decided to accept it.

It was a wonderful moment when theory met practice. Never have I forgotten the lesson of reframing a proposal so that it can be experienced as a gain rather than a loss, thus avoiding loss aversion. I have also continued to try to find opportunities to chat with parties during my mediations to learn more about their lives and circumstances.

SECOND THOUGHTS:

Decision-making concerning settlement in mediation is multidimensional. A totally rational model would have parties making decisions based solely on their chances of prevailing at trial. But as numerous commentators have pointed out, decision making in this context also has strong psychological and emotional components. Understanding this and paying attention to the wider personal universe in which parties find themselves, however seemingly random that information might at first blush appear, can often provide valuable building blocks for settlement.

We often hear presentations at conferences and other meetings of alternative dispute resolution professionals about psychological concepts that affect decision making in negotiation and mediation. Loss aversion is high up on the list, i.e., the concept that people ordinarily will go to much greater lengths to avoid a loss than they will to achieve a gain. I, like many mediators, absorbed this given wisdom intellectually, and went about my mediation practice pretty much as I always had, crossing my fingers when the moment came that the parties either got to yes or reached impasse. George provided an important lesson for me in applying theory to practice.

PART V

Staying in the Middle Without Judgment or Favoritism

Judge not.

"Only connect . . ."

E. M. Forster, Howards End

15.
Compassion in Action

Eleanor Barr

An Unexpected Defense

It was a regular Tuesday night, and I was preparing for a mediation of an employment matter. I had mediated previously with the lawyers on both sides—both men in their fifties, both seasoned lawyers and negotiators. I read the plaintiff's brief, and it seemed as if I would be embarking upon a garden-variety sexual harassment and pregnancy discrimination lawsuit.

But when I read the defendant's brief, I was startled. Instead of focusing on the facts, the defense brief discussed at length the young woman plaintiff's lifestyle: she was promiscuous, she subsequently became pregnant by one of her two boyfriends, her life was in chaos, and now she was trying to get money from the defendant to pay for her poor choices. In short, the defense was putting forward the classic "loose woman" defense.

Now, as a woman, this defense pushed just about every button in my book. Like the plaintiff, I remembered what it was like to be in my twenties and trying to make my way in my profession. When I complained about my contracts professor's sexual advances toward me, for example, I was told that I had a crush on him, as if his inappropriate behavior were somehow my fault. But I knew that in order to be effective in this mediation, I would have to make a conscious choice to not act out of my own biases and to remain truly neutral.

To make things even more interesting, the defendant was a Sri Lankan man of Indian descent. Having lived in India myself during my twenties to study yoga, I suspected that deep-seated cultural differences might be playing a part in the conflict as well.

PREPARATION: TEXTUAL AND SUBTEXTUAL

I set aside the briefs and thought about how to approach the mediation. If my time in India taught me anything—all those hours practicing yoga and studying Indian philosophy—it was that compassion is a critical part of any true healing. And my experience as a mediator had taught me that developing a true, compassionate connection with each participant in the case, including the lawyers, not only helped me remain neutral but often led to settlement—and sometimes even to a bit more peace of mind for everyone.

My attitude of compassionate connection—and all the cultural, spiritual, and sometimes personal ideas that informed it—would never be made explicit to the participants. It was simply how I prepared my own mind for the rigors of mediation. Put another way, it was, for me, the "subtext" of the mediation, with the "text" being largely about facts, law, risk/benefit analysis, and, ultimately, money.

THE PLAINTIFF'S STORY: AN ILL-FATED BUSINESS TRIP

I began the mediation with the plaintiff, Catherine, and her lawyer. Catherine was an attractive, likable, enthusiastic woman in her mid-twenties who worked as a manager of a boutique hotel. She sued the hotel and the owner, Sam, claiming that he sexually harassed her and that after she confronted him about the harassment, he retaliated against her by reducing her salary. Catherine also claimed that Sam subsequently discriminated against her by discharging her after she told him that she was pregnant.

Catherine alleged that Sam lured her to San Francisco on a purported business trip and then made the trip into a date, replete with dinner, a show at a strip club, a failed kiss, and an attempt to spend the night in her hotel room. She claimed to have felt trapped by her boss in San Francisco and was devastated by the setup.

After laying out the basics, Catherine and her lawyer went into the details. Catherine was hired originally as a front desk supervisor, but Sam, who owned various hotels in the area, quickly promoted her to manager. When Sam asked Catherine to join him on a trip to San Francisco to help make choices about the decor of a hotel he was planning to open there—and even indicated that Catherine would manage his new San Francisco venture—Catherine jumped at the opportunity.

Sam told her that he would give her a room at the hotel and that he would be staying in the apartment he leased there. He also told her not to tell anyone at the hotel about the trip because other employees would like this position and he didn't want to upset them. Catherine agreed not to say anything to the other employees.

They flew to San Francisco and took a cab to her hotel. Since they were running late for dinner, Sam asked if he could leave his bag in her hotel room rather than go to his apartment first, and Catherine agreed. At the restaurant, Sam told her that he and his wife were unhappy in their marriage. He then took Catherine to a "show," which turned out to be a topless performance, something that made Catherine very uncomfortable.

After the show, Sam invited Catherine to a bar. When she told him that she didn't want to go, Sam insisted, saying that he wanted her to study the bar as an example of the decor for the new hotel. At the bar, he tried to dance with Catherine and then tried to kiss her. Catherine, upset, pushed him away and ran into the bathroom.

After gaining her composure, Catherine told Sam that she wanted to be taken back to her hotel. When they arrived at her hotel, Sam said he needed to get his bag out of her room. As he entered her room,

Catherine went straight to bathroom and stayed there, waiting for him to leave. But Sam did not leave. Instead, he lay down on one of the beds and turned on the TV. Reluctantly, Catherine emerged from the bathroom and asked him when he planned on leaving, and he said right after the TV show. She lay down on the other bed with her face to the wall. At some point during the night, Sam left.

The following week, upon their return from San Francisco, Catherine told Sam that what he did to her was wrong and that he should never do that again. He apologized to her.

But the following week, he reduced her salary; and a few months later when she told him she was pregnant, he fired her.

In the room, I summarized Catherine's story to be sure that she knew I'd heard it, and I acknowledged how difficult it must have been to be in that situation with her boss.

As we discussed how to begin the negotiation, I knew that as a result of my own experience as a woman, I already had a compassionate connection to Catherine. I remembered that in my twenties, I, like the plaintiff, dated a variety of men. In our culture, this period of dating was considered a normal exploration as we chose our mate.

THE DEFENDANT'S STORY: A LOOSE WOMAN

When I went to the defense room, I went not only with a dollar number to begin the negotiation but also with an informed curiosity about Sam and his position.

Sam was a middle aged man with a pleasant demeanor. For his part, Sam didn't entirely deny the plaintiff's allegations. But instead of focusing on the facts, the defense brief discussed at length Catherine's lifestyle: her life was a mess, she slept around, she had a baby with one boyfriend and now was living with another boyfriend, and she was suing him to get money to take care of her baby. He asserted that she was lying about what happened in San Francisco and that he never came on to her.

At that point, it was very clear to me that the plaintiff and the defendant were coming from very different cultural orientations, and I suspected that this cultural difference may have contributed to the misunderstanding. She was from America, a low-context culture where people generally mean what they say and where there is little subtext or code that one needs to decipher. He was from India, a high-context culture where people are not as explicit and where they extrapolate meaning from subtext and code. I knew that in India, where marriages are often arranged by the parents, a woman who dates or lives with a man is considered "loose." To Sam, a young unmarried woman who was not living with her family, had multiple boyfriends, and agreed to go alone to San Francisco with him had made a "coded" statement that she was willing to be with him sexually on this trip.

I chose to keep this cultural perspective to myself and use it only as a way to shift my own consciousness: to understand—and feel some compassion for—the defendant, who was mistakenly acting out of his own cultural bias.

I summarized Sam's perspective without judgment, and Sam relaxed a bit after I let him know that I understood his story. I never explicitly stated that he might be seeing the situation with a different cultural lens.

THE DYNAMICS INVOLVED WITH COUNSEL

I also took time to connect with the litigators, too, because they were experiencing the conflict in a particular way as well. They were the ones who were fighting the battle for their clients and thus dealing with a whole range of dynamics and emotions. Was the client paying? Was the client unreasonable, perhaps even lying? Was there a barrage of endless motions and discovery disputes? Was there a conflict between the values of the lawyer and the values of the client?

By the time this case got to mediation, the lawyers had each focused so thoroughly on his client's position and fought so many battles for his client, that each lawyer had now projected his perception of the opposing party on the opposing lawyer. The lawyers' communication was rife with hostility and distrust.

When hostility and distrust dominate a relationship, the parties tend to act from the fight-or-flight response, and meaningful dialogue becomes impossible. I began this process first by making a connection with each lawyer and letting him know that I wasn't judging him personally. This was especially important in the case of the defense lawyer, whom I knew well enough to know that the legally irrelevant arguments in his brief—the so-called loose woman arguments—were not what he wanted to be remembered for. He had to make those arguments because both the facts and the law were not in his client's favor; he did not advocate the behavior. From my own days as a litigator, I could relate to the predicament that a lawyer finds himself in when he is expected to ignore parts of his value system in order to zealously represent his client.

SETTLEMENT ISSUES

In Southern California, participants have grown to expect that they will meet with the mediator alone—in private caucuses rather than joint sessions. As a result, I played a significant role in managing the legal, factual, and emotional discussions, as well as the negotiation.

In Sam's room, I gingerly began walking through the plaintiff's allegations with him and his lawyer and explained how a jury in Los Angeles might construe his conduct. Since there was a risk of a plaintiff's verdict and a damage award, would it make sense to settle this matter for a manageable number and avoid the risk of losing more at trial? I learned that Sam wanted to settle this case, but he would need to pay a settlement over time. He made a credible counteroffer to the plaintiff's opening demand.

I told Catherine and her lawyer that any settlement would need to be structured over time. They seemed open to this arrangement as long as the settlement amount was secured by an adequate asset.

The distributive bargaining progressed nicely. The parties finally agreed on a payment plan.

The harder issue was finding agreement on the security to be pledged. This was the most difficult term to mediate because Sam's assets consisted of shares in his privately held businesses, and they were difficult to value. Catherine's lawyer was concerned that Sam would provide an inadequate asset and then fail to pay the settlement. Sam was concerned that Catherine would force him to pledge his most (and likely only) valuable asset, one that he believed had a value far greater than the settlement amount. This made Sam feel that his livelihood was being threatened.

The parties prepared an initial settlement agreement setting forth the payment plan with a term that Sam would pledge an asset sufficient to cover the debt. They intended to enter into a more detailed settlement agreement after the mediation that included identification of the pledged asset, a note securing the debt, and a stipulated judgment in case of default.

The lawyers continued to work out the settlement documents over the course of several days after the mediation. But they quickly reached an impasse, and Catherine's lawyer threatened to move to enforce the settlement agreement signed at the mediation. At that point, the lawyers moved away from problem solving and back to fight-or-flight mode. Distrust set in, communication broke down, and I received a call from the defense counsel to mediate the impasse.

I sensed that the defense lawyer was troubled because he felt pigeonholed by the plaintiff's counsel's perception of him as untrustworthy—a perception grounded not in fact but projected on him because of the perceptions that the plaintiff's counsel had of the defendant.

At that point, I set up a joint conference call with the lawyers and asked them to share with each other their efforts to make this deal work. The plaintiff's counsel reiterated his concern that the pledged asset must be sufficient to cover the debt. The defendant's counsel explained in detail his proposal for determining the amount and value of the pledged shares. Once the plaintiff's counsel heard the detailed efforts that the defendant's counsel was taking to get this deal done, he began to trust the defense counsel. They began to problem solve and to work together toward the common goal of settlement.

A few days later, I received a call from the defense lawyer, and he appeared thrilled with the progress he was making with the plaintiff's counsel. He told me that at one point, he joked to his opposing counsel, "Hey, man, I love you!" We all knew that he was kidding, but I did think that his statement reflected the shift that this lawyer experienced when he and his opposing counsel began working together to make the deal happen.

The lawyers' states of mind shifted when they began to trust each other. They moved away from anger and fear toward a more peaceful state. And when their minds were in a calmer and more peaceful state, they had greater access to more cognitive and creative abilities. This new state of mind increased their ability to come up with, and communicate, settlement options that promoted their clients' interests.

SECOND THOUGHTS:

I chose to write about an ordinary mediation rather than one that involved explicit transformation or reunion of the parties because truly transformational mediations are very much the exception. For every single mediation that facilitates deep encounter and transformation, there are twenty that focus on factual and legal positions and money; and as the mediator, it's not my role to force a different agenda. Of course, we can and should determine whether the parties would like to engage in a deeper discussion, but, ultimately, my job is to have the dialogue and negotiation that the parties and their lawyers want to have. And it is in this context that I strive to greet all participants as openly as possible so that I can be sure that I understand their perspectives and remain nonjudgmental.

While we mediators seek to be neutral and nonjudgmental, we must often have a dialogue with the participants about the possible ways in which a judge or a jury may rule on their case. It is critical for a mediator to understand how to have this dialogue with the particular parties of the case. My approach is to make a personal connection with each participant before I begin to evaluate the merits of the case so that they are in the most relaxed state possible before they hear information with which they may not agree. If they are agitated, then they're less likely to think cognitively and more likely to act out of fear or anger.

I also chose a case that had a factual scenario that was somewhat similar to situations that I experienced as a younger woman in order to explore how mediators manage their own potential biases. It was easy for me to connect with the plaintiff, but I made a conscious decision to connect with the defendant as well.

Finally, I chose this case because the lawyers' relationship did transform, if only subtly, during the course of the mediation. In the beginning, they did not trust each other, but, over time, they gained trust and were able to work together and promote their respective clients' interests in resolving the case. In this way, the relationship of the lawyers transformed more than that of parties. I enjoy seeing lawyers feel satisfied with their work when they've done a good job in representing their clients while also maintaining a respectful relationship with their opposing counsel.

Perhaps after all there was a grain of truth in the defense lawyer's choice of the word *love*. Compared to the angry and volatile interactions that the lawyers previously experienced, their current interaction, based on mutual respect and trust, enabled them to reach a deal that promoted their clients' interests.

That seemed like a win-win to me.

16.
Doing Something

Peter Miller

JUAN AND MIRANDA

The mediation took place some years ago at a community mediation center in the greater New York City area. The two participants were a man and a woman in their early to mid twenties, Juan and Miranda. Juan and Miranda were both hearing impaired, so the mediation center had provided an interpreter to transpose their words, spoken in American Sign, for my benefit and my words back into American Sign for theirs.

Juan and Miranda were both clients of a social agency with an encompassing array of services designed to assist members of the deaf community. It was this agency that had referred Miranda to the mediation center. Later, in talking with a staff member of the mediation center, Juan decided to honor Miranda's request that he take part in a supported conversation with her and so had agreed to participate in mediation.

The center that housed Juan and Miranda's mediation had a mediation room that was singular for its informality. Rather than sitting on opposing sides of a conference table with a mediator virtually interposed at the head of the table, people sat as they chose to arrange themselves on a couch or armchairs that collectively surrounded a coffee table. Here, mediators sat where clients chose not to.

That room was not available on the day that Miranda and Juan came for their mediation. They each seemed ill at ease as they were ushered into the replacement mediation room. In retrospect, it seems likely that finding themselves across a conference table from one another, with a mediator and an interpreter between them, contributed to their sense of being unsettled, on foreign ground, beyond the familiar.

MIRANDA ADDRESSES JUAN

It is not my custom, in concluding my introductory remarks, to invite a particular participant to speak. Rather, I simply ask people how they would like to begin. It took Miranda several moments to gather herself before she began to unfold her story. (In response to my query, Juan affirmed that he was content to let Miranda have the initiative.)

At first, her remarks were directed either toward me or toward the room in general. She told a story of herself and Juan without addressing Juan or directing her remarks toward him. He was an active character in the story, but, in a sense, he was less than fully present in the room for her. Gradually, though, across the telling of her lengthy narrative as Miranda depicted what had happened and her feelings about what had happened, her posture and the direction of her gaze became focused on Juan. She began to say *you*, addressing Juan directly rather than referring to him by name or in the third person. (I began changing the little introductory phrases that I used to reflect what she was expressing from phrases such as "You're saying ..." or "For you ..." to phrases such as "You're wanting Juan to get ..." or "You're wanting Juan to see ...," in order to remain consonant with her evolving intention.)

Miranda described how fractured and without center her life had been in recent years. She told about how she and Juan had become a couple and about the strength and focus she had derived from being

182

in relationship with him. She spoke of how essential he had been to her in recent months as she worked to reconfigure her life so that she could become a better parent to her small daughter.

MIRANDA'S ISSUES WITH JUAN

Miranda's difficulty with Juan, and the source of much hurt, was his uncommunicativeness: even when things between them had gone well, he had never given her a clear sense that being in the relationship was, for him, meaningful; he never told her that he valued her. Now she was hearing from others in the community that Juan was saying that their relationship was over—that they were, in her exact words, "no longer an item." What was really painful, Miranda averred, was the knowledge that Juan was being voluble about her in a public way while choosing to adopt a stance of silence *with her*. Others seemed to know precisely where she stood; however, despite her repeated efforts to gain from Juan an understanding of her situation, *she* remained in the dark.

There were other points that Miranda wanted to raise and talk through with Juan. In attempting to solidify the newfound sobriety (from drugs) that she enjoyed, she was about to place herself, as a patient, in a treatment facility in upstate New York. The course of treatment was to run for six weeks. When she returned, the custody action that her daughter's father had initiated in family court was scheduled to resume. Would Juan, as a friend or as something more, "be there for her"? Would he act as a resource?

And there was the matter of Miranda's automobile. At a point in the recent past, Juan had borrowed her car and gotten into an accident. The initial estimate of $3,000, it turned out, was inadequate. Miranda now understood that a total of $6,000 would be required in order to effect repairs. Thus, the $3,000 that Juan had already given her would not make her whole. Would he give her the remaining $3,000?

JUAN JUST LISTENS

Throughout all that Miranda had said and then through my lengthy reflection of her narrative interspersed with her responses to the reflection, Juan had been both attentive and impassive. Now, in response to my invitation to speak—"You've been following along with what Miranda has been saying; you've certainly heard yourself described. Are there points you want to make?"—he declined, saying something like, "I'll just listen at this point."

Miranda did not seem discouraged by Juan's decision not to respond. Rather, she used the space that his inactivity afforded her to elaborate. As she coursed again over ground that she had previously covered, she became more precise in her description of that ground and, it seemed to me, more clear in understanding what aspects of her situation mattered most to her. Her speech was now expressly directed at Juan, and the forward thrust of her posture reflected this focus. When there were spaces or breaks in her narrative, I would reflect what she had said. Frequently her response to these reflections was to offer further elaboration; sometimes she merely nodded or said, "Exactly." Throughout this long sequence, Juan remained both receptive and silent.

There came a point at which Miranda said to Juan with simplicity and directness and calm, "I do love you, and I want our relationship to continue, but I understand that you may be somewhere else. What I really do require of you is that you tell me where I stand with you. It just hurts too much not to know. And I feel demeaned that you're talking about this to other people."

Here again, Juan was receptive and attentive as he held Miranda's gaze, nodding as if to say, "I do hear what you are saying." But, once again, his feelings were contained, and he articulated no response.

A Single Communication from Juan

At one point, however, while Miranda was complaining to Juan about his persistent failure throughout the relationship to communicate with her, Juan offered a comment. He said, more to the room than to Miranda in particular, that it was very difficult to function in a conversation with someone when the only thing that a person was permitted to do in that conversation was defend himself. And, he went on to say, being thus restricted, his motivation to participate in conversation with Miranda had become pretty thin. (This was the sole statement that Juan initiated of his own accord during this entire phase of the session.) In the aftermath of Juan's comment, Miranda seemed to become thoughtful.

MIRANDA CONTINUES TO ADDRESS JUAN

Nevertheless, the mediation proceeded much as before Juan's single communication—Miranda revisiting their history, her current confusion as to where matters between them stood, and her feelings of being diminished and hurt by Juan's refusal to inform her. Beyond the need for clarity, Miranda again spoke of wanting Juan to be present in a supportive way during the coming contest for the custody of her child. (Clearly, she envisioned this approaching struggle as a crucible that she might have to endure by herself.)

I continued to reflect Miranda's remarks, and she continued to respond to those reflections. Sometimes during pauses I would query Juan as to whether he wished to speak or whether just listening worked better at his end. Juan always replied that he preferred to listen. But he remained connected to what amounted to a conversation between Miranda and me, sustaining focus and visual contact with Miranda.

QUESTIONABLE MOTIVES

My own reactions and impulses during this phase of the mediation are, in retrospect, not entirely clear to me.

I happen to be a transformative mediator. A key aspect of transformative practice is that all choices relating to if, or how, clients participate in mediation, moment to moment, belong wholly to clients. The mediator's task is to support this unfolding of self-determination by articulating those choices as they become manifest. Doing this well means presenting moments of choice in ways that consciously avoid trying to influence the decisions that participants make about those choices. In this sense, apt transformative interventions are divorced from the future; they contain no tactical or strategic element. Thus, a mediator's motive in offering a particular intervention is vital; if a given intervention is intended to open up choice and do nothing further, that intervention supports transformative aim. If an intervention is intended to stimulate or inspire certain responses, that intervention has lost transformative aim and is, in fact, working in the service of something else.

I must confess that I am uncertain about my own motives regarding my periodic invitations to Juan to speak or to continue in a posture of listening. Juan's sustained decision not to speak affected me. I experienced his ongoing failure to participate as a sort of escalating pressure having to do with the quality of the encounter between him and Miranda. Thus, I am not entirely sure whether my interventions were wholly inspired by the desire to articulate in a neutral way a choice that periodically presented itself, which would further transformative aim, or simply by a desire to induce talk from Juan, which would counter transformative aim.

A VISIBLE CHANGE

At a certain moment, while Miranda was speaking, Juan's posture changed. The quality of relaxed attentiveness that had been characteristic of his demeanor after his initial discomfort had dissipated and was now supplanted by restive squirming as if he were in physical struggle with someone or something. Turning to Juan, I said something like, "You seem restless with the conversation."

(Again, the motivation behind my question was murky. If the intention of this intervention was to restore a posture of attentive focus, it was not a good transformative intervention. "Attentive and focused" is certainly a laudable and productive stance for a participant to adopt in mediation. But for me to promote that stance at the expense of Juan's discretion would thwart transformative aim. On the other hand, the same intervention could be intended to simply give voice to a discomfort that I saw in Juan in order to give him a chance to advocate for some sort of change in the conversation if he so wished. An intervention that fostered that sort of exercise of discretion would support transformative aim.)

Juan looked at me and said, "I'm thinking about what to do about the money." I apologized for intruding upon his thoughts.

Miranda continued to articulate the theme that she had been developing.

A PRODUCTIVE BREAK

The mediation had been in progress for some sixty or seventy minutes at this point. Juan turned toward me and asked if he and Miranda could take a break in order to smoke a cigarette. (During my initial remarks, I invite people to take breaks.) Miranda, too, wanted a break. They left the mediation center together.

Some twenty or thirty minutes later, a staff member of the mediation center informed me that Juan and Miranda had returned. Accompanied by the interpreter, I went to the center's waiting room in order to greet them and renew the mediation. As I approached them, Juan declared, "We've worked it out."

A NEW EXPERIENCE

Hearing this, I congratulated them. But I also asked them if they were okay with going back into the mediation room for a few moments: there was a choice that I wanted to present; and if they were all right with one or two questions, I had some that I wanted to pose. They both said that they were fine with my proposal, so we all returned to the mediation room. (It is quite possible that neither one actually wanted to go back to the mediation room with me, but saying so would have required more impoliteness than most people choose to muster.)

There was a quality in Juan's demeanor that was different. He seemed both more present and firmer in ways that I could feel but probably could not have specified. I understood, or at least sensed, that it was he who had initiated whatever the changes were that had "worked things out." In that moment, I knew with certainty that unless I probed, I would never hear the details of those changes; I also understood that the decision to keep those details discrete had originated with Juan. I could sense in Juan the feeling that he owned those changes, and I understood that it was this sense of having himself been the generator of change that was responsible for the change in his whole being. (In fact, I had been hesitant to even suggest that we continue discussing the situation because I wanted to honor and support that shift.)

When we were all seated again, I confirmed with Miranda that she, too, felt that they had "worked it out."

I asked Miranda and Juan if they wished to keep the understanding that they had reached as an oral understanding or if they wished to capture that understanding in writing. I noted that if they had decided that money would change hands, putting that agreement in writing might make the agreement more enforceable by a court.

Miranda thought for a moment and then stated that she would like to commit their understanding to writing. Juan, too, appeared thoughtful. After a short pause, he said, "I'm more likely to keep it if it's not in writing." Miranda paused and then said, "Okay"—meaning "Okay, we'll do it your way."

I asked Miranda and Juan, if in scanning their understanding, they thought that it had sufficient detail as to how and when the things that they had put in place would happen. Were there circumstances that might cause that to change? Or, in thinking about their understanding and how it would work, was it detailed enough as it was? After considering for a moment, both said that it was fine as it was.

I asked if they had conducted as complete a conversation as they wished or if there was something further that either of them wanted to put in words. Miranda spoke orally for the first time that day. She said to Juan, "It feels like *we* did a lot today." Juan also employed oral speech for the first time in answering her. He said simply and without irony, "Yeah, for the first time in my life."

As they were leaving, just after they had passed through the doorway to the mediation room, Juan turned back to me, pointed in my direction, and said, "I like mediation!" Then he left.

Just after they departed I heard the full import of Juan's final reply to Miranda, "Until today, I'd never done something. Now I have!"

SECOND THOUGHTS:

More than fifteen years ago, I began to evolve my practice of mediation. There was a particular impetus behind my desire to create a change.

I had started noticing that people frequently became, in audible and visible ways, more centered, more expansive, and somehow more present in the early stages of the mediations that I conducted. This seemed to happen independently of movement toward or away from resolution. I also starting noticing that these nascent qualities of strength in participants somehow dissipated in the latter stages of these same mediations. I concluded that something in my early interventions was supportive of the changes I was witnessing; conversely, some competing quality (must have) entered into the interventions I employed at later stages that somehow discouraged or undermined these shifts.

I did not have a vocabulary to describe those early-in-the-mediation shifts, but I did value them highly. So, when I discovered transformative mediation, itself nascent at the time, the doctrine had no element of the hypothetical; rather, the theory echoed my own experience. It provided a frame that placed those changes that I so valued within an articulated context.

The story that I related above has a hero beyond its two protagonists. That hero is the phenomenon called *empowerment*. I'm not going to elaborate on transformative theory other than to say that it posits the stitching of connection with the self (here, evident in Miranda but luminous in Juan) as an essential core human response to the disruptive effects of conflict. It was this act of connection that I witnessed in those early mediations, and it is this same act of connection that transformative technique is expressly designed to foster and support.

Doing transformative mediation requires a mediator to make empowerment the supreme desideratum. Empowerment's prominence challenges other considerations that benefit parties and, in doing so, creates dilemmas that may not exist for mediators who do not give it preeminence. I did have internal tensions about Miranda, the surrender of rights, and justice, as well as the solidity of the understanding that she and Juan reached; after all, fairness, justice, and durability of agreement all matter. But so, too, does the agency that Miranda and Juan found in themselves and deployed. When transformative mediation's progenitors wrote of conflict as a crucible from which "moral growth" could emerge, they were referring to precisely the sort of growth exhibited by Juan. Rather than merely making restorative strides as a response to the debilitating effects of conflict, he carried himself, through action, to a new experience of his own capacity. It is to the proclivity of people to do conflict repair that transformative mediation and its practitioners are allied above all other things.

Transformative mediators respect and follow the choices that parties make precisely because we believe that doing so supports their efforts to gain clarity and strength and that not doing so undermines those efforts. Thus, in pursuit of fairness and durability, I could have inquired about the understanding that Juan and Miranda had reached, and I suspect I would have been successful in learning of its details even though their first choice was not to disclose them. But I could not do that without taking something precious away from Juan and Miranda.

In writing this piece, my aim has been to capture, in a vivid way, the generative force toward connection that exists in a conflict's participants. I wanted the reader to see it. Why? Because none of us practices mediation in Heaven, nor do we practice in Plato's republic. Encounters with dilemma are endemic to the practice of mediation. (My definition of *dilemma* is a thicket from which all avenues of escape do damage to something of value.) Thus, all mediation models are imperfect in the sense that none of them can meet every eventuality without sacrifice. About the best we can do is to be clear with ourselves and with others as to why we choose to emerge from the thicket by a particular route above all other routes. It seems to me that reflective practice, which is to say responsible practice, demands that of all of us have clarity about what we value most and why.

PART VI
Momentous Shifts

Alice laughed. "There's no use trying," she said: "one can't believe impossible things." "I daresay you haven't had much practice," said the Queen. "When I was your age, I always did it for half-an-hour a day. Why, sometimes I've believed as many as six impossible things before breakfast."

Lewis Carroll, *Through the Looking Glass*

We are continually faced with great opportunities which are brilliantly disguised as unsolvable problems.

Margaret Mead

Ring the bells that still can ring. Forget your perfect offering. There is a crack in everything—That's how the light gets in.

Leonard Cohen, *Anthem*

17.
Becoming a Believer

Russell Brunson

A Pivotal Mediation Experience

My upbringing developed in me an understandable skepticism about the effectiveness of mediation and other alternative dispute resolution processes. A pivotal experience changed that, and now I have a different orientation.

A Background in Physical Response to Conflict

I grew up in the 1980s in Queens, New York, a community ravaged by the crack epidemic of the time. This drug trafficking was facilitated by a violence that was pervasive in our everyday lives. Even as young children, we had to be well versed in the fight-or-flight response. We had no role models or institutions that taught us a different set of skills to prevent or resolve conflict. In one instance, my brother, who was bullied his entire childhood because he was overweight and an immigrant with a British accent, confronted a neighborhood bully by responding to his taunts with a bat while my family and several neighbors verbally encouraged his every swing. Most fights in our neighborhood had the same result: cheering spectators encouraging the fighters to escalate the conflict until one or both drew blood. The bully with whom my brother fought unfortunately had more than blood drawn: he was knocked unconscious before neighbors intervened.

Like most children in my neighborhood, I grew accustomed to the rules of survival in the street but never became accustomed to the ways in which conflict was handled in my home. My father used intimidation and violence to manage disputes with family members, often targeting my mother and brother. While my sister and I were usually spared from his assaults, we unfortunately witnessed many of his acts of violence. We felt powerless to intervene because our bodies were just too small to step between our father and his selected target for the night.

Fortunately, my mother received support from members of the community and removed my father from the home. However, a significant amount of damage had already been done, leaving my mother to raise children who learned to fight or provoke fights as a first instinct.

SKEPTICISM ABOUT MEDIATION

I entered law school intent on ensuring that the civil rights of individuals were protected. I also became interested in family law, specifically in the areas of abuse and neglect. It was not until I began my work in alternate dispute resolution as a community mediator, though, that I was introduced to a set of skills that was not contingent on physical strength or adversarial prowess but on my ability to understand and engage in dialogue with a person with whom I differed.

Through the law school's mediation clinic, I mediated cases diverted from small claims courts in Brooklyn and Manhattan. Because of the history of violence in my community and home, I was skeptical about alternative dispute resolution and its ability to address an actual conflict rather than a mock mediation in a classroom. There was always a nagging feeling in my mind that these techniques might work in a judge's chambers, but that outside of a controlled setting, the disputants would rely on tried-and-true methods of escalated aggression or angry silence.

A COMMUNAL SPACE MEDIATION

One of my first mediation cases involved two individuals living together in a housing complex in Manhattan. The initiating party, Jane, alleged that her neighbor, Bill, repeatedly harassed her when they were sharing communal space. Bill wanted Jane to simply keep to herself and do her part to keep the communal space clean and functional. He would scold her when he thought that she had not cleaned up after herself in either the kitchen or the bathroom, and the conflict escalated.

When my co-mediator and I began to get a better understanding of each party's perspective, I thought that we had the case figured out. I thought that we would have a fairly easy mediation in which we would discuss the major issues of how each person wanted to be treated when interacting in communal space and their obligations to keep the space clean. Although the parties seemed to be worlds apart, I believed that we would be able to bridge the gap by listening actively, identifying interests, and reaching a resolution.

UNDERLYING ISSUE

I believed that a solution was at hand until the real issue surfaced: Bill kept addressing Jane as "Mr. Jane," "him," and "that." Puzzled and noticing the impact of Bill's words, we clarified with Jane that she wanted to be addressed as "Ms. Jane" or just "Jane." We asked if Bill could follow Jane's request and address her as she wanted. He refused and said that he was simply addressing Jane as "what he actually is." Jane clarified that she was transgendered and it was this type of harassment that she could no longer tolerate from Bill.

With this new issue voiced, I felt myself break into a sweat, realizing that this conflict was challenging my neutrality because it recalled the cultural norm of my childhood, the use of insulting and angry aggression to humiliate and dominate another.

My doubts about the effectiveness of mediation immediately surfaced. This conflict involved more than a noisy neighbor or barking dogs. It involved personal identity, prejudice, deep-rooted cultural differences, and volatile emotions. It also involved the seemingly overwhelming task of moving people from diametrically opposed positions that were tied to deeply held beliefs about gender, culture, and identity.

THE JOINT SESSION

Recognizing Jane's intense emotions, we asked her to speak first. She discussed her desire to have no interaction with Bill in their housing complex. She cried when relating the impact of Bill's treatment of her both in the complex and earlier in the mediation. She avoided Bill as much as she could, scheduling any of her activities that involved common areas around minimizing her contact with Bill. She would eat, shower and engage in recreational activities only when she was sure to not encounter Bill. She was infuriated because a bigot was seemingly dictating how she lived her life: when she showered, with whom she interacted, whether or not she could watch television or when she could do something as essential as cook and eat a meal in the peace of her home without a person yelling or intensely glaring at her. She expressed frustration because she could not afford to move. Her interaction with Bill caused her to feel powerless and desperate for something to change.

We asked Jane how she wanted to be treated by others in the complex and elsewhere. Her responses indicated a deep need to be treated with respect and to have her current identity acknowledged. Further discussion revealed that she understood how challenging it was for Bill to accept her as a person and a female because he had first known her as a male. The issues with respect to the common kitchen and bathroom seemed manageable for Jane, but the disrespect and the way that Bill addressed her were not.

We then asked Bill to explain his perspective. He mentioned that in his culture, people who change gender do not deserve respect. From his perspective, Jane would always be a man and should be addressed as such. Bill admitted to gossiping with others at the complex about Jane and her lifestyle, and to greeting her with intense stares and silence when they encountered each other at the complex because of her orientation. He was generally disgusted with Jane and was very happy to express it with her or other residents at any time.

Internally, I struggled with my disgust for Bill's behavior and my role as a neutral mediating the dispute before me. As we continued to explore Bill's underlying need to be true to his cultural values and his strong sense of right and wrong, I was reminded of my father using a raised voice and other acts of violence to dominate others because he lacked the ability to respond in another way. I fought to suppress my internal instinct to silence Bill's bigotry and allow Jane the space to give voice to her pain. Luckily, I was able to stay with the mediation process, trying my hardest to remain outwardly neutral, relying on my co-mediator to take the lead, and allowing Bill the space to express himself.

When asked to think of the conflict from Jane's perspective, Bill understood how she might feel but focused on his value system as a justification for his actions toward Jane. Given my life experience, I was worried that the parties would freeze in their positions due to deeply held beliefs and different value systems. However, Bill's body language and demeanor changed when we asked him to think from Jane's perspective. He leaned back, looked to the left and right to visualize Jane's perspective, and seemed more contemplative. He became less energetic and more empathetic as he acknowledged that Jane was probably interested in being treated respectfully. This perspective shift or role reversal that many mediators use as a tool to help parties discuss underlying interests appeared to help Bill make a significant change. Although he held to his value system, he began to understand, simply by placing himself in her shoes, that his behaviors were having a detrimental impact on Jane.

Thankfully, our perspective-sharing exercise worked with Bill. Jane, however, was slightly turned from the table and did not make eye contact with any of us, signs that she remained unconvinced of both Bill's empathy and the potential of mediation to change things.

My co-mediator and I felt that caucusing would be a beneficial next step in exploring the belief systems at play because it would allow the parties to express their perspectives and feelings, analyze their own motivations, and create a face-saving space to allow each of them to begin to empathize with the other and decide how they wanted to proceed.

A ROUND OF CAUCUSING

So we called for caucuses to address Jane's discomfort and to explore Bill's ability to empathize. We started with Bill to continue the momentum from the joint session and to give Jane a chance to compose herself and self-reflect while she waited. We asked Bill what he hoped to accomplish with Jane. Bill emphasized the cultural differences at the root of his conflict with Jane but reiterated a desire to move forward with Jane in the future. We closed Bill's caucus with a commitment to share his vision with Jane in joint session.

I feared the upcoming caucus with Jane, assuming that she would erupt with anger resulting from her mistreatment during the session. A small part of me hoped that she had left the building in frustration while we met with Bill because I could not see a way for these people to pull themselves out of the tailspin that their lives had become.

With as much professionalism and enthusiasm as I could muster, I invited Jane to caucus. She entered the room with a lack of energy, indicating that she was resigned to her fate to live with Bill for the near future. We asked Jane how she was feeling about the mediation. She was reluctant to make eye contact and spoke with her head held low, almost as if she were addressing the table. Jane reflected on the many instances of disrespect that she had experienced during the mediation. She had experienced similar disrespect in her interactions with Bill in the apartment complex and expressed a level of hopelessness with him and with the mediation. She questioned how this procedure could help an aggressive bigot become more accepting of her or empathetic enough to leave her in peace. My co-mediator and I reassured her that this process could not help Bill change his values, but we could give them both a safe space to discuss how to change their behaviors with each other. After sharing that Bill was interested in attempting to work with Jane to create new rules governing their interactions in the complex, we asked Jane if she could do the same. She accepted our proposal to return to joint session.

My co-mediator and I returned to the joint session and asked the parties to share their thoughts. Bill remained reluctant to talk openly with Jane and repeated his desire that Jane stay away from him in their housing complex. However, Jane expressed her feelings, saying that Bill's actions made her feel powerless and invisible. These feelings were exacerbated because the actions took place in her home, where she wanted to be secure and safe. She shared that she simply wanted to be left alone and live without harassment, respected as a person.

FINDING COMMON GROUND

The issue between Bill and Jane was not only about shared space and chores but also about communication and interaction that had become deeply destructive. However, my co-mediator and I were able to change the dynamic with a simple reframing of the core issues and a challenge to look at the situation through the eyes of the other person. If this conflict had continued in a style similar to my upbringing, the parties would have stopped their discussion and continued to escalate the harassment until one party was forced out of the housing complex.

Capturing all of the issues and acknowledging each person's values allowed the parties to find common ground—the need for recognition of their identities and beliefs. Working from this shared interest, they were more open to discussing other needs. They shared their mutual desire to refrain from living a life of fear and harassment, retaliation, and conflict escalation. They discussed a potential future where they could maintain their cultural and personal differences but agree on a means of civil engagement to avoid the behavior that brought them to the table. Finally, Bill apologized for using slurs against Jane and promised to address her respectfully in the future as "Jane." Jane remained guarded with words and body language but continued to share her feelings as we progressed. Bill's apology and willingness to acknowledge Jane's interests led to a simple but powerful gesture from Jane—a "thank you." We then explored and tested other options that addressed the need for clean common areas and respectful interaction.

While drafting and clarifying the final agreement, I hoped that the dispute resolution norm of my family and culture would not emerge and erase any progress made in the mediation. Instead, the parties left with an agreement between them and a modicum of understanding and respect. The interaction had shifted. The air was clearer. It felt great!

SECOND THOUGHTS:

That moment was pivotal in revealing to me the power of mediation. Mediation was not a classroom game. It was not limited to courts with powerful judges making people behave. As mediators, we had helped two parties with strongly opposed beliefs discuss and end behaviors that negatively impacted their lives. Two remarkably different people recognized that they held some similar underlying values. Bill and Jane were enmeshed in a deeply personal conflict using aggression and avoidance as the primary tools to resolve conflict. With my limited upbringing, I had never envisioned the true power of communication in mediation to allow people to engage in more productive behaviors. The parties here raised their voices, expressed extreme emotions, and yet were able to come to a resolution that worked for them with the help of neutrals and the techniques of active listening, caucusing, reframing, role reversal, and interest-based discussion.

Drained, yet also energized from the experience, I envisioned how I could incorporate the skills and momentum from the session with Bill and Jane into other areas of my life. I taught and worked with at-risk youth to help keep my sanity during law school and saw a natural fit in helping teens navigate social issues while also improving academically. I designed workshops on language, social and emotional learning, and diversity issues for youth, mostly in circumstances and neighborhoods similar to mine, grounding my materials in the theory and experience that I received from the mediation clinic and work in the community mediation centers. My first effort, a workshop called "What's Up, Nigger," addressed the expanding use of that charged word among all youth in an after-school program. Conflict among males in this program was escalating because Latino youth were frequently addressing friends as "nigger," while also using the word as a slur against African-American students. In a manner similar to what occurred in the mediation with Bill, I asked both Latino and African-American youth to engage in a perspective-sharing exercise. As a result of this workshop, the youth developed new expectations of each other based on shared pain and hope for improved relations. Tensions between the youth groups decreased, and, most importantly, the students took ownership of the problem and their role in ending the hostility. As in the situation with Bill, I had to simply give the students an opportunity and structure to discuss their behavior and its impact. They engaged in the hard work of self-reflection, discussion, and decision-making about their own future.

I have since trained youth and adults in the use of these skills in the community, in schools and universities, and in workplaces across the country. I have consulted with schools, government agencies, and community-based organizations to establish conflict resolution systems to better resolve disputes, provide guidance to work teams, and engage in dialogue. I assisted four workplace teams that all faced the same challenge that my father and I both faced: an inability to constructively manage conflict. One situation involved members of a team targeting a newer staff member using exclusion and gossip because they thought that she did not "know her place." The isolated team member also escalated the conflict by ignoring others, refusing to speak, and complaining to supervisors and union representation when other members of the team attempted to hold a direct conversation with her. While my work with this group successfully ended with the team establishing new norms of behavior, not all conflicts reach a successful conclusion because some parties cling to old, destructive habits. Regardless of the outcome, I am grateful to be able to share mediation techniques with those who are interested in a different means to resolve conflict but have, like I had in my youth, limited exposure to positive ways of handling disputes.

While I have engaged in this work with many trainees, I am most thankful for the use of these skills with my family members. I have found that my skill level and frequency of intervention in family conflicts have increased. I no longer am subject to my father's unbridled methods of brutal fighting or complete avoidance, and I look forward to creating a different norm for my wife and newborn son: respect for differences of opinion and use of dialogue to deal with conflict.

I am forever grateful to those who have helped me learn these skills and values and to Bill and Jane for showing me that people experiencing pain and hate can create a new future defined by respect and hope. I have become a believer that through mediation, we can all live in a world that is less chaotic and threatening than the one in which I grew up.

18.
A Day in a Life

Lee Jay Berman

On Her Way

Beth awoke anxious, excited, and scared to death. This was the day she had been awaiting for more years than she could remember. She had wanted to do this—no, needed to do this—since she was a young woman. And it was here at last.

Oh my God, she thought. I can't get out from under the covers. I have to, but I can't! Finally, she drew a slow, deep breath and mustered all of the courage that had made her get on a plane and fly all the way to Los Angeles, to Hollywood, to claim what was rightly hers. It was almost a ten-hour flight from Europe. God, this had better be worth it, she told herself.

It was a spring day like any other. As she rode in the taxi to the mediator's office, she watched the people out the window and wondered if any of them were about to confront anything as big as she was going to confront today. She thought for a minute that she should go over the facts again to make sure that she didn't freeze or forget any details but quickly reminded herself that she had lived them. There was no reason to worry. This was her story. It was her life.

Arriving more quickly than she expected, she paid the cabbie and wandered into the office building, having memorized the suite number. She had looked at that letter a hundred times, praying that this mediator would be her savior. He had been recommended by her lawyer, the lawyer she had found on the Internet. Lord almighty, this had better work. She would only be more of a laughingstock if it failed.

The receptionist pointed her to the conference room to her left and told her that her lawyer had phoned and said he was just a couple of minutes away. Starting to get nervous now, she made a cup of tea and went and sat alone in the large, empty room.

MEETING THE TEAM

Eventually her lawyer arrived. Smiling, he introduced himself. He seemed nice enough. How odd to have only emailed and talked once over the Internet before such a big day. She felt better that he was here. It was also just nice to have someone on her side for a change.

They reviewed their discussions, and before long I entered, saying "Good morning" and introducing myself. I shook the lawyer's hand and then Beth's hand. Beth seemed to feel comfort with the team that she had picked to help her.

The chitchat ended, and Beth's lawyer and I began talking about putting everyone in the same room. Sh*t, the same room, Beth thought to herself.

Beth's lawyer turned to her, smiled, and asked her if she was ready. Beth had wanted this her whole life but wondered if she was ready *right now*. "Sure," she told the attorney, faking a smile. Hearing her answer, I nodded at her and left.

MEETING THE FAMILY AND PRESENTING THE DEMANDS

After a few minutes, I returned with the family, closed the door, and began introducing them. Beth met Patty and her two daughters, Trish, the oldest, and Becky. The family resemblance was obvious. Beth met their lawyer, a man in his mid-fifties. Beth didn't hear his name.

I began talking about confidentiality and about the process, and Beth's mind began to drift again, looking at the women across the table. So, she thought, these are *them*.

"If you think about it, each of you came here today looking for something," I said. "Even if that something is just a release, it's the people sitting around this table right now who have what it is you came here for today."

When I finished, I mentioned that the parties involved had chosen not to submit briefs. Beth remembered her lawyer discussing that with her—a choice to save money and also to let Beth tell her story rather than the lawyer doing so.

I invited Beth's lawyer to start things off. He began by explaining that this was a case about music royalties and that his client, Beth, had been denied her rightful share to the songs written by her now-deceased father, Jerry. He detailed the amount of these royalties, somewhere between $100,000 and $130,000 annually, and said that Beth was entitled to her rightful 25 percent share as his daughter. He went on to explain that Jerry had been an early rock star in the late 1950s and early 1960s whose music was still popular today and that Beth, as his daughter, was entitled to 25 percent of those royalties for the past twenty years since Jerry had passed away. The lawyer said that this amounted to somewhere between $500,000 and $650,000 and that they were seeking that amount plus interest and legal fees and costs, or somewhere around $750,000. In addition, they were seeking a one-fourth share of the royalties going forward into perpetuity.

Glancing across to the other side of the table, Beth saw Patty looking down; the two grown sisters, each in their thirties, looking with dismay at the numbers they had just heard; and their attorney taking notes.

BETH'S STORY IN HER OWN WORDS

At that point, as they had prepared, Beth's lawyer turned to Beth and said that with everyone's permission, it would probably make sense for Beth to explain the rest. I nodded and Beth began.

"I remember my father. I remember playing with him with a ball in my yard. I remember the bicycle he gave me for my seventh birthday—it was pink and white with streamers coming from the handlebars, a white basket in front, and pink and white pedals. And I remember him sitting on the edge of my bed and telling me that I was his daughter and that he would always be there for me and that he loved me and would always love me."

Beth went on to explain that her father had left her and her mother in Europe to go and make it big as a pop music star in America and how they were brokenhearted to learn of him marrying an American woman and starting a family there with her. This American marriage happened when Beth was very young—long before the bicycle on her seventh birthday and long before her father telling her that he would always be her father and would always take care of her. Beth's mother had explained to her that out of respect for his American wife and her children and to keep his wholesome reputation (something that pop stars required in those days), he could not publicly acknowledge Beth as his daughter or she and her mother as his family.

After his death, Europe mourned as much as America did, and Beth explained how she went to the press there and told them that she was his daughter. They asked for evidence, and she gave them what she had. They asked her a million questions and took some pictures of her. But she never saw the news article. Instead, the tabloids put her on their front pages as a fake, a phony, a loon who was so starstruck with this pop idol that she claimed to be related to him. They made her out to be a crazy person, a gold digger, and they soon had people believing that she was out of her mind.

A NEED FOR ACKNOWLEDGMENT

As she was telling the story, her quiet tears turned into sobbing, but she wouldn't stop. After a couple of moments, she continued.

She said that she filed this lawsuit because she and her mother could use the money, as they were facing very difficult times financially, but mostly because it was time that the American family rightfully acknowledged their presence and her position as his legitimate daughter. She said, "I'm not going to let this go until justice is done and somebody—you all or some court—acknowledges that he was my father and sets the record straight."

At this point, her lawyer reached over and put his hand on her forearm to calm her. Sniffling, she blew her nose and began to compose herself. I asked if she would like a moment, and she shook her head no. Her lawyer gave me that long blink and slight head nod as if to say, "Let's keep pushing on."

I asked if there was anything else they wanted us to know at this point, and her lawyer said, "No, that'll do for now." I turned to the defense counsel and invited him to go next.

WELCOME TO THE FAMILY

The defense lawyer said, "Well, while we can certainly sympathize with her feelings, there simply isn't any evidence to support her claim. Counsel, if you have anything concrete that you can show me, birth records or the like, I'd be happy to consider them and review them with my client, but to date, we have seen nothing and only have her word to go on."

Beth glanced across the table and noticed Patty. Her head was down, looking at her hands in her lap. This was more than empathy for the crying woman across the table from her. It was more than discomfort with the palpable emotion in the room. This was a deep head hang, eyes closed. This was guilt or shame. Beth stole a long look at the American wife and then looked down into her own lap, rubbing her hands as though she had arthritis.

The family's lawyer noticed Beth's eyes, which had left him while he was speaking, and followed them to Patty.

Then Patty's daughters seemed to step out of their own processing, trying to decide what to make of what they were witnessing as their attention also drew to their mother and the strong energy that she was giving off in her silence.

Patty clasped her hands together in her lap and raised her head. She looked for a long moment at Beth, tears still dripping down her face. Then Patty's eyes went to Beth's attorney. Patty put her clenched hands on the conference table and without looking their way, said, "Girls . . ." Her daughters both looked at her profile as she kept looking at Beth. "There's something I have to tell you."

Beth and her attorney looked up at Patty. She looked at both of her daughters and then down again into her lap. She reached out to her daughters on either side of her and said in a low, weary voice, "I knew." They both gasped. She continued softly, telling her daughters that their father had told her a long time ago, after Trish was born, that he had a little girl in Europe but that he never mentioned it again. Patty said that because they never talked about it for all of those years, it was almost like it wasn't real. Because they never heard from the daughter in Europe, Patty said that she thought maybe the girl didn't even know. "So we just went on with our lives," said Patty. "But I knew." Then Patty said that when she first saw the lawsuit, she figured it had to be a fake. She Googled Beth, and everything she read convinced her that Beth was another crackpot and that the suit was frivolous, maybe even an attempt to get more attention.

"But when we walked in here," Patty continued, welling up with tears, "the moment I saw Beth in person, I knew. I knew it had all come back. There she was in the flesh. This was her. That little girl had grown up." Patty was now crying with her eyelids pinched tight together, as if hoping that she could keep the tears from coming out.

Trish and Becky sat stunned. They each had a hand on their mother's shoulder, but they were in shock.

"Girls," Patty said, "she's your sister."

At that point, all three of them looked at Beth, who had stopped crying but still had pink, wet cheeks. Beth sat strong, lips tight, her expression matter-of-fact, as if saying, "Well, there it is." With a hint of sadness or empathy, Beth watched Patty as Patty dropped her head and the tears silently rolled off of her cheeks into her lap.

With Patty's head down, Beth looked at Trish. The two women had a long moment where it sunk in that they were now sisters. In a moment, Trish stood up and started around the long table toward Beth. Beth did the same, and the women met at the far end of the conference table and embraced in a tight, crying hug. Becky, only a couple of steps behind Trish, wrapped her arms around them both. Slowly, Patty pushed her chair back and walked over to the girls and gave them all a mama bear hug, holding them while they all four sobbed and heaved. After about a minute, they laughed at themselves and then cried more. Eventually, Trish's muffled voice from under the huddle. "Welcome to the family," she said.

At the other end of the long table, the two lawyers looked at me and at each other and then back at the women.

When the girls eventually separated and finished their individual hugs with Beth, the defense lawyer said, "I think I'd better talk with my clients for a couple of minutes." I took them out of the room and down the hall to where they had started the day.

While they were gone, Beth could only cry—tears of joy, relief, exhaustion, and disbelief.

FAMILY BONDS

After about twenty long minutes, the family returned. The family's lawyer said that the women had agreed to give Beth her rightful one-quarter share of the royalties going forward. While they were not in a position to do anything financial about the past payments, he said, they hoped that by welcoming her into the family in the truest sense and wanting to get to know her and begin to build a family bond with her, starting with dinner tonight, Beth would be happy and dismiss her lawsuit.

Beth started nodding her head vigorously yes before Patty had even finished. When Patty finished, Beth said that the whole process wasn't really about money for her; it was about family and connecting to the other family that she had in the States. And, she said, it was about sanity—knowing that it was all true and having someone acknowledge it. "I appreciate the royalties," she said, "but I just need you to know that it's about more to me than getting a check. I want to get to know you all, and it's like I'll finally be receiving a check from my Daddy, like I should be, and like I know he would want me to. I hope that makes sense."

Trish said that it definitely made sense. "I can't believe you waited this long and fought this hard," she said. "You're a strong woman. I'm glad to call you a sister, and I can't wait to get to know you better!"

With that, the ladies all looked at each other, smiling and wiping their cheeks. Then finally they looked at their lawyers and me, giving us the cue to get busy and get the settlement agreement done so they could get to dinner and move on with their lives. Together.

SECOND THOUGHTS:

What makes mediating so challenging and so interesting is that we never know which days are going to end in crying group hugs and which won't, but we have to come to work each morning allowing for the possibility that this could be one of those days. We have to come ready with both the tools from our training and our personal characteristics—like our optimism; we have to come ready as if each day could carry the importance in the lives of our participants that this case did because each day actually can. Whether it reveals itself to us or not—well, that part is not up to us. A mediator who sees his role as limited and narrowly defined cannot see the infinite possibilities that are available. A mediator who is open-minded, creative, and without boundaries sees more possibilities.

Some of what mediators bring to the table can be described as "process," including deciding when to use joint session with all parties present versus private meetings or caucuses with smaller groups. But much more of what mediators bring into the room comes from our deep intention and our beliefs about this process that we carry with us as our compass. There is a lot of debate in the mediation world about whether mediation is a tool for settlement of a litigated case (usually a compromise between parties who are deep into a conflict) or for resolution of a dispute (oftentimes offering deeper resolution of relationship issues, both past and future). I think about mediation as an opportunity to help people get as much of what they came there for as they can. I take my lead from the parties because it is, after all, their dispute and their resolution. In this case, Beth came for a deeper meaning—almost to justify her very existence and to claim her rightful share, not to the money but to ownership of her father. And not to her father the famous performer and songwriter, but to the father who sat on the edge of her bed and tucked her in at night and gave her the gift of her first bicycle.

Mediators must pay deep enough attention to those people in front of them to catch the subtleties of their message, spoken or not. How we learn these things from people is all about how we listen (and sometimes about how we read the lawyers' briefs). It follows logically that how we listen is determined by how we define our role and our goal. Mediators who listen for settlement are listening for liability, causation, and damages and for hints of flexibility and firmness in order to help the participants formulate offers of financial compromise. Mediators who see their role as something deeper tend to listen for misunderstandings, needs (spoken and unspoken), hurt feelings, and the keys to unlock blame and begrudging at a deeper level in an effort to bring about a more complete resolution and perhaps a more lasting peace.

Many who read the last paragraph just chose one or the other of those options. The hard thing about mediation is that if we want to be effective, we don't get to choose. Mediating is about helping the people in front of us to understand the choices they have available to them and to assist them in making those choices. The decision about how deep to go and how much healing people desire is up to them. So, essentially, mediators must come equipped for dealing with different levels of resolution, and ultimately the parties decide what sort of agreement they want. My dear friend and colleague Richard Millen, who mediated until he was eighty-eight years old and passed away this year at eighty-nine, would quote a line from a poem written by another colleague, Tap Steven, that ended with the following prophetic words: "[A]nd they came and did for themselves what they had come for the mediator to do for them."

How mediators let the participants decide this is as much about our presence as it is our direct dialogue. Mediators have to bring an approachability, and people have to feel from them a deep caring and compassion, a sense of feeling protected, and some level of intimacy before they will give the mediator permission to spend their time on noneconomic issues. Friend, colleague, and mentor Randy Lowry used to tell people in a mediation training course that some people have offices where intimate problems are regularly shared, but that others have never been told a secret in their lives. He said that the number of secrets people tell us in life is an indicator of how approachable we are and of how much others want to confide in us. He said that good mediators must have a quality that invites openness if they are going to get into deeper discussions with people, discussions beyond settlement offers of money alone. Some mediators have offices with a revolving door, i.e., people go in all day to tell them their problems; others have never heard a secret in their lives. This is an indicator of how approachable a person is and how much others want to confide in that person. Mediators must have this revolving-door quality if they are going to get into deeper discussions, discussions beyond settlement offers of money.

It also helps if a mediator has a couple of secret weapons. My conference table in the main room where I do most of my joint sessions is actually my grandparents' old dining room table. One of the other conference tables is my parents' old dining room table. The special sentimental value of these tables and other items in the room help me to remain in that open and helping place, even in the heat of high conflict.

On the particular day of the music royalty conflict involving Beth, the kind of approach described above is likely responsible for the direction that this mediation took and the outcome achieved by the participants. Of course, there is no way to know for sure. Perhaps Beth would have headed in this direction with any mediator or with no mediator at all. What I do know is that all of what I brought with me into that room on this day was intentional: my hope and dream was to help the participants achieve the very outcome that they did, if possible.

In this mediation, I believe that Patty and her daughters came to this process prepared to defend their family unit from invasion, both emotional and financial. By the time I had finished setting the tone with them for collaboration and trust, both in their private room and in the joint session with Beth and her lawyer, I think their minds were opened a bit, allowing them to hear Beth just a little bit differently. That is what was needed—a crack of daylight in the steel walls that they had built to keep out intrusions like the one presented by Beth.

As the day went on, there was such emotion and energy filling the room that my most effective role was to lead from behind. Some days, the mediator needs to take charge and be out in front like a museum docent leading a tour ("Next, we'll head in this direction. . . ."). Other days, like this one, the mediator's more effective place is behind the pack, letting it go the way it wants to go and acting more like a shepherd, making sure that nobody detaches or strays from the group and going and getting anyone who does.

A good mediator needs to recognize when to disappear, too. When it came time for Patty and her girls to speak privately with their lawyer, I took them back to their private room and left them alone.

Most people are averse to conflict and, given the choice, will pick any option that keeps them from having to confront another person. Sometimes the mediator needs to encourage participants to take calculated risks by stepping into potentially confrontational situations in order to try to get a better, more lasting resolution. When the defendants' attorney told me that they had an offer to convey, I told the attorney that while I could definitely convey that offer and see if it would resolve things, it would be much more genuine, sincere, and persuasive if Patty and the girls offered it directly to Beth themselves. I discussed with a reluctant Patty and her daughters that their relationship with Beth was just beginning and given that they were going to have an ongoing relationship, it was important to begin to build that trust and foundation right here.

Eventually, they agreed that it would be best to return to Beth's room and have that discussion with her directly. When they did, and when it triggered the response that it did, the two attorneys and I sat there unmoving and knew that this was the ladies' moment. We were suddenly like uninvited guests in their room. I don't think that the women even knew we were there in that moment. We men talked about it later and all felt the same, i.e., that if we could have disappeared at that moment and left the four of them together, we would have.

It was later in the day when I learned that Beth had found her attorney via an Internet search and that this was the first time that they had met face-to-face. I realized that if her Internet search had turned up one of the other 40,000 members of the Los Angeles County Bar Association, the odds were that I would never have gotten this case—and what a loss that would have been.

Looking at days like this, I thank God and the powers of the universe for bringing me to this chosen field. Whether my role on any given day is that of an architect or a conductor or more closely resembles that of an observer or a passenger on the train, I am grateful that this is how I get to spend my days at "work."

19.
All in the Family:
A Story of Transformation
through Mediation

Kenneth Cloke

The oldest sister finally couldn't stand it anymore. She telephoned and said she was sick of the conflict, that her parents were in their eighties and not in good health, and that she had a horrifying dream of fighting with her siblings over their grave site.

The entire family had not been together for over fifteen years as a result of their conflicts, though they all lived in Los Angeles, and the children were all in their late forties or fifties. There were even grandchildren who had never met, or refused to see, their aunts, uncles and cousins as a result.

THE WISH LIST

The family members were resistant at first to the idea of mediation, and it took some conversation and problem solving over the telephone to get the two brothers and two sisters to agree that they would meet together, along with both brothers' wives, but without the mother and father.

As they walked into the room, they did not say hello to each other and avoided eye contact. The siblings sat as far apart from each other as possible.

I began the mediation process by welcoming them, thanking them for being willing to come together to talk about their problems, explaining mediation, and reviewing the ground rules. I then asked them to introduce themselves by telling me their name, their place in the family, one problem they would like to see addressed in the mediation, and one wish they had for an outcome to this process. I recorded their responses on a flip chart, and their answers were as follows:

PROBLEMS	WISHES
Ongoing conflicts back to age two. Telling lies and untruths.	To live like a family.
Mother always looked the other way. The family is into avoidance.	To all get along, tell the truth, and accept each other.
Feeling like an outsider in my own family.	To be respectful and involved in the same activities and share caring for our parents as they get older.
A lack of sincerity and sensitivity— being superficial.	To make our relationship better.
We have never been open and are too much into competition.	To respect each other and put the conflicts behind us.
Our mother uses rivalry to divide us.	To discuss issues respectfully, and immediately, and be a happy family.

After completing their introductions, I asked them to look back at the list I had made to see if they could find any commonalities. When conflicting parties are asked to perform this exercise, they immediately slip out of their conflict roles and emotional processing and are actually able to see their conflict as an "it" rather than as a "you." They also gain process awareness and may be able to identify what they have in common without the mediator pointing it out to them. Everyone agreed that all the problems that had been mentioned were true and accurate and that their conflicts made them feel superficial and dishonest and like outsiders in their own family. They also agreed that they were in complete unanimity about what they wanted, which was to be a family again.

THE TRANSFORMATION BEGINS

I then decided, based on the tone of the conversation and the fact that we had only two hours to complete the mediation, to take a risk and open the conversation to a deeper, and potentially transformative, level quickly. Instead of inquiring about their issues, I asked whether any of them had anything for which they wanted to apologize.

After a few moments of silence, the older brother spoke and apologized to his siblings for having stolen money from their parents several years ago and having lied about it. He said he felt horrible inside for having done this and had apologized to their parents, offered to sell his house to pay them back, and been paying them back each month for some time.

At this point, I could have thanked him for his apology and gone on. However, it was clear from the energy in the room that a major shift had started, and I didn't want to leave it before opening the door a little wider so the family members could shift their direction, open their hearts to one another, and begin a new family process that was based on honesty and acceptance.

To enlarge this opening, I asked the other members of the family to respond to what their older brother had said. The first to speak was the youngest sister, who complimented him for his courage in making the apology. I asked the oldest sister to speak, and she also thanked him and accepted his apology. The youngest brother went last; he said that since he had been two years old, he had doubted his older brother's integrity, and now was the first time that he had seen him behave in a morally responsible way.

He then said, "I just have one question to ask you." I started to worry that he would return to some unresolved issue before completing the resolution of this one. Instead, he asked, "If you were in so much trouble, why didn't you come to me for help? I'm your brother." At this point, it was clear that the conflict had been broken and the transformation of the family had begun.

MORE APOLOGIES

The oldest sister also wanted to apologize. She was their stepsister and had come into the family after her father married their mother within a year after each of their respective spouses had died. She said that at the time she joined the family, she was still mourning the death of her mother and did not feel she had really given the rest of them a chance; that she had been deeply unhappy and had not been a real sister to them.

Again, I asked the others to respond, but this time their response was one of disbelief. None of them had felt what she thought they had felt. I then turned to her and asked, "Isn't there someone else you have to apologize to?" She asked, "Do you mean me?" She and her siblings agreed that she had been too hard on herself and if she had slighted them, it had been by not asking them for support when she needed it.

The youngest sister also had a number of things to apologize for and was similarly accepted and welcomed with open arms by her brothers and sisters.

CURTAINS AND KITES

We next turned to the question of whether they were ready for a resolution. I wanted to know whether there was anything holding them back from creating the family that they had wished for; and since the youngest brother had twice referred to his distrust for his older brother as something that went back to the time when he was two, I asked him to describe what had happened.

The youngest brother said that when he was two (though it is more likely that he was three or four), his older brother had taken a pair of scissors and cut a pattern out of the living room drapes. Their mother had been furious; and when they both denied having done it, she announced that no one would eat dinner until someone confessed. The older brother threatened his younger sibling and told him to confess or his kite would get broken. The younger brother confessed to save his kite, but his respect and trust were broken instead.

I asked the older brother to respond and he apologized, but the absolution by his younger sibling was not complete. The anger over this betrayal was still in the tone of his voice. I asked the younger brother what it would take for him to let go of this anger that he had been carrying for over fifty years. Finally, he said, with deep emotion, "I want him to buy me a kite," and it was clear that his response was exactly the right one since it came not from him on that day, but from him as a child fifty years ago. The older brother agreed to buy the kite, and the younger brother agreed to let go of his anger in response.

A COMMON STRATEGY

In retrospect, the siblings all agreed that their mother must have known who had actually cut the drapes and should not have accepted the younger brother's confession. In fact, she had routinely divided them against each other rather than uniting them. They agreed that they needed to develop a common strategy to use with her—and with their father, who basically bowed out of their conflicts and spent most of the time with them in silence.

Their common strategy was to go to their parents' house together and say the following: "We want to thank you for everything you have done for us. We have decided that what is most important to us right now is to have a family again, and we need your support to make it happen. We want to ask you to help us by asking us if we complain to you about each other to go to the person we have the problem with and to help us try to see the problem from that person's point of view."

As we began to run out of time, I asked when they would go to see their parents and how they wanted to tell them what they had done. I urged them to do so as soon as possible. One of the brothers agreed to cancel a previous engagement, and they decided to go immediately to their parents' house to tell them what they had decided and to plan their first family get-together in fifteen years for the coming holidays.

I told them the change would not be total or immediate for everyone but that they should be persistent and remember, if things got rough, how much they had achieved in just a few hours.

Finally, I returned to their list of wishes and asked them how they felt about each other right now, and whether their wishes had already begun to come true, just in the way they were talking to each other. They agreed, and the older sister said she hadn't thought it was possible that her family might celebrate together over the holidays.

As we ended, I reached over to hold hands with those who were seated next to me, and the circle of hands grew until it joined. The two brothers then got up and hugged and kissed each other for the first time in fifty years, then they were all kissing and hugging and crying, and set off to tell their parents what they had done. In that moment, they were a family again.

SECOND THOUGHTS:

Clearly, not every family dispute will end in such a heartfelt way. All families are different, and as Leo Tolstoy observed in the opening lines of *Anna Karenina*, "every unhappy family is unhappy in its own way." Yet there are countless processes that can be used to encourage a wide range of heart-based responses in people who, no matter how unhappy their family has been, want a deeper conversation than one that is oriented solely to settling the issues. For example, here are some approaches that can be used to create deeper, sometimes risky and dangerous, conversations in family disputes:

1. Ask family members to introduce themselves by name, birth order, and describe the role they play in their family, or indicate how they think other family members see them. This may help clarify family system dynamics.

2. Ask each person the following questions:

   - "What word or phrase you would use to describe the kind of family you most want to have?" I write each word or phrase on a flip chart. Notice that the one who says they want a family that is honest feels lied to, and the one who wants a family that is respectful feels disrespected.
   - I next ask, "Does anyone disagree with any of these words?" No one ever does, but if they did, I would search for an acceptable euphemism. I then congratulate them on having reached consensus, and they are sometimes shocked to hear it.
   - The next question brings them right into the present: "Are you willing to start right now living up to those words and use them to guide our conversation?" No one has ever said no.
   - Finally, I ask: "Does everyone here have permission to call us on it if we move away from those words, and remind us of them?" Again, no one has ever said no.

3. If you want to get even riskier, you can also ask, the following questions:

   - "What stereotypes, images, or false expectations do you think other members of the family have of you?"
   - "What would you like them to know or understand about who you actually are?"

- "What is one thing you would like to be acknowledged or thanked for?"
- "What is one thing you would like to acknowledge or thank them for?"
- "What is one thing you wish you had done differently, or that you would like to apologize for?"

4. And if you want to get *seriously* dangerous, consider asking a version of these questions (based partly on ideas by Peter Block):

- "What have you done to create the very thing that you are most troubled by?"
- "What have you been clinging to or holding onto that it is now time for you to release?"
- "What are you responsible for in your conflict that you have not yet admitted or acknowledged to other family members?"
- "What do you most want to hear other family members say to you that you haven't mentioned?"
- "What do you long for most in your relationship with your family?"
- "What is the refusal, or 'no,' that you have not communicated to them? Would you be willing to do so right now?"
- "What is the permission, or 'yes,' that you gave in the past that you now want to retract? Why did you give it, and why are you now taking it back?"
- "What is the resentment that you are holding onto that the other person doesn't know about?"
- "What do you never, *ever* want to hear again?"
- "What did the other person do to you that you are still unwilling to forgive?"

- "What price are you paying for your conflict? How much longer are you willing to continue paying that price?"
- "What gift could you give to the other members of your family that you are withholding?"
- "What is one thing you are willing to do for the other members of your family with no acknowledgement or expectation of return?"

There is no single correct answer to any of these questions. To ask them at the right time and in the right way, the mediator needs to be completely present, open-hearted, and courageous enough to take the conversation to a deeper level if that is where the conflict is located.

20.
Conflict Stories: Three Case Studies in Mediation

Kenneth Cloke

A version of these stories was first published in *The Crossroads of Conflict: A Journey into the Heart of Dispute Resolution* (Janis Publ'ns 2006) (www.janispublications.com).

1.   BLINDED BY CONFLICT

Sara had been blind from birth. She had also been a victim of childhood sexual abuse, and while she had gone on to become a champion downhill skier, karate expert, and horseback rider, she had not been successful in establishing a satisfying sexual relationship.

She met Bill in 1978. They did not marry or live together, but dated for about six months. She said she had not wanted a sexual relationship with him. Nonetheless, according to Sara, Bill had raped her, and she had become pregnant. Bill denied doing so but did not provide an alternate version of their sexual encounter.

Sara said nothing to Bill about the pregnancy and had the baby, Scott, alone. While undergoing counseling regarding the aftereffects of her rape, Sara decided, when Scott was two years old, to confront Bill with his child. At first Bill denied paternity, though his son looked a lot like him. He asked Sara how she knew Scott was his. It took him awhile to accept that Scott was his son, and he had many misgivings about Sara not telling him. Eventually, though, he began to see Scott for a couple of hours on Saturdays and then steadily increased the time they spent together. He began to pay child support, and Sara felt that he had "stuck in there."

Two years before the mediation, at a workshop for single parents and their children attended by Sara, Scott drew a picture revealing sexual content and suggesting possible sexual molestation. An allegation of possible sexual abuse was filed against Sara's mother, who had been Scott's primary caretaker, which both Sara and Bill felt was unfounded. Scott was taken from his home and from his father and mother and was eventually sent to Sara's sisters, who refused to allow Bill to even see him. Sara and her mother hired an attorney. Bill felt he had been supportive of them. He discovered in court, however, that his paternity was not established and that he was not recognized as Scott's father. All the latent hostility that Sara and Bill felt toward one another came out in court, and the child abuse case turned into a bitter custody battle. Bill hired an attorney and was finally able to secure a joint custody order with visitation every other week. Scott began spending one week with his mother and the next with his father.

Sara began a relationship with another man, Ted. They discussed marriage, but Sara had been troubled throughout the relationship, and in the course of several years together they had not had sex with one another.

In August, Sara and Ted decided to move to a small town about four hours from Los Angeles, where she and Bill had lived and worked and where Scott, now age seven and a half, had gone to school. She gave brief notice to Bill of her decision to move and none to the court.

Bill applied for and received a temporary restraining order preventing her from removing Scott from Los Angeles and applied for sole custody, alleging that Sara was in violation of the court's prior order regarding joint custody and visitation. Sara appeared in court to oppose the order and lost. School was due to start in one week, both sides were at complete loggerheads, and a trial was set for October, long after school began. They had each spent tens of thousands of dollars on legal fees and were no closer to a solution.

MEDIATION

In desperation, Sara's attorney recommended mediation. At first, Bill was reluctant to go to mediation and refused to pay for it. Sara said she was unable to pay. In order to get them started, I agreed to begin the mediation and indicated that if they felt I had not been helpful at the end of two hours, they would not be required to pay. I have done this on several occasions when a couple's conflicts prevented them from agreeing on who would pay for the mediation, and I have always been paid at the end of the session.

I asked Sara to start because she seemed the most agitated and untrusting, but she deferred to Bill. But as Bill spoke, she continually interrupted him. Bill threatened to leave if she continued, which created a difficulty because she was unable, due to her blindness, to take handwritten notes for later reference.

I shifted back to Sara, but she was less talkative when initiating dialogue than in response to Bill's narrative.

CUSTODY ARRANGEMENT

I asked her how she felt about the one-week-on/one-week-off schedule, and she said it was not working for her or, she thought, for Scott because the transitions were difficult. She expressed concern over changes in Scott's behavior after returning from Bill's place, where there were constant videos and nonstop talk about Ninjas, He-Man, Superman, and other escapes into fantasy. She felt that these activities were excessive and interfered with Scott's emotional development.

I asked her what she wanted. She said she wanted Scott to be with her for nine months during the school year and was willing to give up all holidays and vacations to support Bill's relationship with him. She said she wanted them to be close and did not want to interfere with their relationship. I asked her to speak directly to Bill and tell him what she wanted and why. She turned to him and repeated what she had said to me, but more directly and emotionally and in a heartfelt way.

I then asked Bill to tell Sara directly what he wanted and how he felt about what she had said. He said that he loved his son and wanted to see him all the time but recognized that Scott needed his mother and was willing to do whatever was necessary to help him. In fact, he had moved a few months earlier to an apartment only a block from Sara's house so that Scott could walk between their homes. He had agreed to joint custody because it was a compromise that would help Scott, but acknowledged that the every-other-week schedule was not perfect. He appreciated Sara's acknowledgment of his relationship with Scott, but felt that Sara should have given him more notice and consulted with him rather than just announcing her move. He told Sara that he still loved her but recognized that they were unable to get along. He regularly invited her to talk, but she always hung up the phone or walked out on him.

A WORKABLE SOLUTION

I thanked them for the honesty of their statements and their willingness to acknowledge their son's need to spend as much time with each of them as possible. I pointed out that they had a much harder time reaching agreements when they discussed what had occurred in the past than when they focused on their son and his future. I summarized their requests and asked whether they would be willing to agree on a solution that would reflect what was best for their son. They agreed.

Sara and Bill also agreed that many parents lived apart and exchanged children during school holidays; that many psychologists counseled against switching children too frequently or from school to school; that children generally prefer not to switch schools before graduation; that courts often prefer mothers as the primary custodial parents for younger children and fathers for older children, especially boys; and that as Scott grew older, he would probably want to have a direct say in where he would live during the school year.

We discussed a number of possible solutions, and they agreed in general that Scott would need to spend his school year with one parent and holidays with the other. We also discussed travel arrangements, improving their communications, and increasing child support. In the end, though, Sara and Bill still each wanted Scott during the school year.

I asked whether they would consider dividing the elementary school grades into two sets: Scott would spend third and fourth grades with one parent and fifth and sixth with the other. Bill said he was willing to work things out with Sara and be more generous than he had planned before coming to the mediation. He offered to let Scott live with Sara for two years and then with him for the next two years, and Scott would spend school holidays and every other weekend during that time with the non-custodial parent. Sara felt relieved and quickly agreed.

I wrote down their principal points of agreement, which included specific drop-off times and places, making these agreements flexible, making the exchanges a priority, taking Scott's wishes into consideration in selecting his junior high and high schools, meeting again to discuss their communication problems and child support issues, and returning to mediation if there were any future problems.

A UNITED FRONT

Bill suggested that they see Scott together after the mediation to tell him together what they had decided. Sara agreed. They agreed to tell Scott that they had resolved their differences and were going to support each other more in the future. They agreed that they would do more things together with Scott and not let their past disagreements get in the way of their future cooperation. They agreed to let bygones be bygones, recognize that they both loved Scott more than anyone, and discuss any issues regarding his future and well-being with each other before jumping to conclusions.

I congratulated them on their success in reaching these agreements and their willingness to compromise and acknowledge each other's love for Scott. I told them how lucky I thought Scott was to have two parents who loved him so much. They both began to cry and talked about how much they loved him and wanted the best for him. I said I hoped that they would continue to acknowledge and respect each other and recognize how difficult the past few years had been for both of them. I suggested some ground rules for their future communications, and we set another date for mediation. Bill offered to pay for the mediation and, as they left, reached over and hugged Sara, who hugged him back. They both stood and cried for a while and left arm in arm.

EPILOGUE

The mediation succeeded because it encouraged them to recognize that in spite of their opposing differences, they had one powerful interest in common: their love for their son. As a result, they were willing to sacrifice their anger at each other for his welfare and commit to finding a solution, albeit imperfect, outside the legal system and making it work. This result was encouraged by their experience with the costs, delays, uncertainties, and emotional damage they had suffered in the courts.

The mediation allowed them to express their emotions and anger at each other, yet recognize that their anger would not help them make decisions regarding their son. At various points, I made them aware of specific communication problems by asking them to focus on the future rather than the past. I stopped their circular arguments periodically with process interventions, pointed out specific communication problems as they occurred, and occasionally said, "Let's take a look at what just happened in your conversation with each other," in an effort to increase their awareness of *how* they were communicating. I worked with them to create a common agenda, refocused their attention on problems rather than each other, and provided them with information regarding criteria other parents had used to solve similar problems.

The mediation did not become sidetracked in endless, collateral arguments over whether Bill had actually raped Sara years earlier, whether their son had been molested, etc., since none of these issues, in their minds or mine, ought to have determined where Scott would go to school. Sara's blindness was acknowledged and addressed openly, but not allowed to dominate or distort their negotiations.

In closure, I encouraged them to acknowledge their mutual love for their son and suggested that they might actually become friends over time. While the session began with acrimony and accusation, it ended with both of them speaking from their hearts to each other. They started to reach forgiveness and reconciliation the moment they agreed to tell their son together what they had decided and try to minimize his feeling that one of them had been treated unfairly or had greater power than the other. In this way, they took a small, significant, collaborative step toward joint parenting, transcended the issues and conditions that had led them into litigation, and learned the power of collaboratively negotiating their interests and communicating from their hearts.

In short, they were able to transform their conflict and successfully create a collaborative parenting relationship in place of the competitive one that had developed over time—not just as an idea, but as a real experience. They were able to break through their animosity and re-establish a more integrated family system, even at a distance. Finally, they were able to speak honestly to each other, deepen their relationship, and transcend the centripetal orbit of their earlier relationship.

In a follow-up mediation I conducted several months later, Bill and Sara both reported that their agreements had held up, and their communications had never been better. Scott was doing well, the transitions had become less difficult, and their new relationship had reduced his level of anxiety, hostility, and acting-out. They both felt they were starting to become friends again.

2. WEEDING OUT CONFLICT

Ramon moved to California from Mexico and spent twenty years doing odd jobs as a gardener to feed his family. Finally, he received the offer of a lifetime: a full-time gardening position on the estate of a wealthy retired businessman named Sam. Ramon worked for Sam for several years and received frequent accolades for his devotion and responsibility.

THE BEGINNING OF THE END

Sam hired a manager, Luis, to oversee Ramon and other employees. On one occasion, Luis told Ramon to clear away some wood and take it to the dump. Ramon asked if he could have the wood since it was of very high quality but not useful on the estate, and Luis told him that he could.

Ramon and Luis got along fine until Luis decided to bring in a subcontractor to trim some ailing trees. Ramon did not like the way the subcontractors attacked the trees and noticed that the truck they were using did not have a license plate. He checked and found out that they did not have a license to trim trees. Ramon reported this information to Luis. Luis became furious and told Ramon to mind his own business. After that, their relationship deteriorated.

One day when Luis was on vacation, Ramon decided to take three pieces of wood that had been thrown away and could not be used on the estate to repair the house. When Luis returned, he complained to Sam, who called Ramon into the office and summarily fired him. Ramon was shocked and tried to explain, but Sam would hear none of it. Ramon returned the three pieces of wood but felt so humiliated by the experience that he decided to sue for wrongful termination.

AN OPPORTUNITY TO BE HEARD

At the mediation, both attorneys began by indicating that neither they nor their clients would make any opening statements but wanted to move directly into separate rooms to conduct settlement negotiations. I met with each side privately and recommended against this process. Based on my observation of the discomfort their clients were experiencing and my intuitive sense of what lay beneath the surface of their dispute, I asked if there were things that the clients wanted to say to each other that had not yet been said. Both said that there were, and the attorneys agreed to allow Sam and Ramon to speak directly to each other.

Sam asked to go first and told Ramon how disappointed he was in him. He said he liked Ramon and felt his gardening work was excellent, but his trust had been shattered and he could no longer keep him on the estate.

Ramon asked Sam why he had not allowed him to explain what happened at the time he was terminated. Sam said he had asked if Ramon had taken the wood, heard that he had, and that was all he needed to know.

Ramon told him the circumstances that had led him to take the wood and said he had never stolen anything in his life. He agreed that he ought to have waited for Luis to return from vacation to ask permission as he had done in the past; but he knew the wood was being thrown out, and Luis had given him permission in similar situations before.

Sam thought the unresolved conflict between Ramon and Luis made the whole situation impossible and felt he had to accept what Luis had told him. I asked whether either side would like to bring Luis into the mediation to tell his story, but both sides felt there would be no point since Ramon had found a new position and did not want to return to working at the estate.

Based on an empathetic sense that had I been in their shoes, I would have wanted to say more, I asked them if there was anything either of them wanted to apologize for. After a moment of silence, Ramon apologized to Sam for not having checked with him before taking the wood and not being able to resolve his conflict with Luis. Sam then apologized to Ramon for jumping to conclusions and said he now understood that Ramon had not stolen the wood. He said he felt sorry that he had not listened to Ramon when he tried to explain what happened and asked if there was anything he could do to make up for it. Ramon told Sam he had found another job but wanted to be paid for the six months he had been out of work and receive a positive letter of recommendation in case his present job did not work out. Sam immediately agreed.

CLOSURE

To give them an opportunity to reach completion, I said that this was probably the last time they would see each other and asked if there was anything else either of them wanted to say in parting. Ramon said he had really appreciated working on the estate, that it had helped him provide security for his family and purchase a home of his own. He said he wished Sam well. Sam thanked Ramon for all the work he had done to make the estate a beautiful place to live. He said he had no problem writing a very positive letter of recommendation because Ramon had really been a wonderful employee. He wished him well and said he would miss him.

To move the conversation further in the direction of learning, I asked them each to identify one thing they would do differently as a result of this experience. Sam said he would communicate better and not avoid difficult conversations that could require him to change his mind. Ramon said he would not ever take anything that belonged to anyone again because it wasn't worth it. He said he would not let future conflicts with coworkers go unresolved but would work hard to prevent bad feelings from building up.

I asked them, if they now felt the conflict between them was really over, whether they would be willing to shake hands as a way of symbolizing that it was ended and wish each other well in the future. They shook hands, then hugged each other with great emotion, cried, and spoke privately and intimately for several minutes while their attorneys sat wondering silently what had happened.

Had the mediation been conducted as the attorneys originally wished along the lines of power or rights, none of this could have happened. No amount of simply shuttling between the parties could have conveyed the open, honest, heartfelt spirit they brought to their communications, a spirit that could only have emerged between them in person. While the litigation might still have settled, the underlying reasons for the dispute would have gone unresolved, and the parties would not have reached forgiveness or negotiated an agreement that was very different from what each side initially demanded. Only their direct communication, heart-to-heart engagement, willingness to

234

apologize for what they had done, and genuine appreciation for each other as human beings allowed them to walk away feeling good about themselves and each other, and reach genuine closure in their conflict.

By speaking honestly and empathetically to each other, they were able to transform their intentions and attitudes toward each other, and their conflict became a direct, open, honest, empathetic conversation, a vehicle of learning and increased awareness, a way of evolving in their understanding and approach to conflict and resolution, and a means of transformation and transcendence.

3. WASHING AWAY SINS

Roberta was driving home from work on the freeway when her windshield suddenly shattered. She slammed on the brakes and narrowly averted a collision with the cars around her. A police investigation revealed that two young kids, ages twelve and fourteen, had been throwing rocks at passing cars from a freeway overpass.

REFERRAL TO MEDIATION

They were arrested, but because it was their first offense, the prosecuting attorney's office referred the case to a juvenile victim-offender mediation program as part of a pilot project to determine whether mediation could produce better results than the criminal courts.

It took some effort to convince Roberta to mediate, as she was afraid at first to meet her attackers. Ultimately, she agreed to mediate with the two juveniles, Phil and Tim, together with their aunt who was raising them because their mother was working out of town and their father had disappeared. Phil and Tim were also reluctant to meet with Roberta, but their only alternative was to face prosecution in juvenile court and a possible jail sentence.

I opened the session by thanking everyone for being willing to meet and talk honestly about what had happened. I expressed a hope that we would be able to achieve something more through direct conversation than through formal court proceedings. We agreed on a set of ground rules, which included everyone's right to stop the conversation if it was not working and either correct it or end the process and return to court, where we would lose the ability to speak confidentially and directly to each other.

HONEST FEELINGS

I asked Roberta to begin and be completely honest in telling Phil and Tim what they had done to her and how it made her feel. She pointed a finger directly at them and said in a tense, angry, accusatory voice, "You little sons of bitches, you almost killed me! I am going to be a grandmother next month, and you almost killed me, you little sons of bitches." She began to sob. Phil and Tim, who were frightened just to attend the mediation, were now completely terrified and also began to cry. The victim they had never stopped to imagine, except as a faceless nonentity, had suddenly turned into a real, angry, frightened grandmother whom they had nearly killed.

On seeing Phil and Tim burst into tears, Roberta realized that the "hardened criminals" she had imagined were just children. She softened her tone and told them more openly and vulnerably about her fear and sadness and asked them, "How could you have done this to me?" Their aunt tried to enter the conversation to defend them, but I did not want to let them off the hook and asked her to hold her comments and let Phil and Tim answer the question themselves. I said, gently and calmly, that Roberta was entitled to hear directly from them why they had done it.

It took several moments of silence for them to recover enough to speak. At last, Phil, the fourteen-year-old, spoke. Sobbing, he told Roberta that he was sorry, that he hadn't meant to hurt anyone, that they had just been playing, and that he hadn't thought about the harm they might cause. Tim said, "It's all my fault. I was the one who threw the rock. I'm sorry." And they both began to cry again.

On hearing their willingness to accept responsibility for what they had done, Roberta softened even more and began to speak to them directly in a sympathetic tone about what they had done, insisting that they take responsibility for the damage they had caused.

I asked the aunt if she wanted to speak, and she said that Phil and Tim were good boys but were having a hard time as their father had disappeared and their mother had to work full-time to support them, which was why she was not present. Roberta was sympathetic but did not feel that this excused their actions.

I asked Roberta what she thought Phil and Tim might do to prove to her that they were willing to accept responsibility for what they had done. She said what she really wanted before the mediation began was for them to pay for a new windshield, but she now understood their circumstances and saw that they were not old enough to find paying jobs.

A TRANSFORMING OPPORTUNITY

She thought for a while and offered instead that they might come to her house once a week for three months and wash her car. I asked Phil and Tim what they thought about this idea, and they eagerly agreed. We set a date, wrote up their agreements, and ended the mediation with the idea that it was now up to them to reverse the harm they had caused by being responsible for repairing the damage as best they could. I made a point of telling them that the criminal case would not be dismissed until Roberta certified that they had fulfilled their agreements.

At first, Roberta was anxious about inviting Phil and Tim to her house, but when they came, behaved respectfully, and worked hard to clean her car, she began to relax. It became clear to her that while they were washing her car, they were also washing away their sins and cleansing their guilt; and she began to experience forgiveness. The second time they came, she offered them some milk and cookies. The third time, she invited them into her house, and they talked about school and their lives. At the end of the three months, they had begun to be friends, and Roberta decided to pay them an allowance to take out her garbage and perform small tasks around the house.

Several years later, when Phil was about to graduate from high school, Roberta asked him what he was going to do, and he said he didn't know. She encouraged him to go to college, but he said he couldn't afford it. Guess who agreed to pay his tuition.

EPILOGUE

Now imagine the same story without mediation. Imagine what might have happened to Phil and Tim in the criminal justice system. Imagine them in prison and what their lives would have been like afterward. Imagine how Roberta would have felt about the trial and sentence and what the lack of real closure would have meant to her life, as opposed to what actually happened.

It would have been impossible for any of the participants to imagine at the beginning how this conflict would end—not just with restitution but with redemption, transcendence, and real forgiveness. By communicating deeply and honestly and with open hearts, they were able not only to resolve their personal conflict but to transcend the conditions that had created it, revealing the possibility of a far greater social evolution.

Their resolution revealed in miniature how mediation can produce far more effective results in criminal cases than those obtained by prosecution. They were each able to find at the center of their conflict a path leading directly to conflict transformation and personal and social transcendence.

SECOND THOUGHTS:

Each of these very different case studies begins with a story about someone who did something wrong, or something that was perceived to be wrong by someone else. In each case, my task was to deconstruct the stories they told about their conflict and reveal that a story with a completely different ending than the one they had imagined was possible. Looking closely at how people construct their conflict stories can help mediators see how to transform their stories.

In the stories we tell about our conflicts, every word we select, every fact we recite, every transgression we recount, indirectly chronicles our life choices. Every detail in our stories provides a clue to who we are, what we think, how we feel about ourselves and others, what we have done and failed to do, what we fear and hope will happen to us, why we remain stuck, and what we might be willing to do to transform and transcend our conflicts.

If we listen correctly, every conflict story allows us to reach deeply into the subconscious mind of the storyteller. Every conflict story exists on three levels: there is the *external story* that we tell to others; the *internal story* that we tell ourselves; and the *core story*, which consists of the reasons why we made up those other two stories. A single story, properly understood, reveals not only the facts about what happened and their emotional meaning to the storyteller but also the reasons the storyteller believes the conflict remains unresolved, the emotions and assumptions that lie at its core, and a deeply hidden set of vulnerabilities and desires that can be read as instructions for how the parties might live happily ever after.

The core story on conflict often begins with assertions of facts or declarations of feelings. These nearly always take the form of an *accusation*; yet beneath every accusation is a *confession*, and beneath every confession is a *request*. Hidden within conflict stories are also requests for acknowledgment, cries for help, confessions of powerlessness, and requests for forgiveness.

In conflict stories, the cunning or depravity of our opponents is simply the flip side of our own powerlessness, pain, sadness, and frustration. Because we feel powerless in conflict, we seek comforting explanations, justifications for our failure to do more, and rationalizations for our adversarial reactions. When we experience pain at the hands of others, we are drawn to ask what could possibly motivate someone to harm us. We want others to respect us as decent people who do not deserve this kind of treatment, and we are therefore drawn to characterize our opponents by contrast as wicked, malicious, evil people who intend us harm for no good reason, which also offers a backward justification for why we can do nothing to prevent or resolve it, and why we should not be blamed for harming them.

In these ways, conflict stories "dress up" the facts regarding upsetting events; yet, in so doing, they create signposts pointing inward to the hidden sources of conflict within the storyteller. Each story directs the listener's attention outward toward what the perpetrator did, partly out of a desire to minimize or deny the storyteller's own complicity, fear of confrontation, or wish to prevent future attacks through the deterrent of a well-timed counterattack. The perpetrator's perfidy is magnified in proportion to the storyteller's desire to appear innocent. In these ways, conflict stories "protest too much."

Yet conflict stories can also be heard as *invitations to resolution*—and as calls for the storyteller to transcend the story by:

- developing a more constructive attitude toward one's opponent,
- confronting and overcoming one's own inner demons,
- taking collaborative responsibility for resolving the dispute,
- transforming the antagonistic elements in one's relationships, and
- transcending the conditions that made it irresolvable in the first place.

Conflict stories are parables in which we describe how someone broke our hearts or caused an emotional or spiritual crisis in our lives. These stories are communicated not only externally to our listeners but also internally to ourselves, and not simply to ameliorate the crisis we are facing but to disguise its significance, demands, and potential consequences. The tone, metaphor, and symbolism of our stories are shaped by our needs, and we use the music, rhythm, and dramatic tension of the story to evoke and excite resonant emotions in others and soothe our own anxieties.

Conflict stories are also fairy tales in which the storyteller becomes a princess (victim) describing the actions of a dragon (perpetrator) to someone that (he or) she hopes will become her prince (rescuer). In the fairy tale, the princess is primarily responsible for expressing feelings and being emotionally vulnerable, the prince is responsible for coming up with solutions, and the dragon is responsible for directing attention toward problems that might otherwise go unnoticed. In order to elicit sympathy and support from the listener, the storyteller must be seen as powerless in the face of evil. The action of every conflict story is therefore to trade power for sympathy. Instead, the mediator offers empathy and empowerment and shows both parties how they are playing all three roles. This means refusing to become a rescuer, asking the princess to accept responsibility for part of the problem, helping the dragon become more open and vulnerable, and encouraging both to participate in solving the problem.

Every conflict story, at its core, expresses a heartfelt desire. It is a "cry of the heart," a protest against the absence of other, infinitely more desirable, stories—not about the pain of conflict, but about the longing for resolution, intimacy, compassion, forgiveness, and reconciliation. Each story is a hypothesis hoping to be disproved, a child's plea for comfort and mutual affection, a wish for the world to be different, a list of what most needs changing.

Marina Warner wrote regarding fairy tales that "[i]n the kingdom of fiction, the tension between speaking out and staying silent never eases." The same can be said of conflict stories, which walk a delicate line between what people desperately want to say and what they are afraid to hear and therefore try to ignore, suppress, or disguise. The mediator's object in using these techniques is to locate that line, take both storytellers by the hand, and formulate questions that will encourage them to cross it so that they can discover on the other side who they really are and what they really want.

PART VII

Self-Reflection and Reflection on Practice

[T]he very first requirement in a Hospital [is] that it should do the sick no harm.

Florence Nightingale

They were careful
as someone crossing an iced-over stream
Alert as a warrior in enemy territory.
Courteous as a guest.
Fluid as melting ice.
Shapable as a block of wood.

Lao Tzu, Tao te Ching 15 (Steven Mitchell trans., 1991)

21.

Mediation as Parallel Seminars: Lessons from the Student Takeover of Columbia University's Hamilton Hall

Carol B. Liebman

This is a modified version of an article that appeared in *Negotiation Journal* Volume 16, Issue 2 (April 2000). It is reprinted with the permission of *Negotiation Journal*.

THE CRISIS

In April of 1996, a faculty colleague and I spent four days and all of one night mediating the student takeover of Hamilton Hall at Columbia University. The building takeover was the culmination of a year-long debate about whether or not Ethnic Studies should become a formal part of the university's curriculum. When I was called in (by the university) to mediate, three students had been on a hunger strike for twelve days and were approaching what I was told was the point at which they were in danger of long-term damage to their health. Two days earlier, the university had called the New York City police, which resulted in the arrest of twenty-two demonstrators at another of the university's main buildings. In short, the debate over Ethnic Studies was rapidly escalating.

BACKGROUND

Throughout the 1995–1996 academic year, students—primarily, but not exclusively, students of color—had been urging the addition of the field of Ethnic Studies to the curriculum at Columbia University. In February, they briefly occupied the office of the dean of Columbia College, Austin Quigley. By spring, students were demanding that the university establish a separate Department of Ethnic Studies.

In a four-page leaflet (called "What Is Ethnic Studies?") that the students circulated around the campus in March, they drew on language from a University of Colorado at Boulder document to explain the field:

> . . . Ethnic Studies comprises a series of distinct approaches, and theoretical analysis of the historical, political, social and cultural forces and phenomena that have shaped the development of America's diverse racial-ethnic peoples over the last 500 years and which continue to shape our future. The focus of Ethnic Studies has traditionally been on marginalized and largely powerless groups which have been racially constructed as "non-white" or "people of color," and socially constructed as "minorities," that is, not part of the dominant society. As such, these communities of color have been denied the full benefits and opportunities that U.S. society has held out to European immigrants and their white descendants.

The document went on to state that even though the field was called Ethnic Studies, scholars in this area

> ...recognize distinctions [among] race, ethnicity and culture. Racially defined groups in the U.S. have a social trajectory and outcome quite distinct from white or European ethnic, religious or cultural standards, such as Irish Americans, Jewish Americans, Italian Americans [and] Polish Americans. Ethnic Studies scholars understand that race is not just another type of ethnicity, and that the social phenomena of institutionalized racism maintains a sharp divide between "whites" and "peoples of color" in the U.S.

This approach to the study of the experience of racial groups in the United States differed markedly from traditional academic analysis of the subject.

On April 1, four students began a hunger strike to draw attention to the Ethnic Studies cause. One of them quickly dropped out for health reasons.

In an April 5, 1996, letter to Jane Bai, one of the leaders of the Ethnic Studies movement, Columbia President George Rupp indicated support for the goals of the students but rejected the proposed means for achieving those goals. Specifically, he indicated that he saw no possibility for a separate department devoted to Ethnic Studies.

Thursday, April 9, was a day filled with meetings and negotiations aimed at finding a solution to the Ethnic Studies debate and an end to the students' hunger strike. From all accounts, the meetings were not a success, although for a time university officials believed that an agreement in principle had been reached to end the hunger strike. I was told that communications during at least one of the meetings on April 9 were difficult and that, at one point, a high-ranking administrator lost patience with the students and walked out.

At 4:00 p.m. on April 9, students rallied at the sundial at the center of campus. Then, more than a hundred demonstrators moved into

Low Library, the university's main administration building and the focal point of student demonstrations in the late 1960s, where they spent the night. On Wednesday morning, April 10, the police were called in to remove the students. (When I later asked why mediation had not been tried at that stage, I was told that administrators felt they were faced with an emergency situation in which people's physical safety was at risk because of the crush around some of the Low Library entrance doors. Supporters of the students doubted that claim and suspected the administration of wanting to show its toughness.) When the police arrived, students were given the opportunity to leave the building or stay and be arrested. Twenty-two of the student demonstrators chose to be arrested. It seemed as if the crisis had passed.

However, during the late afternoon of Thursday, April 11, approximately one hundred students took over Hamilton Hall, the main academic building of the university and the place where many of the classrooms and a number of department offices were located. The students lined up along one side of the hallways and chanted quietly so that those with business in Hamilton could pass by and so that classes could go on. Thursday night, other students joined the Hamilton demonstrators. On Friday morning, April 12, the nearly 200 students in the building barricaded the doors and would not allow anyone else to enter.

MEDIATION INQUIRIES

Early on Friday morning, April 12, the dean of the law school was attending a meeting at Low Library. As he was leaving, the provost asked him if anyone at the law school knew about mediation. The dean gave him my name. Later that morning, while I was teaching a class on negotiation, the dean's office received a call from Low Library asking that I come immediately to meet with the president of the university and others responsible for dealing with the situation.

At that time, I had limited information about the issues underlying the conflict. I had, of course, read about the Ethnic Studies debate in the *Spectator*, Columbia's student newspaper; had seen the tent where the hunger strikers were staying; and had read press accounts of the student arrests on Wednesday. The beginning of April was quite cold, and I remember thinking at the time that if the demonstrators were staying out all night in a tent in such weather, this was more serious than the usual spring student protests.

I ended class early on Friday, April 12, and went to the president's office in Low Library, where eight to ten university officials were gathered. After introductions, various university representatives briefed me on the background of the situation from their perspective and indicated their most pressing concerns: the health of the hunger strikers, fear of physical confrontation between the demonstrators and unsympathetic students trying to force their way into the building, and disruption of classes and other university business. They also asked me what a mediation process might involve and, ultimately, asked me to try to mediate.

ADDING DIVERSITY TO THE MEDIATION MIX

I replied that I was willing to try, but I thought that I was the wrong person for this job. I doubted that a white, middle-aged faculty member who was married to a dean was going to have credibility with the students. I knew there was no chance that I would be accepted if I went on my own to propose mediation to the students. Thus, I suggested that I try to locate one of my law school colleagues, Kellis Parker, an African American who, over the years, had served as a counselor for Columbia College students of color, and ask him to introduce me to the leaders of the student group. I also said that I would try to locate other mediators who might be more acceptable to the students. I left messages for Kellis at his office and home and then began trying to contact other possible mediators.

Kellis and I finally made contact about 2:00 p.m. He agreed to introduce me to the student leaders. We walked together from the law school across Amsterdam Avenue to the main entrance of the campus at 116th Street. There, we had to stop and show our university IDs. All of the gates to the main campus (an area six city blocks long and three blocks wide) had been locked except for the two main gates at 116th and Broadway and 116th and Amsterdam. Columbia IDs were required to gain entrance to the campus. This had the effect of barring outsiders from augmenting the ranks of the protestors, and it had the indirect effect of keeping out the press.

As Kellis and I walked down the steps from College Walk toward Hamilton Hall, Carlton Long, a young African American political scientist, joined us. Carlton and I had never met, but I had heard good things about him. We walked together the short distance to the front entrance of Hamilton. It was a beautiful day, chilly but sunny. The student protestors had inscribed the names of critical race theorists on the front of the building, in chalk not paint. Some students were inside the building; others were gathered outside.

Kellis introduced me to six students who were described as the leaders of the demonstrators. It was never clear to me how they were designated as the leaders. As far as I could tell, neither the demonstrators nor the six leaders had much time to jell as a group. As a result, I was concerned throughout the mediation that their leadership was precarious.

Kellis spoke briefly to the six student leaders while Carlton and I chatted. He then brought them over to meet me. When I was introduced to the students, I told them that I taught mediation at the law school, that I had met with university officials in Low Library, and that the university was willing to try mediation. I said that I was willing to mediate, but I was not sure I was the right person because of the same reasons I cited to university officials: I was a white, middle-aged woman faculty member married to the law school dean. The students asked several questions about mediation and then walked a few yards away and talked. They came back and, pointing to Kellis and Carlton, said, "We don't want you. We want one of them." I responded, "That's not going to happen. This is too hard. This is too complicated. You need somebody with training and experience. I can help you find someone else if you want, but it can't be somebody who doesn't know about mediation." They withdrew to confer again. After about five minutes, they returned and asked, "What about you and one of them?"—meaning Kellis or Carlton. I took a deep breath and said, "We can make that work."

Kellis, Carlton, and I talked briefly about my view of the role of the mediator and then discussed which of them should mediate. We decided that Carlton Long, the young political scientist whom I had known for about ten minutes, and I would be co-mediators and that Kellis would remain available to the students as an adviser. My anxiety level was high as I agreed to team up on what was clearly the most difficult case that I had ever mediated with a person whom I had just met and who had no background as a mediator. But it was necessary to take that risk in order to get the mediation going. The decision worked out well. I could not have hoped for a better partner; it was as if Carlton and I had worked together for years.

THE STAKES

Once the students agreed, at mid-afternoon, to try mediation, it took until well into Friday evening to start the first formal mediation session. The students wanted time to meet and talk with their constituents.

As the mediation began that Friday evening, all of the participants were under a fair amount of pressure. At this stage, the three students had been on a hunger strike for fourteen days. We were told that they were entering the danger zone where they began to risk long-term damage to their health. The information we all had was that healthy young people can go about two weeks without eating and that, while there was no bright line, there was more and more concern day by day once the two weeks were up. That information made all of us—the student leaders, the university representatives, and the mediators—feel that it was urgent to find a solution.

In addition, if the mediation did not succeed, the university faced the prospect of having its students very publicly arrested for the second time within a week, and the students were facing the risk of damaging their academic careers and acquiring a criminal record. The sense of those close to the scene was that if the police were again called, students were not going to have the opportunity to avoid arrest by choosing to leave. For students of color, many of whom had overcome significant obstacles to reach Columbia and whose families were sacrificing to support their children's education, a criminal record would be an especially heavy burden on their futures.

Moreover, as the weekend went on, I was concerned that there was less and less chance that a second round of arrests would occur as peacefully as the first. Certainly, New York City police were better trained for dealing with demonstrations than they were in the 1960s. The university people who watched them carry out the arrests on Wednesday morning told me that the police had been "professional" and "very kind" in their interactions with the students. But a week later, the police might be less patient, and they would be dealing with students who had not had a lot of sleep in that period. So the odds of avoiding a serious confrontation the second time around did not appear to be good.

THE OPENING SESSION

When the first formal mediation session began, the students were represented by the six student leaders. Two of them were African American, two were Latinos, and two were Asian American. The university team was represented by two white women, two white men, and an African American woman who was unable to join the negotiations until Saturday morning. I had not met any of the students, but Carlton knew most of them. I was aware that one member of the student team had been a controversial figure around Columbia after writing an anti-Semitic article in the *Spectator* earlier in the year that was so virulent that it attracted notice in the national press.

We started the mediation Friday evening with the traditional mediators' opening: We reviewed our understanding of the process and our role in it, explaining that we were there to help the two teams work out a resolution that met the interests of both, that we were not judges or arbitrators and would not be deciding who was right or wrong or telling them what the solution should be. We also explained confidentiality. This seemed especially important for the student negotiators, who would probably face disciplinary charges and were sure to be concerned about whether the things they said in mediation would come back to haunt them at a later date.

We wanted to underscore the fact that mediation was a different process. Therefore, while waiting for the formal mediation to start, I made some quick amendments to the Columbia Law School Mediation Clinic's standard agreement to mediate. After our opening statement, we asked all of the participants to sign the agreement to mediate.

The students caucused to discuss the agreement and came back with the request that the following one-sentence paragraph be added: "In the event that any individual or group decide to withdraw from mediation he/she/they will communicate the reason for that withdrawal in writing to the other participants in the mediation." At the time, my reaction was that this was just a move by the students to establish control of the process. Probably because I was extremely anxious to get all of the participants to commit to the process and to start discussions, it did not occur to me to use a standard mediator move of exploring what underlying interest of the student team was represented by this requested addition. I did not appreciate the value of that paragraph until after the mediation, when one of the university negotiators told me that having the requirement of a written explanation before withdrawing kept them going at times when they were ready to give up. In addition, I did not understand until after the mediation that the paragraph was a way for the members of the student negotiation team to bind themselves to each other and to the process.

MEDIATION AS PARALLEL SEMINARS

Once the agreement was signed, Carlton and I indicated that we intended to start by having everyone who wanted to speak tell us his or her view of the situation. This request was greeted with a fair amount of eye rolling by members of both teams. I had the sense that they were thinking they had already told their stories ad nauseam. They were right, but, as in so many mediations, stories had been told but not heard.

A great deal of what we did as mediators during the first few hours was basic clarification of exactly what the parties intended by various phrases or actions. We asked the students such questions as, "When you say *Ethnic Studies*, what do you mean? Why is it important to you?"

We asked the university representatives questions like, "When you say it [Ethnic Studies as a department] can't happen in the university, tell us how the university works."

We were really conducting two parallel seminars the whole four days, but especially that first evening. In one, the members of the student team taught us what they meant by Ethnic Studies, why it was important to them as a way of addressing the alienation they felt, and why it should be important to the university. In the other seminar, the members of the university team taught us how universities are governed, how change comes about in the university, and how faculty are appointed.

There is a third seminar that takes place during mediation, and it is a crucial component of the process. Most mediators use discussions aimed at getting the parties to the table and the opening statement at the beginning of the mediation to explain the process. But those explanations are, as in the Hamilton Hall mediation, only the first steps in teaching the participants about the process and, thereby, empowering them to use it effectively. One of the most important responsibilities of the mediator in this, and in most mediations, is to anticipate the training needs of the participants, providing them with on-the-spot training throughout the mediation process.

We started in joint session, and it was there that the third seminar first came into play. One of the students began, mainly reading from a list of demands. It was a positional statement. At the end, the student speaker, in a fairly confrontational manner, demanded a response to the list from the university team. This presented another opportunity to educate the parties about the mediation process as we intervened and suggested that it would be helpful to us to hear from more people so that we had a better understanding of the concerns before moving on to discuss the issues. Everyone at the table was invited to contribute his or her view of the situation.

The opening statements continued for several hours, with the students taking several breaks for discussions within their group, which the mediators were not invited to attend. After a few hours, tempers began to fray, so we decided to caucus.

254

BUILDING TRUST: PART ONE

One of the challenges in any mediation is to establish trust between the mediators and the participants. In the Hamilton Hall mediation, we needed to build trust between the mediators and both negotiation teams and, at some points, among individuals on the same team. We mediators and the university team obviously started with some common perspectives. Furthermore, establishing trust among the members of the university team was fairly straightforward: the university administrators had worked together in the past, and most were experienced negotiators. Trust issues with the student team were more complicated, however. Establishing trust with the student team was more difficult; we faced the challenge of working with a group of student representatives who had a limited history of working as a group and, therefore, needed to establish trust with each other.

As I had realized from the beginning, the profile I presented was not one designed to produce immediate trust with this group. My partner, Carlton Long, was trusted more because he was a person of color; because many of the students knew him as a teacher; and, possibly, because as an untenured junior faculty member, he seemed less a member of the power structure. Gaining the trust of the student leaders was an issue we continued to work on over the four days. We never reached a satisfactory resolution of this issue, and the lingering lack of trust complicated our jobs. I believe that this lack of trust also made it difficult for the students to use us and the process to maximum effect.

While earning the trust of the student team was an underlying issue throughout the process, it became an explicit issue early in the mediation. We had taken a break so that the student team could confer. I had gone to my office in the law school, where the mediation sessions were being held. Carlton was elsewhere. The students and Kellis came to my office and asked to meet with me. One student said that they thought that I had cut him off when he tried to take the discussion in a certain direction, saying that we were not ready to talk about that topic. He charged that, fifteen minutes later, another student brought the same topic up and I had not objected. He accused me of trying to split the student group.

Frankly, I did not remember the exchange and said so. I also said that I was sorry if I had given that impression. I acknowledged that sometimes mediators looked for differences within a negotiating team but told them that I had realized early that such a tactic was not going to be a useful approach in this situation. I paused, and then my mediator instincts took over: I addressed an underlying issue by saying to the student who had challenged me, "If what you are really asking me is, 'Have I heard about you as a controversial student?,' the answer is 'Yes, I have.' I have been told that you can be pretty wild, but I haven't seen that here, and I am going on what I have seen."

I had felt the tension in the room go down a little when I said that I was sorry if I had given the student the impression that I was trying to split the group. However, when I acknowledged the underlying reputation issue, the decrease in tension was remarkable. I knew I had made a small inroad toward establishing trust. Mediators talk about the importance of addressing underlying issues, and we talk about how discussing explosive issues can make them less scary. But I was still stunned by the impact of the use of those basic techniques on my interactions with the students.

THE MEDIATION CONTINUES

It was clear to me quite early that there was a deal to be made. The challenge for Carlton and me was to find a process that would let the negotiators work through what they had to do themselves as individuals, as members of a negotiating team, and with their constituencies so that the deal could happen.

We met in joint and individual sessions until midnight on Friday and then started again at 10:00 a.m. on Saturday and went until after midnight. On Sunday, I was beginning a thirty-hour mediation training for lawyers at the Association of the Bar of the City of New York, so we did not resume meeting until 5:00 p.m.

A detailed account of what happened Saturday and Sunday would not be particularly useful. However, as a general observation, it was especially interesting to work with the students who were putting into practice what they had been learning in the classroom. Universities are, in some ways, the most radical institutions in society. In the classroom, students and faculty are constantly pushing at intellectual boundaries, questioning conventional wisdom, challenging the orthodoxy of those in power. The student demonstrators seemed to have learned some of those lessons well. But universities are also among the most conservative institutions in the country in terms of institutional change. It may be that intellectual radicalism is possible because institutional structures change so slowly. The student demonstrators embraced the task of challenging the existing assumptions of the university, but they did not, at the beginning, have a realistic idea of what could be achieved and how fast it could happen. That was something that they needed to understand before agreement could be reached. Similarly, the university team needed to hear and appreciate the sense of alienation, lack of respect, and separateness that had led the students to take action, as well as the relevance of the student concerns to real and deep university goals.

LESSONS LEARNED AND RELEARNED

Saturday was the kind of day most mediators would expect: joint sessions, caucuses with the mediators present, caucuses without the mediators. On Saturday, I learned one important lesson and relearned another. The lesson I learned was about the importance of food in mediation, and the lesson I relearned was about ways in which a mediator's personal stake in the outcome of a dispute can interfere with her effectiveness.

A Lesson Learned: The Role of Food

Before the Hamilton mediation, the only time I had thought about the role of food in mediation was when a student from the Middle East mentioned, in a class discussion about cultural differences and conflict, that in his culture if you broke bread in public with someone with whom you had been having a dispute, it was a signal that the dispute was over. When Carlton and I began the Hamilton Hall mediation, we had been authorized to order refreshments as needed. We had a local provider (the aptly named Hamilton Deli) send over soda, juice, chips, cookies, and fruit.

Once the mediation sessions began, normal eating schedules for all of the participants disappeared. I realized that when members of the negotiation teams had not eaten for a long time, their morale dropped, they became pessimistic, and it was difficult to get them to consider new options. Then they would eat and would experience a surge of energy that allowed us make some progress for about an hour before they began to sag again. Often the two teams were eating on different schedules. We would break for caucuses or meetings with constituents. During the break, one team would grab a bite while the other would return to the table hungry and dragging.

A Lesson Relearned: The Risks When the Mediator Has a Stake in the Outcome

The principle of mediator impartiality is one of the first lessons in any basic mediation training. On Saturday afternoon, I gained new insight into the reason that an impartial mind-set can be so important.

As the day progressed, we were getting resistance from both teams. At first, I could not figure out what was going on. Then I realized that I had been pushing both teams too hard and that the pushing was occurring because I had a stake in the outcome.

One of my standard "lines" to the parties when a mediation seems stuck is "I am here to try to help you work out a solution to the situation that brought you to mediation. I have no stake in the outcome. If we work it out, I'll be pleased. If we don't work it out, you will go on living with the dispute, while I shall feel a bit sad but then just move on with the rest of my life." I finally realized that was not the situation I was in during the Hamilton mediation. As part of the university community, I had a stake in the outcome, and as a result I had been pushing too hard to reach an agreement. Once I realized what was happening, I actually told the negotiators from both teams what my standard line was. However, I went on to say that this situation was different, that as a member of the university community I had a stake in finding a solution that would resolve the crisis. I told them that because I did care a great

258

deal about finding a way to resolve the situation, I had been leaning on them and that I would try to back off.

Articulating what was going on for me, first to myself and then to the negotiators, enabled me to back off and lower the temperature of the mediation. While the voicing of these feelings was in no way intended as a mediator tactic, in retrospect my admission did help me establish credibility, especially with the members of the student team who identified me with the administration. I simply told the truth, i.e., that I cared very much about helping find a solution. It may have built another layer of trust.

BUILDING TRUST: PART TWO

Progress on Saturday was slow. The teams needed frequent caucuses during which they worked through issues within the team. These caucuses were especially important for the student team. The students first had to decide what the group's position was going to be and then decide who was going to speak for the group when they returned to joint session, and then the spokesperson needed to practice the statement to be sure he or she said it with the nuances that other members of the group wanted. The members of the student team varied in their sophistication, eloquence, and articulateness as well as in their views about the situation. This meant that they spent a large amount of time in caucuses.

While the university team generally allowed Carlton and me to sit in on its caucuses, the students were often reluctant to have us there when they met. Kellis Parker, who served throughout the mediation as an adviser to the students, was generally present at their meetings, many of which took place in his law school office but, appropriately, respected the students' desire for confidentiality.

When the students were meeting privately, Carlton and I would stop by to see how things were going. Often we would stay for a while and then go check on the university team. Gradually, either we gained enough trust to be allowed to sit in during most of the students' caucuses, or everyone was too tired to notice or object. Even so, we were never able to develop enough trust to allow the student team to use our services to maximum effect. One result was that much of the mediator's "reality tester" role was left to Kellis.

Sunday, we started again in joint session at 5:00 p.m. We began with a summary of our understanding of the interests, issues, and feelings on both sides of the conflict. We also recapped the progress we had made and indicated our confidence that the participants would be successful in finding a resolution. We worked through the night.

At one point in the middle of the night, Carlton and I were in Kellis's office with him and the six student negotiators. The students were talking as a group and also having side conversations. One of the students came over and said to me, "I'm sorry, but we are not comfortable having you here," and asked me to leave. The students were willing to have Carlton stay. Carlton told me that we needed to talk, and the two of us went to another room to speak privately about what to do and about my reaction. Neither of us was happy with the situation, but we agreed that Carlton should return to the student caucus. I proposed that Carlton tell them that I was disappointed (I wanted to say I was hurt but reframed my reaction), that I did not think they completely understood my role or the mediation process; but if this would work for them, I could live with it. Carlton agreed but added that he was also going to tell the students that we were partners and there were no secrets between us. When he returned to the caucus and spoke to the students, they kicked him out, too.

We could work more easily with the university team. The members allowed us to sit in during most of their caucuses, seemed comfortable letting us see some of their differences, and shared with us their predictions of university decision makers' reactions to various proposals. The members of the university team let us work with them to "think through" the strengths and weaknesses of various topics being discussed and how best to present proposals both to the student team and to the university decision makers. They seemed to trust us and to have a clear understanding of how to use our services. In addition, Carlton and I went with them to Low Library at various stages to meet with university decision makers to give our assessment of the status of the negotiations and to argue for keeping the mediation process going. We never spoke directly with the students' constituency.

KEEPING CONSTITUENCIES INFORMED

On Saturday, the issue of how to keep the constituencies informed became an important and time-consuming piece of business for the mediators and the teams, especially the student team with its larger and less-defined constituency. Carlton and I heard that there were rumors that the mediation had broken down and that the university had pulled out. In response to that rumor, for the first time in the process, we issued an informational memorandum from the mediators. It was short and factual, stating the following:

> We want you to know that we began mediating yesterday afternoon with student and university representatives. The times of our meeting have been Friday, 4/12/96 from approximately 8.00 p.m. until 11:30 p.m. and today (4/13/96) from 11.00 a.m. until 6:45 p.m. Our mediation is scheduled to resume tonight at 8.00 p.m.

We took copies of this memo to several heavily trafficked places around campus, including Hamilton Hall.

While we were distributing the memo, we decided to visit the hunger strikers. Because we were going to call on the strikers, we were allowed into Hamilton. The visit to the hunger strikers let them know that we cared about their well-being; it also let us show the students occupying Hamilton Hall that we were concerned and working to resolve the situation without undermining the authority of the student negotiating team. We made several other visits to the hunger strikers during the remainder of the mediation.

In retrospect, it would have been a good idea to issue a statement on the first day of mediation, simply saying that the process had begun, and to continue with brief releases throughout the mediation, letting people know that the process was continuing. Doing so would have cut down on the rumors. It might also have kept us from failing to have an agreed-upon statement for release at the end of the mediation.

THE ALL-NIGHTER

When I had been introduced to the students on Friday, one of the questions they asked about the mediation process was whether mediating meant that we would meet all night. I answered no and said that I did not believe in all-night sessions because that too often meant people were making decisions when they were tired and under pressure. I had added that I was too old for all-nighters. However, on Sunday, the president of the university was quoted in newspapers as saying that students would be out of Hamilton Hall "one way or another" by the end of the day on Monday. With the added pressure of the university's implied threat to call in the police if no agreement were reached by the end of Monday, there seemed no choice but to continue mediating until we reached an agreement or the police arrived. Thus, after going back to work at 5:00 p.m. on Sunday, we continued straight through until an agreement was finally reached at ten minutes before 7:00 p.m. on Monday evening.

THE TENTATIVE AGREEMENT

At 6:00 a.m. on Monday, we reached a tentative agreement with the following provisions:

- Instead of amnesty for the demonstrators from all disciplinary action, students would be censured, which was, in effect, probation for two years.
- Two tenured faculty and two untenured faculty would be appointed in the field of Ethnic Studies. Prior to the Hamilton Hall takeover, the university had indicated a willingness to make Asian American and Latino Studies tenure track appointments and to add a Latino Studies nontenured appointment. During the negotiations, the university agreed to make this a firm commitment and added an Asian American nontenured position.

- The tenure track slots were to be dedicated for ten years to appointments in the specified fields.
- The university would establish an Ethnic Studies Center.

"Selling" the Agreement

The university team called the university decision makers and arranged to meet to review the proposed agreement. The university quickly agreed to the proposed settlement.

The student team faced a much more difficult task.

Community mediators are familiar with the phenomenon of parties arriving accompanied by a number of supporters. The mediator or staff person explains the process and asks the "cheerleaders" to remain in the waiting room. After several hours with the mediator, during which the parties may have gained new insights into the source of their conflict and recognized the needs and interests of each other, they reach agreement. The parties sign the agreement and may shake hands or even exchange hugs. Then they go out to the waiting room where their friends and families are still ready for battle. I usually discuss options for handling this situation with the parties at the end of a mediation and often offer to have the supporters join us at the end so that we can explain what has happened and ask them to support the agreement.

The student team members faced this problem on a grand scale. The approximately 180 demonstrators who were not present at the mediation continued to demonstrate, rally, and hold fast to their vision of needed change. Their representatives needed that commitment to give credibility to their efforts during negotiation and as a source of energy. But, as the negotiations progressed and it became clear that not all of the goals would be achieved—especially the goal of a separate Department of Ethnic Studies—the task of communicating with their constituents became more complex and difficult for the student team.

The student team members needed to sell the deal to the 180 demonstrators occupying Hamilton Hall but were not prepared for that challenging role. We mediators fell short in training them how to handle it. Even though it would not have been easy, given the limited trust between the mediators and the students, we should have tried to talk to the students about the role they were facing and offered to brainstorm with them about how to handle it.

Those with experience in the labor field are familiar with the phenomenon where the workers are in the streets or on the picket line riled up and demonstrating. The negotiator gets the best deal she can at the bargaining table, using the noise in the streets as one of her persuasive tools. Then she has to go back and calm the troops down and tell them that she has gotten far less than they were demanding but that it is a fabulous deal. The student negotiators had no experience in this role. They were tired and, while they knew (given what they had heard during the mediation) that they had obtained a reasonable package, they went to meet with a core group of the demonstrators feeling that what they had achieved was not a victory or even close to a victory.

The student team met at the law school with a core group of about thirty or forty of the Hamilton demonstrators. After meeting with the core group, the student team went to Hamilton Hall to meet with the larger group and present the proposed agreement. At 10:00 a.m., we got word that the students had voted it down.

This was crushing news. Carlton and I were exhausted, and the words of the university president that the demonstrators would be out of Hamilton "one way or another" began to loom large.

THE BLUE RIBBON COMMITTEE PROPOSAL
We decided that it might be helpful to meet and brainstorm with a small group of faculty members who were sympathetic to the students and had been around during the demonstration to lend moral support and guidance. We hoped their input would help us find a resolution to the impasse. That meeting produced an impasse-breaking proposal, i.e., that the president of the university appoint a "blue ribbon" committee to study the future of Ethnic Studies at Columbia.

It was decided that two of the professors at the meeting should write a letter to the president proposing the special committee as a way to end the confrontation. Carlton and I took the letter to Low Library and presented it to the negotiating team and to the university decision makers. After some discussion and editing, the university agreed.

We took the proposal back to the student team members who were gathered outside of Hamilton Hall. They and the three hunger strikers and several of the supportive faculty members who had stayed around outside of Hamilton discussed the proposal with us. It was about 2:00 p.m. The discussion was emotional. Then the student team and the hunger strikers withdrew to discuss the proposal among themselves.

I was starting to feel that time was running out because of the threat implied in the university president's statement that the demonstration would be over by the end of the day on Monday. I felt enormous pressure because of the sense that the arrival of the police on campus again was just around the corner. The tactic of "locking yourself in" is well known in negotiation literature. It can be an effective tactic and, no doubt, was a factor in reaching resolution in this dispute. But at the time, it did not seem as if we had been mediating very long, and I wished that the president had not, in effect, "thrown the steering wheel out the window."

At about 2:30 p.m., the student team members informed us that they and the hunger strikers had voted the proposal down again. At that point, my co-mediator decided that he could no longer continue to mediate. Carlton had become involved because the students trusted him as their teacher, and now, as their teacher, he was being rejected. He was particularly upset because he felt that by rejecting the latest conciliatory proposal, the students were being disrespectful of his senior colleagues of color who had paved the way for him and for the students. So he left.

As a mediator, I viewed my job as keeping at it until one side withdrew or until the police arrived. Because I saw myself as a mediator—not as a teacher, mentor, or friend—for the most part I was not personally hurt when the participants challenged me, kicked me out of their caucus, or voted against what I thought was a good package. Mind you, such behavior did not thrill me, but I knew that it wasn't personal. Thus, it was perhaps easier for me to stay than it was for Carlton.

A LAST-DITCH EFFORT AT AGREEMENT

As it turned out, Carlton's departure probably had a positive impact on the resolution process. It had shock value, and it may have added to the sense of urgency. Once the student team and I recovered somewhat from the initial shock of Carlton's leaving, we talked more about the idea of the blue ribbon committee. The student team then rewrote the university's proposal. At times, we were talking about punctuation or about capital *E* versus little e, seemingly small details but details that had enormous symbolic importance to the students. Finally, the students came up with a draft that I thought might also work for the university.

I called the university team, which had moved to Low Library, and said I was coming over with a new version. The team members' reaction was negative; in effect, they said, "Don't even bother." I responded, "Fine, I'll be there in a few minutes."

As I headed back to Low Library, I noticed students leaving Hamilton Hall with their bedrolls under their arms and realized that this had been going on all day. I did not understand the significance of this phenomenon at the time. In retrospect, I realized that as the university president's deadline approached, the more moderate students were leaving. They may have wanted to avoid being arrested or arrested again or to avoid the more serious university discipline that would be imposed on those still in Hamilton when the police arrived. The students who remained in Hamilton were the "true believers," who would be less willing to accept a compromise. The challenge for a mediator when a decision-making constituency is not constant is to find a way to increase the likelihood that the moderate, more settlement-oriented participants are present when critical votes are taken.

I reached Low Library and met again with the university team members. Even though they were close to giving up, they had invested a huge amount in the process. They wanted the mediation to work and had developed a commitment to and investment in the process. As

266

frustrating as it was for them—spending all night negotiating a deal, then selling it to the university, then having the students say no—my sense was that the university team had developed an allegiance to the process and to making it work. In addition, I believed that the university team had developed respect for the student negotiators. And, of course, the university team members were also aware of the dire consequences for their students and their university if the mediation failed. So, while their initial reaction when told of the new student draft was not to bother bringing it to them, they took it, went off, and rewrote it in a way that they thought they could sell to the university. Once they obtained approval, they gave it to me with a note saying, "Take it or leave it by 5 o'clock."

It was about 4:00 p.m. when I got back to the courtyard outside of Hamilton Hall. Faculty sympathetic to the students and several deans had gathered there. It seemed that everyone had a sense we had reached a dangerous point. The student negotiators, the sympathetic faculty and deans, and I gathered in the lounge of a dorm next to Hamilton.

One of the students reached for the revised proposal and demanded that I give it to him. I said, "No. Sit down. I am going to talk to you; I am going to read this to you. I have tried to respect your doing it your way even when I thought that it wasn't the best way to do it. But it is too late in the game. You are going to listen." Then I went back to basics and started talking about the interests of the participants. As I did so, I choked up. When I finished reading the last revised proposal, one student said, "This is all garbage." I wondered how I was going to reframe that.

After I went over the proposal with the student team, I asked if they would allow some of the faculty who had been supportive to go into Hamilton Hall and speak to the students. The reasoning behind the proposal was twofold: it was clear to me that the members of the student negotiating team were too conflicted about the terms of the proposed agreement to be effective salespeople for it, and I thought it might be useful to have others share the responsibility of urging

267

agreement. The students inside Hamilton voted against hearing from the faculty. Then they voted down the revised proposal.

It was close to 5:00 p.m. and the take-it-or-leave-it deadline set by the university. The students were asking for more time. They did not have an efficient decision-making process. From 5:00 p.m. on, I was on the phone to members of the university negotiating team every ten minutes or so saying, "Please don't do anything yet. I'll call you back. Don't do anything for ten minutes."

The student demonstrators continued their discussion and finally decided to allow the sympathetic faculty to come in and speak with them. I was not invited in. After about twenty minutes, one of the faculty came back to the lounge and reported that my law school colleague, Kendall Thomas, had given an inspiring talk, that the students were clapping and crying, and that movement seemed likely.

The faculty were asked to leave, and the student discussions continued as the handful of faculty members and deans waited with me outside Hamilton. It was starting to get dark. I kept saying to myself that this had to work, but I wasn't sure if the students could accept the proposal. One of the students, the one who seemed to shoulder the burden of reaching agreement during those final hours, kept coming out saying, "I need more time." And I kept making phone calls to Low Library begging for time.

SUCCESS

Finally, at ten minutes of seven, one of the students came out and said, "We are going to leave." It was an extraordinary scene. The students marched out of Hamilton Hall chanting, some crying. Most of those who were standing outside—administrators, faculty, security—began applauding, and many of us were also teary. I know that mediators are not supposed to cry and applaud at the end of a case, but I did.

PROCURING SIGNATURES

Part of the agreement was that all members of both negotiating teams had to sign the agreement. The university negotiators had already done so. As the student demonstrators marched out of Hamilton

268

Hall, I needed to stop each one of them to secure their signatures. They were reluctant to separate from their friends, but four were persuaded to stop and sign. Two refused to sign. At that point, almost everyone else—faculty, administrators, demonstrators—was gone, the building was vacated, and everyone was relieved and happy.

But my job was not finished: I had to find those last two negotiators and get their signatures on the agreement. I was not happy. Luckily, my colleague Kendall Thomas was still there. He went with me to find the two students, who ultimately signed—after writing out a statement saying that they were doing so "under duress." This addendum was a way of providing a face-saving explanation to the constituents of the two negotiators.

Accompanied by Kendall, I took the signed agreement to Low Library.

"SPINNING" THE NEGOTIATION STORY

Once the students agreed to accept the proposal and vacate Hamilton Hall, there was no opportunity to talk about how to present the successful outcome to the public even if we had recognized the value of having such a discussion. But I wish now that, earlier in the process, I had put communication with both constituencies and with the general public on the agenda of issues that we were going to need to address.

If we had stopped periodically to consider that communication, the postdemonstration stories might have been more neutral. The *New York Times* carried a story the next morning about the end of the Hamilton Hall takeover. The headline read: "The Students at Columbia End Battle for Ethnic Studies"; the carry-over headline read: "Their Goals Unfulfilled, Columbia Students End Two-Week Battle for Ethnic Studies." In the text of the story, university officials insisted that they had made no concessions and that they had already begun to pursue most of the proposals contained in the agreement. They said they did not negotiate about academic issues. The *Wall Street Journal* ran a pro-university editorial, "Times Are Changing," praising the president for having the backbone to stand up to the students.

These stories satisfied important university interests, but I was concerned that this one-sided spin would undermine the hard-earned student trust and their sense that their interests were better understood that developed during the mediation and would taint future communication about implementation.

THOUGHTS ABOUT GATES AND ROSES

The takeover of Hamilton ended Monday night. Wednesday morning, I had an early morning meeting on the main campus. I had to go to my office before the meeting and left the law school building at 117th Street since the main entrance at 116th Street was closed due to renovations. There was a gate to the main campus directly in front of me across Amsterdam Avenue. Out of habit developed during the five days of demonstrations when only the two main gates to the campus were open, I started to turn left toward the main entrance at 116th. Then I realized that the 117th Street gate was again open. It struck me that much of what we do as mediators is opening gates. When mediators help people talk to each other and hear each other and understand their own and others' interests, they symbolically aid the participants in unlocking the positional or emotional gates that have stood as a bar to settlement.

The day after the mediation, I received a dozen long-stemmed roses from the university negotiating team. Carlton received phone calls from the students. When we met in my office that afternoon to debrief, Carlton saw the roses. I had the sense that he would have liked roses, too. There is no question in my mind that I wanted the phone calls from the students.

SECOND THOUGHTS:

Although this story included implied and sometimes explicit thoughts about what I learned from the Hamilton Hall mediation, it seems useful to recap the major lessons here.

MEDIATION AS PARALLEL SEMINARS

The notion of the initial stages of the mediation—the party opening statements and mediator clarifying and summarizing—as parallel seminars may be a useful way to conceptualize the beginning stages of all mediations. Perhaps it was the academic setting in which the Hamilton mediation took place that let me see—that taught me—that mediation involves multiple seminars. In the best seminars, all participants—teachers and students—are learners. When mediators describe their role, they often talk about wanting to understand the parties' concerns, wanting the parties to understand each other's concerns, and helping the parties obtain clarity about their own and the other participants' goals and interests. The techniques used by the mediator, such as summarizing issues and interests, reframing, probing for underlying interests, and acknowledging feelings, are tools that enhance the learning process by making information available in a way that allows it to be heard by the participants.

When the mediation process works best, parties not only find a resolution to their conflict but also acquire information and insights about their own goals, interests, and priorities and about the goals, interests, and priorities of the other participant that may empower them to avoid similar conflicts in the future. In the Hamilton mediation, the student negotiation team and the mediators learned more about university governance while the university negotiators and the mediators learned more about the interests that drove the students' protests. It is unlikely that an agreement could have been reached without this learning.

The third seminar in the mediation process, when successful, enhances the parties' ability to use mediation. One responsibility of a mediator is to determine, and throughout the mediation process reassess, the training needs of the mediation participants and to decide how best to deliver that information. Mediators also provide training about the process by modeling useful problem-solving techniques, especially those that aid parties in hearing each other.

In the Hamilton Hall mediation, Carlton and I were only partially successful at leading the third seminar. At critical times, we did discuss the process, but doing so more often and more directly, especially with the student negotiators, might have been helpful. Our experience suggests that it could be useful for mediators to spend more time thinking about what each party needs to know about the process, i.e., about their training needs, and how best to provide that information not only during the initial stages of the mediation but throughout the process. Mediators are trained to "return to the process," that is, to talk about the way mediation works, when the mediation hits rocky moments. It could be useful to think about these moments not so much as indicators that the parties do not understand the process but more as indicators that the mediators need to do a better job of explaining, of teaching, of leading the third seminar.

IMPORTANCE OF FOOD IN MEDIATION

Both the energy-giving and symbolic aspects of food played a role in the Hamilton mediation. Becoming aware that parties' moods and energy levels will fluctuate greatly depending on when (and what) they have eaten helped Carlton and me be more effective facilitators. As mediators, we had to be aware of where the teams were in terms of their energy levels. We needed to pay attention to when people were eating and manage the additional tension that was created when one team returned to the table full of energy after a meal while the other was dragging. If both teams had "refueled" at about the same time, we had the opportunity to take on tough issues and make progress. When they were eating at different times, we needed to use caucuses to take advantage of the opportunities for movement presented by the high-energy team while encouraging the team that was dragging. Mediators need to structure discussions to capitalize on the surge of energy and optimism that follows a meal and to avoid the clashes that may occur between recently fed, momentarily upbeat parties and parties whose energy level is dragging because they need to eat.

Mediators also need to monitor their own need for fuel and, especially in a prolonged mediation, to refuel regularly with food that is likely to let them maintain a steady energy level rather than food that produces quick highs followed by crashes. I had been on a weight loss program for several months and decided to see if I could stick with that regime during the mediation instead of doing what would have been more typical for me—going for the chocolate and junk food. As a result, I ended up (until Monday afternoon) staying away from junk food and sweets, instead eating a piece of fruit, a yogurt, or half a sandwich every two or three hours to maintain a steady energy level. Also, in the months before the mediation, I had not been drinking much caffeine; so, when I started to drag, a Coke or a cup of tea had much more than the normal impact.

It can be tempting, especially in an extended mediation, to tough it out and push toward agreement without taking a break to eat. This can be an effective tactic, but it runs the risk that neither the mediator nor the parties will be at their best and that the resulting decisions will be of lower quality than they might have been.

BUILDING TRUST

One of the critical tasks for a mediator is building trust with the participants in the mediation. Trust building starts as mediators (and others) explain the process to the parties, explore with them whether the mediation process is a good fit for their dispute, and agree to try mediation and the guidelines that will govern the process. Mediators continue to build trust throughout the session through their opening statement, repeated explanations of the mediation process, and their behavior during the mediation. In the Hamilton mediation, the initial trust-building activities—explanation of the process and assessment of the appropriateness of the process—were compressed because of the crisis atmosphere. While the sense of urgency prevented a thorough discussion of these issues, it also created an energy for doing something to end the impasse that may have aided the decision to try mediation.

I have noted a number of instances in which I feel that I—and, to a much lesser extent, Carlton—failed to gain the trust of the student negotiators. Initially I raised, with both the university administrators and the student leaders, the question of whether I was the right person to mediate this confrontation because I appeared to have more in

273

common with the administration and its negotiators in terms of race, age, and institutional position. The student team's response—that they wanted one of the two African American professors who participated in the initial discussions with the students about the administration's offer to act as the mediator and their subsequent request that one of them co-mediate—was a clear, early confirmation of my instinct that building trust would be a major challenge.

Subsequent events, including the early questioning about whether I was trying to split the student team and the request in the early hours on Monday morning that I leave the student negotiators' caucus, showed that I, at least, was not entirely trusted. In retrospect, I wish that I had taken time when the students asked me to leave the caucus to ask them about their concerns. I often find it useful in mediation to ask questions to which I already know the answer on the theory that having concerns or information made explicit can help the participants and the mediators gain clarity about the issues and spot nuances that they may be overlooking. Even though I knew why the students wanted me to leave, I should have asked them to articulate their concerns. Maybe I could have addressed some of the concerns and maybe not, but it would have been worth a try. It may have been that subconsciously I was afraid to engage the students about how to use the process for fear of alienating them and driving them away. The crisis atmosphere and the stakes if mediation failed created pressures that may have made us shy away from process discussions with the student leaders, discussions that might have built trust or, at least, increased their ability to use us and the process to achieve their goals.

IMPACT OF THE MEDIATOR'S PERSONAL STAKE IN THE OUTCOME

I have described the way that, as a member of the Columbia community, my personal stake in the outcome of the mediation led me to press the participants too hard on Saturday. Once I recognized what was happening, I acknowledged it to the participants, a move that I think may have gained some trust both because of my owning up to my investment in the outcome and because my reaction showed how much I cared about finding a way to end the crisis. Unlike most cases that I mediate, failure to help the negotiators find a solution in this situation would have been very visible. I tried to maintain my normal mind-set of measuring my success in a mediation by looking at whether I have helped the parties identify and clarify interests and issues and not by whether I have notched another agreement on my mediator belt.

MANAGING INFORMATION FLOW TO CONSTITUENTS AND THE PUBLIC IN A HIGH-VISIBILITY DISPUTE

One of our biggest deficits as mediators was in the way we managed the flow of information to those not directly involved in the mediation.

From time to time, we made several visits to Hamilton to see the hunger strikers. While our informal visits to Hamilton Hall may have helped the demonstrators there put a human face on the mediation process, Carlton and I did not suggest a meeting with the students occupying Hamilton to explain mediation and what would be happening during the process. My thinking was that leaving this communication to the student negotiating team was a way of supporting their position as leaders. This approach may have had some merit, especially early in the process. But we should have made repeated offers throughout the mediation to participate in a meeting with the students occupying Hamilton Hall. In contrast, when first called to Low Library on Friday, I did have the opportunity to explain the mediation process to the university decision makers, and Carlton and I were able to reinforce that explanation during visits to Low Library when we encouraged the administration to stick with the process. Had we provided a similar description of the mediation process and the expected give-and-take to the students in Hamilton at the beginning of the process, it might have been easier to obtain acceptance of the final proposal.

We also failed to work with the student negotiators on how best to present the agreement to their constituents. Once a tentative agreement was reached early Monday morning, we should have initiated discussions about the challenge they were about to face in selling the agreement.

Furthermore, we failed to do an optimal job of handling information flow to the public. We issued brief statements that the mediation was under way or that it was continuing in order to counter rumors that the process had broken down. While our ad hoc responses seemed to work out, it would have been wise to include early in our negotiation a discussion of how to communicate to the university community and to the press. Similarly, though I am not sure how we could have avoided it given the way the end played out, we and the participants in the mediation did not agree on how to release information about the successful end to the negotiations.

CONCLUDING THOUGHTS

I realize that each participant in the Hamilton Hall mediation has his or her own perspective on the reasons for the crisis. The members of the student and university negotiation teams would no doubt tell very different stories about what happened during the mediation, as well as during the events that led up to the takeover of Hamilton Hall. I have told this the story of my mediation experiences in the hope that both the lessons about mediation and the questions that remain about how I could have done better will be of use to the mediation community.

22.
A Blunder

Eric R. Galton

SMOKE SCREEN

Kenny's hand appeared out of the customary cloud of smoke and beckoned me to come out on the deck. Kenny Vacco, the city's preeminent plaintiff's labor and employment lawyer, was on his second pack of Marlboros and it was only midafternoon. As the smoke cleared, Kenny's creased face gave it all away: he was having his usual great day and terrible day all in the same moment, and he needed his mediator to rag on and ease his pain. I stepped outside into the gorgeous central Texas spring day that Kenny had failed to notice. I was ready for Kenny's speech. I had heard the speech about fifteen times before.

"I freakin' hate the practice of law. You know, Eric, you mediators got it made. You got out. I'm still in it. You know I hate the freakin' practice of law. If I wasn't makin' so much money slamming tech companies, I would get out in a New York minute and do what you do—whatever that is," Kenny rasped through a newly lit Marlboro.

"I feel your pain, Kenny. I really do," I said sarcastically. "But right now you've got 40 percent of $350,000, the case is only two months old, you have no money or time in it, and you are unhappy. Frankly, Kenny, I am having a hard time feeling sorry for you right now."

"And I thought you mediators were supposed to be the sensitive type and allow people to vent and such," Kenny said.

"The clients are the ones who are supposed to vent, Kenny. The clients! Not the lawyers," I responded.

"Hey, we lawyers have feelings, too," Kenny sighed, "but as always you put that mediator finger right on the problem. You know, Eric, that is why I come to you. You always spot the problem," Kenny said as he exhaled a steady stream of smoke.

As is commonly the case, I had no idea what my finger was on, so I resorted to my favorite tactic: the mediator-pretending-to-be-perceptive gambit. "You caught me again, Kenny. I don't know how you do it. But, while I get it, lay it out a little more specifically in case I missed a detail or two," I said.

Kenny laid it all out: His clients, the Wilsons, were the problem. They were wonderful people, but James was as stubborn as a mule. Kenny had spent four hours with them the day before telling them that they should take any number over $200,000. The offer was now $350,000, the most Kenny had ever been offered in a race-based discrimination case, and James still wasn't biting.

"So, your client won't take a premium settlement, you are on your third pack of smokes, and you don't know what to do?" I asked.

Kenny told me that this was why he paid me big bucks—so I would get his crazy clients not to blow great deals for irrational reasons that Kenny did not understand or frankly care about. "The Wilsons love you, Eric. You let them talk all day. So go in there and get them to take the 350K," Kenny demanded.

"Okay," I replied. "Let's go in together and see if we can reason with them."

"I ain't going in there with you. Are you crazy? I'm sitting out here and smoking some more. Take your time and make it happen, Eric. You're the best! So get it done," Kenny said.

PIECE OF CAKE

James Wilson had worked for Dynabit for eight years, had survived eight rounds of layoffs, and had been denied three promotions because "he was not qualified," according to junior, less experienced, white coworkers. As an assistant supervisor earning $85,000 a year, James had twenty employees on his team and had negotiated over fifteen million in sales the past year. Robin, his lovely wife, was the principal of Murchison Middle School and had found a way to navigate around James's occasional angry outbursts for twenty-two years.

James smiled broadly as I entered the conference room. I could tell that he knew why I was there and had been looking forward to this moment. "So, did my terrific lawyer send you in here alone and tell you that I was stubborn as a mule and that I wasn't accepting this 350K?" James asked without breaking eye contact.

"Well, there was a reference to a mule, James, and he might have used the word stubborn," I replied. "But you know, James, the offer is about $150,000 over par and is a great offer."

Incensed, James roared that the company was offering that because it thought that it could just overlook black men and get away with it. "They just messed with the wrong black man in this case!"

"You seem to be enjoying this," I noted.

"Oh, he is enjoying this," Robin interjected. "It's the lawsuit over coffee, it's reviewing depositions at lunch, it's Googling other cases at night. I just can't wait for summer break to be over so I can get out of the house."

"So, are you saying I'm no fun, Robin?" James asked.

Cleverly evading the question, Robin told James that she loved him and that the company undoubtedly had wronged him. However, she added that he had stood up and made his point for long enough, that she and James could pay off a chunk of the mortgage and have money for their son's college education.

"Well, I know all of that! I have factored that in already. I have listened to the advice of my excellent lawyer. Our mediator has allowed me to blow off steam. But, Eric, I need something else. I'm choking on this big fat pill. I need another reason. Give me one really new good reason to take the deal. Can you do that?" James asked.

I think that all mediators have moments like this. You know, one side of your brain is suggesting something that sounds good until the more sensible side of your brain speaks up and says, "Don't do that!" Well, at this moment, that side of my brain wasn't speaking to me. I was just hearing the little devil in there who was whispering, "Come on, Eric. Just do it!"

I straightened myself and looked James straight in the eye. "You want a really good new reason?" I asked.

"Lay it on me, Eric," James replied.

I told James that I didn't know if he'd been paying attention to the political realities in the great state of Texas these past fifteen years, but in case he'd been sleeping, I felt that I should point out that we'd been living under Republican rule. And that meant that all the appellate judges were Republican, and they'd never met an insurance company or big business institution they didn't like. I told James that a jury might give him a lot of money, but three years later those Republican appellate judges would devour him and spit him out and he would walk away with nothing! "Is that a good enough reason, James?" I barked.

"Eric, I am really offended," James said, miffed.

"Offended?" I asked. "How can you be offended?"

"Well, you might have wanted to know before you began that ugly rap that I am the current vice-chair of the Williamson County Republican Party," James proclaimed in a huff.

You know those Southwest Airlines commercials? The ones where somebody does something really stupid, and the tag line is "Wanna get away?" That was how I was feeling at that moment. I began babbling an endless stream of apologies—"I'm sorry, I'm sorry, I'm sorry, . . ." —and mea culpas. I kept apologizing until I noticed James's mouth moving, although I wasn't really hearing anything.

"You can stop," James said.

"I am so sorry," I said.

"You already said that a few hundred times. I am offended—but, Eric, you are right! I'll take the $350,000! Now go tell my lawyer," James decided.

Kenny was still smoking on the deck. "Get 'er done, Eric?" Kenny asked.

"Your client will take the $350,000," I responded.

"That's why I always hire you, Eric. You know how to close. You are such a good closer," Kenny laughed.

"Piece of cake, Kenny," I said. "Piece of cake."

SECOND THOUGHTS:

Mediation literature has abundant illustrations of mediator "success stories" in which mediators have made brilliant process moves to achieve a settlement. But if you get a group of "average Joe" mediators together, the conversation inevitably drifts to blunders and mistakes that the mediators have made. Since mediators operate on the stage of live theater, blunders are inevitable. Truth be told, mediators probably learn more from the mistakes that they have made than their occasional moments of accidental brilliance. Admittedly, though, large blunders, such as the one described above, are difficult to 'fess up to.

In this story, your fearless mediator erroneously assumed that there was no chance that an African American plaintiff in a race discrimination case could possibly be a Republican. Some of you may be thinking that was probably not an unreasonable assumption. Some of you may also be thinking, as some of my students have commented, "What's the big deal? The case settled."

I was quite embarrassed by what happened and deeply disappointed in myself. First, I realized that my appreciation of diversity was not as perfect as I thought it was. I was stereotyping, although not in a mean-spirited way. This moment heightened my awareness that I had more work to do in this regard.

More broadly, I realized that many of the mistakes I have made were the product of making assumptions—almost a form of mediator "profiling." For example, in one case, I had assumed that a bald banker in a dark suit was probably an unhappy person and probably difficult to deal with. Several hours later, the banker commented on the Led Zeppelin poster in my office. We had an amazing conversation about the band's first North American tour, and this helped navigate us toward a settlement. But I had assumed things based on appearance and job description and was patently wrong.

I have also met an angry insurance representative on more than a few occasions and have not always made the correct assumptions. In one instance, I walked into a caucus room and heard the insurance representative scream at her own lawyer. I assumed that she was an unreasonable person who was spiteful even to her own able counsel. As it turned out, after I took her outside and asked what was wrong, the insurance representative was terrified that she might be laid off, she was not receiving child support from her ex-husband, and she felt that her decision in this mediation was going to be carefully reviewed.

Assumptions are judgments, frequently wrong, that get in the way of obtaining information that could be helpful in getting a matter resolved. Many years ago, I started saying a private mantra before every mediation. I remind myself that I know absolutely nothing about any of the people I am about to meet and that my mission is to get to know each of them and what is important to each of them. I also think of this story. Politics never belongs in a mediator's toolbox, and I no longer reference it. I also no longer assume anything. I think my blunder actually made me a more effective mediator, more able to look more fairly and openly at the people I serve.

23.
The Broken Family

Jeffrey Krivis

A Perfect Place to Live

The Central Valley of California, known for its good weather and rich soil, is considered a slice of Americana. The many people who live in this agricultural community work hard. They know that the literal fruits of their labors feed people, and they are proud of their role in society. They are also strong believers in family values.

Rocked to the Bone

It was against this backdrop that a stunned community learned of the arrest and detention of local farmer Tom Locke for molesting his seven-year-old daughter Andrea.

Much has been written about the sociopathic behavior of child molesters, particularly if they are adults who molest their own children. Society has been plagued by such behavior both in the family and in the church. When this type of behavior surfaces in a sleepy agricultural town whose family values embody the very essence of its people, the alleged perpetrators are never able to regain their reputation. People begin to look over their shoulders and question whether their neighbors are who they think they are. The concepts of trust and faith are rocked to the bone. This is why few crimes carry as much social disgrace as child molestation. Most people would rather be accused of armed robbery.

MODEL CITIZENS
Tom Locke had lived in the Central Valley his entire life. He married his high school sweetheart and continued to work on the family farm growing various crops that had sustained his family for over one hundred years. He was a deacon in his church and a member of the local city council. When folks needed help in the community, they knew that they could count on the Locke family.

Tom and Mary Locke had been married for fifteen years and had three children, ages four, seven, and eleven. The children were typical fun-loving kids. Annie was the four-year-old who was her sister Andrea's shadow and looked up to her in every way. Andrea was an imaginative seven-year-old who loved the family trips to Disneyland and enjoyed playing with her Barbie dolls. Charlie played Little League baseball, collected Pokémon cards, and spent hours playing games on his Wii. All of the children were healthy and well adjusted at school and did not exhibit any emotional problems.

Neither Tom nor his wife had any criminal record and had been considered model parents by their friends. Until the moment of Tom's arrest, the Locke family lived the American dream: they owned their own home, raised three children, and were well respected in the community.

A CHARGE OF MOLESTATION
All of that changed on September 1, 2006, when representatives of the county district attorney's office came to Andrea and Charlie's school and interrogated them without their parents' knowledge or presence and removed both children from the school without obtaining any

warrant whatsoever. According to witnesses at the scene, the law enforcement officials indicated to the school principal that the children were in imminent danger of serious bodily injury and had to be taken into custody for their own protection.

The facts that gave rise to this unusual set of circumstances were very simple. Andrea had an active imagination. She made unusual statements to family and friends about ghosts and goblins living in the neighborhood and recited to her mother her dreams of being strangled by snakes. One day she brought to school a teen magazine that ran some stories on sexual themes. Just like the game of telephone tag, the children who saw the magazine surmised and gossiped until the message was that Andrea was playing sexually inappropriate games with her father. As a result, the teacher brought her to the principal's office to discuss the matter.

While Andrea was in the principal's office, a social worker was contacted and immediately went to the school to interview Andrea with the principal. Mrs. Locke was not contacted during this entire procedure. Following the interview, the social worker, in a classic rush to judgment, removed Andrea from school; and a meeting was convened among the social worker, the police, and the district attorney to discuss further investigation. The parties agreed to audiotape and videotape another interview with Andrea as well as a separate interview with Charlie. The purpose of the interrogation was to determine if the children were victims of sexual abuse by their father. The interviews were witnessed by a victim advocate watchdog, who reviewed the interviews from a separate room via hidden camera equipment. Based on the interview, Andrea seemed to implicate her father and, to a lesser extent, her mother in sexual assault. In addition to the interrogations of the children, the district attorney prevented the Lockes from entering their home while other evidence could be accumulated.

A collective decision was made to have Andrea undergo further forensic examination at public expense. She was subjected to an invasive forensic vaginal and anal exam without the knowledge, consent, or presence of her parents. Photographs were taken to determine whether there had been any improper sexual activity, and the evidence was then put in a special evidence locker for the district attorney to examine. The physical examination findings were normal, meaning that there was no evidence to confirm or negate sexual abuse. Such findings were considered to be inconclusive.

Despite the lack of evidence from multiple interrogations of the children, the forensic examination of Andrea, and the search of the Locke home, as well as interviews with other children and parents, the county continued to detain the children from their parents and proceeded with legal dependency proceedings based on knowingly deficient and improper allegations of abuse. The children were placed in foster care immediately, and later with family friends. A juvenile court dependency petition was filed, and the allegation of sexual abuse began to wind its way through the legal system. The local newspaper published pictures of the family on the front page, which was tantamount to tarring and feathering the Lockes in their local community.

Eventually, after exculpatory information finally surfaced, the legal proceedings were dismissed due to the fact that there was no corroborative evidence. Approximately forty-five days after the legal proceedings began, the children were given back to their parents. The cost to fight the legal proceedings exceeded $50,000, but the emotional scars and embarrassment were even worse—they have never evaporated. The spirit and the reputation of the family who had been upstanding members of the community for over one hundred years had been broken.

A Sizable Offer

After the initial nightmare was over, the Lockes filed a lawsuit to seek compensation for violation of their civil rights and to protect other families in the future from this type of abuse.

Rather than put the family through additional aggravation, the county decided that it would be in everyone's best interest to sit down privately and resolve the case quietly outside of the court system. Faced with this opportunity, the Lockes were encouraged that the county finally wanted to come clean and accepted the offer of mediation.

The mediation process itself was fairly uneventful. Tom and Mary spent most of the day deferring to their lawyers and politely listening to the mediator as he went through the subtleties of the case and the current state of the law with regard to the county, which was currently in flux. Despite my efforts to engage with the Lockes, they were somewhat distant and demonstratively quiet. I decided to focus on a more conventional approach, exchanging offers and demands in the typical negotiation dance until I was able to obtain a sizable offer that was thoroughly endorsed by the Lockes' counsel. The final offer from the county was so substantial that there was palpable excitement in the room from the Lockes' legal team.

THE "REAL" MEDIATION

It was at that moment that the real mediation began. Mary broke down crying, and Tom looked at her quizzically as if he was confused as to what was going on. He gave her a nod, and they stepped down the hall into a private room to talk without their counsel. After about twenty minutes, the attorneys were looking at me to move things along, so I went down the hall to check on the Lockes. What I found was tantamount to a complete meltdown.

Evidently, Tom had notified Mary that as soon as the settlement was consummated, he was going to leave the marriage. Knowing that was going to occur, Mary decided that she would not agree to the settlement terms as it was clear that reaching an agreement on the money would result in a dissolution of their marriage, which was something she desperately wanted to salvage. While the stress of the criminal case was over, the scars were deeply imbedded; and, for reasons known only to Tom and Mary, Tom did not want the marriage to go forward.

Clearly, this was information that was not presented to me in the plaintiffs' brief, nor had it surfaced during any part of the day as I tried to engage with the parties on various levels. To say that it came as a surprise to me and even to the Lockes' counsel is an understatement.

At that moment, I realized that I had made a terrible mistake by not identifying and addressing the emotional concerns of the family early on in the mediation. I accepted the Lockes' indifference and abstention from discussion as a willingness to put the conflict behind them and focus simply on the financial terms of the settlement. I failed to recognize how the strain of the criminal proceedings had built up a well of anger that was hidden beneath the surface of a rock-hard shell around Tom Locke. What's more, I elevated the status of the lawyers above that of the clients for the purposes of processing the mediation so that I could get to the numbers as soon as possible and consummate the transaction known as settlement. Unfortunately, the pecking order in this case should have been reversed, with the Lockes placed at a higher level along with recognition of the impact that this set of events had on their lives.

Anxious to rewind the tape, I spent the next two hours with the Lockes exploring in detail all of the facts that led to this uncomfortable moment in their lives. I gently prodded the Lockes to accept that, though I was no psychologist, perhaps some family counseling might be in order now that the financial side of their house would be secure. In short, I used the skills I had acquired twenty years earlier to help the Lockes look ahead and be grateful about what they were about to receive in the settlement.

BROKEN, BUT ON THE MEND

While the emotional scars ran deep, litigating the case any longer would prevent the entire family from continuing the healing process. Mary recognized at that moment that it was important to put the children's concerns ahead of hers, and she agreed to accept the settlement on the condition that Tom meet with the family counselor, which he agreed to do.

A term sheet was prepared and the parties signed, but the family was broken. At least, I thought, the settlement offered them a chance to look to the future.

SECOND THOUGHTS:

The dynamics of this case presented a number of challenges on various levels. The primary issues that I had to deal with were

(1) status, i.e., recognizing the hierarchy in the room; (2) intuition, i.e., trusting my gut to deal with the emotional roadblocks that would necessarily result from such a traumatic situation; (3) identification of barriers to settlement, i.e., looking for the strategic and/or emotional barriers that prevent a case from settling; and (4) management of the "transaction versus transformation" components of the mediation, i.e., knowing when to focus on the financial terms of the deal while recognizing the personal healing that needs to take place.

The concept of "status" is something derived from improvisational theater. It is a social position that is defined by the behavior of the parties and the way they interact with each other. In this case, Tom and Mary took a low-key approach to the mediation, acting like everything was fine. Following those cues, I assumed that they wanted to defer to their legal team and treated them as if they were low status, elevating the lawyers to a high-status position. While status can shift during a situation, it requires interaction and changes in behavior to allow for the shift. Here, I maintained a consistent behavior throughout the proceedings, recognizing the high status of the lawyers and low status of the parties until the actual moment that settlement was on the table. At that point, the parties (Tom and Mary) shifted status on their own, completely changing the dynamics of the case.

I had a sense early in the case that there might be an emotional roadblock with the parties. After all, they had been through difficult criminal proceedings and had almost lost their children to unwarranted allegations of child molestation. Nevertheless, I leapfrogged over my own intuition in order to cut to the negotiation chase. In so doing, I missed the cues that were given by the clients, cues that were ever so subtle but glaring in retrospect. Clearly, people who have been through this type of emotional trauma would not sit by idly while their situation is discussed inside and out by lawyers and claims examiners. At a minimum, I should have sat quietly with the clients and had them summarize what this trauma had done to the family and how the family had coped with the huge interference in their lives. By doing so, I would have clearly identified the emotional barrier exhibited by the

Lockes earlier in the session rather than after a settlement had been reached.

People hold private information they want to hide or to use to mislead the other parties in order to get a bigger piece of the pie. These "strategic" barriers need to be identified in order to manage the negotiation transaction, particularly when the approach to settlement is horse trading, i.e., operating within a set routine or pattern designed to maintain rather than change the relationship of the parties. The bigger problem is when people depart from rational behavior, leading to a distortion and misinterpretation of information, resulting in artificial impasse of a case. These "emotional or cognitive" barriers are just as critical to address as strategic barriers, as I discovered in this case.

Negotiations of litigated disputes often have an overarching principle of horse trading. This "transactional" approach to mediation is highly successful but ignores the "transformative" nature of the process. The latter engages the parties in sometimes risky but usually positive work that prompts change in the parties and their positions. The former focuses solely on the exchange of numbers. While a garden-variety personal injury case is a perfect dispute to be handled in a transactional way, it's important to utilize the transformational strategy when adding potential emotional hurdles to the case.

A mediator who is on autopilot can get a case settled but often misses opportunities to use the instruments available to him to create a positive experience for the participants. The most obvious instrument that was underutilized here was listening to what was not said as opposed to what was being said in the negotiation. Had I been sensitive to the lack of client involvement, I would have been able to identify the emotional impediments earlier in the day instead of allowing a complete breakdown when closure time arrived. Luckily, I was able to salvage the settlement late in the day, but only after an artificial impasse was created by the clients. It was at this point that I allowed the process to unfold for all parties involved, not just the people interested in the financial outcome, by shifting from autopilot to full engagement.

Every negotiation is a communication process built on a story. To begin with, the players have to agree to the basic set up; the who, what and where have to be developed so that the stage is properly set for the negotiation. After that, each idea should be met with "yes, and..." By saying "yes, and..." we are not necessarily agreeing with the principles presented by our partners. We are simply developing the scene. First we accept the reality created by our partners, and then we add new information, so that we can ultimately determine what realistic options are available for settlement. Using this principle early on in the mediation with the plaintiffs would have allowed the mediator to address the emotional roadblocks way before the impasse occurred at the end of the negotiation.

24.
Conversational Shifts

Lela P. Love

MAKING MOUNTAINS OUT OF MOLEHILLS

On one side of the table was Ben, a black man, dignified but silent—instructed not to speak by his attorney. Ben had dressed up for the occasion but seemed too respectful to speak, given that his attorney was taking the floor. Ben's attorney, an overweight, red-faced, and bombastic man, was all too pleased to do the talking. As the attorney explained the situation and his positions, it seemed never to occur to him to consult his client Ben.

On the other side of the table was the insurance adjuster, who seemed as if this was his millionth worker's compensation case—he was not that interested. And, of course, there was the mediator, and me—an observer given some license to jump in if needed.

After the mediator's opening, the worker's attorney led off in an angry tone: "Ya'll [referring to the insurance company] were sent a notice that all checks for Ben should be sent to me, not to my client. That's how I do it. Does anyone open mail in your office? You sent the check to Ben here. But he never got it because he moved. It should have been sent to me." The attorney went on about the check. Listening, you would think that the check having been sent to the claimant's address was a criminal offense.

The mistake had been discovered after about a month, and another check was sent promptly to the attorney's office. However, the attorney was still making an issue of it. "The audacity of ignoring notices," the attorney said.

The insurance adjuster apologized—probably not for the first time—saying that he was sorry that the lawyer's client received the check late but noting that the client had it now.

The mediator asked if the amount of the check was correct.

The attorney said, "Yeah, those boys got that right at least. The amount was okay, but it was sent to the wrong place. The insurance company has to learn a lesson about where it sends checks."

What was the big deal? I wondered, as I sat in my observer's chair. And why did the insurance company need a lesson? What kind of lesson would do?

MAKING MORE MOUNTAINS OUT OF MORE MOLEHILLS

The attorney continued to rant, this time on a different topic. He said that the problem wasn't just about the check; it was about the insurance company wanting Ben to see another doctor. The attorney said that the insurance company claimed that it was entitled to an independent medical examination (IME) but that Ben had already seen a doctor—at the emergency room. "They forced Ben to go to the emergency room when he fell," said the attorney. "Forced him! He saw a doctor after waiting three hours. There's their stinking IME. They can have the emergency room doctor's report. Three hours in an emergency room is a nightmare. They're not going to get another IME."

The insurance adjuster sighed. In front of him was a big stack of files. He had a tired and exasperated expression. "Mr. Attorney," he said, "everyone knows an emergency room visit is not an IME. Let's get real."

THE "EASY" ISSUE

So, there it was: two issues—the check and the IME. The mediator picked the "easy" issue, the check, and spent the better part of an hour going over every angle.

It seemed easy because not much money was involved; in fact, it was not clear why any money at all was due. What were the damages? According to the attorney, at a minimum, the insurer must pay interest on the time that Ben didn't have his money. By his calculations, that came to $42. Even accepting the exorbitant interest rate that would be required to reach $42, it was simply not possible to follow Ben's attorney's math. So, the mediator changed tacks.

And how much would it cost to litigate this? The attorney was unconcerned about such matters. "We'll take it to the Supreme Court to teach these guys a lesson," said the attorney. "When I send a notice, it should be obeyed."

The mediator explored various angles to try to resolve the issue. He suggested that a reasonable solution would be to try to prevent this sort of mistake in the future. Was there a way to do that? Yes, there was, agreed the attorney, but he still demanded $42 for his client because that "lesson" would provide the very best prevention. The mediator suggested that perhaps the insurance company was not the only one to blame, asking whether it was the client himself who provided his address on his insurance forms. Yes, the client had provided the address that the check was mailed to, agreed the attorney, but he felt that the attorney's notice should have superseded that.

The insurance adjuster wouldn't pay the $42. He just wasn't going to do that. After all, it was an honest mistake, and there was no call and no precedent for such a payment. In addition, the interest rate that the attorney used to arrive at $42 was ridiculous and incomprehensible.

The insurance adjuster and the attorney went round in circles ad nauseam.

The mediator finally called it a day, saying that he was sorry that he couldn't help them resolve the situation that day.

The "Hard" Issue

Then, as an afterthought, I jumped in and asked about the IME. This second issue—appearing much harder than the first—had seemed futile to address to the mediator given the utter lack of success regarding the check. But, why not try? After this prompt, I resumed my role as a fly on the wall.

The mediator asked about the doctor that the insurance company wanted to use. Since Ben's attorney didn't know the particular doctor, Ben finally spoke up and said that he felt it was a waste of time going to that doctor because "everyone knows that the doctor will say anything that benefits the company." This was enough to begin a discussion about who might be an acceptable doctor. The parties bargained until they found one who was nearby and deemed sufficiently neutral.

The issue of the IME went entirely differently from the issue of the misdirected check. The parties seemed tired of fighting and more willing to consider some sort of resolution.

Who would have thought that the issue could be resolved? It was done. Ben would go to an agreed upon doctor within a week for the IME.

Success Breeds Success

Given this success, when the mediator returned to the issue of the check, things had shifted. In some ineffable way, the one agreement instilled some harmony. The attorney said that he and Ben would forget about the $42 as long as the insurance adjuster made sure that it never happened again. "But Mr. Adjuster," added the attorney as a parting shot, "if it happens again, we'll see you in Supreme Court!"

Second Thoughts:

In Mediation 101, a lot of time is spent talking about structuring the conversational agenda. What issue should be addressed first? What issue should be raised next? When do you shelve a topic and move on? This story illustrates that the agenda and how the mediator moves from one issue to another can allow for unexpected headway and hence success. The mediator here picked what appeared to be an easy issue, but it wasn't easy, at least not until there was some momentum. What made the issue of $42 so hard? I speculate that the attorney wanted to make sure that money reached his office so that he could take his cut before the balance moved to the client, but who can say? Moving to the subject of the IME worked wonders. Why? Just the switch in focus at a point when everyone was worn out may have opened up possibilities. How to find where the river will go is a mysterious process. The mediator needs to keep the conversation flowing as long as possible.

The second lesson that this story held for me was that mediators (in the words of Winston Churchill) should "never, never, never, never give up." After all, a river never gives up—it finds a way in, around, under, and through obstacles, moving toward the sea. If one path is blocked, try another.

25.

The Power of an Authentic Story

Lela P. Love

Not Easily Persuaded

The plaintiff in a workers' compensation case wanted a substantial award due to what she claimed was a severe and debilitating back injury. She was a middle-aged woman who had lifted a carton at work that was just too heavy for her, and her back had "gone out". Sitting beside her lawyer at the mediation, she was attentive. Her appearance was nondescript in many ways. She was not well dressed for this important event in her life, and she did not command attention except when she was finally given the floor to speak. At that point her voice was clear as a bell and transformed the fluorescent lit room.

The professionals around the table each had a stack of files—each file filled with many papers—in front of them. The papers and the

299

routine manner in which the claim was made by the plaintiff's attorney, followed by a predictable response from the insurance adjuster, would make any observer sleepy.

It seemed that the practice in the professional community of lawyers and insurance representatives tended toward insisting that the professionals do all the talking in workers' compensation cases. Hence, the claimant's lawyer took the stage in lieu of the claimant, and he was pressing for a high award based on the medical documentation that he had.

The insurance representative, while willing to pay something, just wasn't buying the story that the back injury was so serious. There are a lot of back injury cases, and the severity of injury in many situations is simply hard to prove.

The mediation was going nowhere fast because the medical reports were not that persuasive to the insurance company representative, who had his own independent medical examiner.

MAKING IT REAL

Progress was utterly stalled until the claimant herself, to the professionals' surprise, broke in. Utterly frustrated by the lack of progress and the sterile way in which her story had been presented so far, she addressed the insurance adjuster. Her own lawyer simply could not stop her. She was like some elemental force.

She said, "Mister, you don't think I have a back injury? Let me tell you what my life is like. I can't even put on my clothes by myself—or do other private things. I have a real nice husband, but I don't like it at all to ask him to help me like this. Can you imagine having to help out when your wife uses the toilet? It's not pretty. When the kids come home after school, my back hurts so much I can't play with them or stand or sit for long enough to help with homework, and I can't make dinner. So, I've had to have my mother-in-law come help. I don't like my mother-in-law. She takes over MY kitchen. To be there with everyone, I have to lie on the floor with my legs up so my back can be flat. Mister, it's hell. She tells them things I don't agree with, and I can't even turn my neck so I can see where everyone is. She's bossy and loud, and the kitchen doesn't seem like my home. It's been that way for a month.

"At night, in bed, I lie there crying because it hurts so much, and I know I'm not getting enough sleep to make good sense the next day. Yeah, I can take the pain medicine, but it makes me so nauseous and out of it that I'm no good to anyone."

"My doctor says there's no end in sight. If you don't get that picture from my doctor's report, why don't you come home with me after this mediation and see what you think?"

TRUE INSIGHT

The insurance adjuster sat with his tall stack of files in front of him. Until that moment, they were all just impersonal cases with people and stories that weren't "real" to him. Suddenly, though, one of the files went from two-dimensional to three-dimensional, and he wanted to help this lady. He sat up. He said he was sorry for what she was suffering, a comment that seemed to everyone in the room like just the right thing to say. He asked some further questions, studied his paperwork again and the case settled quickly for a figure that the plaintiff thought was fair.

SECOND THOUGHTS:

Attorneys can be great advocates. They can make situations clearer. They can listen and be articulate. But they haven't been in their client's life, in their client's skin. There is nothing more persuasive than the real thing. It wasn't just that the claimant became believable due to the details about her life that she provided; it was the way she told her story. By infusing her tale with emotion and passion, the claimant aroused empathy and connection between herself and others in the room. In fact, the insurance adjuster seemed pleased to be able to do something compassionate when he himself was convinced that it was the right thing to do. The lesson? Clients can be the better and more persuasive speaker. They will get satisfaction from telling their story AND they may have the best shot at moving their counterpart on the other side.

26.
Unexpected Events

Margaret Shaw

A Grim Situation

It was the end of a very long day for me. I had sat all day at the head of a large oval table with a glass top, surrounded by adjustable chairs on wheels. Large framed pictures of partners and other notables adorned the walls, all of them with expressions as imposing as those on the living, breathing humans in the room. A plush rug was the only thing that softened what was a rather intimidating atmosphere, typical in many New York City conference rooms.

Ranged around the table were the plaintiff and the defense teams in a case brought by lenders against a hospital which had defaulted on a large loan. The lenders alleged that the hospital had made negligent representations and omissions concerning its operations and performance. By mid-afternoon, after an initial joint session and several separate caucuses, little progress had been made and the

303

parties remained far apart. In desperation I suggested that we all meet together to address several issues I thought could benefit from direct communications. And so we reconvened.

After some communications back and forth between the parties I looked around the group and sensed a grim bleakness. The conference room table was ringed by black suits relieved only by an occasional gray, with the one other woman in attendance dressed in navy blue. There were no smiles and absolutely no signs of movement. I found myself desperately trying to think of what to do next.

A COMPROMISING POSITION

Unexpectedly at that late hour, one of the attorneys made a statement that made me feel there was at last some avenue to pursue, some route toward compromise and accommodation.

Excited about the possibility, I leaned forward, ready to pounce. The sudden movement catapulted the chair in one direction and my body in another. I found myself UNDER the table, surrounded by many pants-covered legs, looking up through the glass top! Wearing a skirt that day, even though it was one of which my mother would have approved, did not help with respect to keeping my sense of dignity. My legs splayed, one shoe dangling precariously off my toes, I was having rather an out-of-body experience.

Fortunately (in retrospect), the situation struck me as so totally comical that I began to laugh as I climbed back up, peering sheepishly over the rim of the table. Fortunately the gods were with me, and everyone around the table began to smile—and then laugh—until we were all in stitches trying to describe our various perspectives of what had just transpired. ("I couldn't figure out where you had gone!" "You had the most amazing expression on your face!" "I was just about to make an important point when you disappeared!")

FROM GRIM TO GRINS

While I would not recommend this as a mediator strategy, particularly if the mediator is wearing a skirt, what happened next is a testament to humor and to people sharing an experience that creates a bond.

The mood shifted. The parties began to ask questions of one another as opposed to just making arguments, and the conversation became much more productive. While the case did not actually settle that day, we gained some much-needed momentum, and the case was resolved after further follow-up telephone calls.

SECOND THOUGHTS:

So often, in the context of coaching mediators, I am struck by how helpful it is to remain upbeat, even to be funny (when there are appropriate opportunities), to maintain a lightness of being, and to resist becoming as unhappy as the parties are. This story celebrates how laughing together—like breaking bread together—creates connections between people and hence a possibility for forward movement. Obviously, I experienced forward movement in a very literal sense in this chair incident, but by using the moment to lighten the mood rather than becoming a victim of an unfortunate circumstance, I was able to achieve another kind of forward movement as well.

PART VIII

Addressing Issues That Litigation Cannot

I was never ruined but twice; once when I lost a lawsuit and once when I won one.

Voltaire

27.
Tony

Joseph B. Stulberg

THE SETTING

St. Augustine was a Catholic parochial school with a total of 450 students in its high school (grades 9–12).

The school was located in Newtown, a suburb of Lyon. The anchor city, Lyon, had a population of 350,000 citizens; another 400,000 residents lived in its surrounding suburbs. The metropolitan area had a strong, diverse economic base comprised of manufacturing and service industry companies; there were thriving arts and cultural institutions in Lyon, and the region attracted many visitors to its lakes and parks during the summer months.

Lyon reflected an African American population of approximately 15 percent and a Hispanic population of 5 percent; the remainder—80 percent—was Caucasian. The suburban areas were, for all practical purposes, entirely Caucasian.

In an attempt to promote racial and economic diversity in its student body, St. Augustine created a scholarship program. The program provided full-tuition scholarships to four qualified students per class (for a total of sixteen students each year). To qualify for these scholarships, a recipient had to be a full-time resident of Lyon and be a student in good standing in its public school system. The scholarship also provided money for books and transportation.

The scholarship program targeted applicants who would enrich the racial and economic diversity profile of the St. Augustine student body. During its fifteen-year program history, there had been only seven scholarship recipients who were not African American. St. Augustine leaders were very comfortable with that statistic.

Tony Shaw was a senior at St. Augustine. An African American, he was born in Lyon, and his mother raised him there as a single parent. He was an only child. He had been a scholarship recipient at St. Augustine for four years. A standout athlete, he was selected to the all-state football team his senior year. Following graduation in June, he planned to attend a Big Ten university on a full football scholarship.

THE ASSEMBLY

Father O'Brien was the headmaster of St. Augustine. On the first Monday in June (that year, June 4), pursuant to St. Augustine's long-standing tradition, he convened a school-wide assembly for high school students.

This assembly, widely referred to as the free-for-all, was the annual occasion in which the headmaster, administration, and faculty invited students to an "open mike" to share what things the students believed should change about school practices to improve the school experience.

For many students, this was their favorite assembly of the year. It always took place on the first Monday of the last week of classes. For seniors, this was their final week of high school before they (and other high school students) took their final examinations. Historically, student comments ranged from spontaneous, individual speeches about the curriculum or school activities to preplanned presentations (skits) by students who tried, through humorous satire, to communicate their ideas.

Father O'Brien convened the assembly at 8:10 a.m., the beginning of the school day. He invited comments. By tradition, he invited graduating seniors to speak first. Tony Shaw raised his hand and was selected to be the first speaker. As he approached the microphone, some audience members started shouting, "Go, Tony! Let's start it right!" Others started applauding in support. Tony took the microphone and said, "Father O'Brien. Teachers. Classmates. I just want to say this: After four years at this place, I think that all of you are still a bunch of motherf****** racists."

Pandemonium erupted. As Tony left the stage, students shouted at him. Many booed. Someone shouted "Go home, n***** [N-word]!" Others screamed comments that were laced with derogatory racial epithets. All comments conveyed the same message: "Tony, leave!"

Father O'Brien quickly went to the microphone and bellowed, loudly and emphatically, "Tony, meet me in my office immediately. Students and faculty, this assembly is hereby dismissed. Everyone should report to your next class, but use the time of this assembly period as a supervised study hall."

People left, bitterly protesting. Tony Shaw went to Father O'Brien's office. Father O'Brien, in strong, angry language said, "You are dismissed from this school. Immediately. Pack all of your things. Get out. You are not to return to take your exams. You are not to be at St. Augustine for any reason. You will not be given a diploma from this school. If you want to finish high school, you will have to get a GED. I am telephoning your mother to tell her about this."

Shaw packed his things and left the building.

ESCALATING TENSIONS

That afternoon, Tony and his mother met with their minister, Reverend Scott. Reverend Scott suggested that the three of them meet with the president of the local chapter of the National Association for the Advancement of Colored People (NAACP) as well as with a lawyer from the local Legal Services office. Reverend Davis, the president of the NAACP and himself a minister, listened to Tony's story; when Tony finished, Reverend Davis instantly stated that he would organize a demonstration at St. Augustine for the following morning.

The next day, sixty people—all African American—walked in front of the entrance to St. Augustine High School carrying picket signs. Their signs read: "Reinstate Tony Shaw" and "We are here to teach you how to be good Christians." Several St. Augustine students joined the picket line. Some turned away from the school, refusing to go through the picket line for fear of hostile taunts, reprisals, or physical fighting. Other students crossed the picket line, later claiming that they were harassed as they did.

A local TV reporter interviewed a picketer. The picketer said, "If they don't immediately reinstate Tony and let him graduate, then we will make certain that St. Augustine's graduation ceremony on June 15 will make the urban riots of the '60s look like a picnic." That quote became the lead story on the local TV news at both 6:00 p.m. and 11:00 p.m.

By 2:00 p.m. on that Tuesday, two "student groups" within the school had emerged: one supported Tony's reinstatement, the other protested it. The editor of the school newspaper developed a "special edition" of the paper in which she called for Tony's reinstatement. The Student Council President quickly responded by circulating a petition signaling support for the School's action towards Tony; 70 students signed it. Students in the school quickly made signs supporting either the school administration or Tony; as they passed each other in the hallways, they would "heckle" one another. No fights, though, erupted.

By Tuesday evening, many parents of St. Augustine students telephoned members of the school's governing board to protest the protestors. Many had seen the local TV story and were both angry and concerned by the reported "threats" to disrupt the graduation. They heatedly urged the school leadership to stand strong behind Father O'Brien. Other parents, however, telephoned board members to express their belief that the school leadership had acted inappropriately in dismissing Tony; those parents encouraged the school leadership to reinstate him.

Tony

On Wednesday morning, the front-page headline of Lyon's major newspaper read: "Race Riot Threatened at St. Augustine Graduation." The story gave a detailed account of events at the school assembly on Monday, described the previous day's picketing, referenced the statement made to and reported by the TV reporter, and contained quotes from students both supporting and opposing Tony's dismissal.

Late Wednesday morning, Tony Shaw's lawyers filed a lawsuit against the school. The legal claim was that the school had violated Shaw's free speech rights guaranteed under the First Amendment of the U.S. Constitution. The court set a hearing date for Monday, June 25.

On Wednesday afternoon, the local reporter who had written the lead newspaper story pursued two additional leads. He contacted the football coach at the Big Ten university that Tony would attend in the fall. In his interview with the coach, the reporter described the events at St. Augustine and asked the coach for his comments. The coach was quoted as saying, "I don't know anything about the situation you describe. We want Tony to be here, but of course, if he does not graduate from high school with his diploma, he will not be eligible for his scholarship."

The reporter also contacted Newtown's chief of police. When asked how the department would respond to possible disruptive demonstrations or other conduct at the school's high school graduation ceremonies scheduled for June 17, the police chief was quoted as saying, "We have a peaceful, law-abiding community. We do not anticipate any difficulties from our citizens. But if anyone appears that day to try to inflame tensions, we will not hesitate to use whatever lawful force is required to quell their efforts."

In Thursday's newspaper, a front-page follow-up story appeared about the Tony Shaw incident; it included the quotes from the football coach and the police chief.

Reverend Davis and his group of protestors continued picketing at St. Augustine on Thursday morning. This time, in addition to television cameras covering the event, eight uniformed officers from the Newtown police walked the sidewalk to monitor student-picketer interaction. When protestors started singing protest songs, opponents

313

shouted loudly, and some passing motorists blasted their car horns in an attempt to drown out the music. No arrests were made, but tensions were clearly mounting and tempers were frayed.

MEDIATION SET IN MOTION

What happened next? The president of St. Augustine's governing school board knew a member of the board of directors of the local community dispute resolution center. At approximately 11:00 a.m. on Thursday, the president telephoned him and asked if the center could be of assistance. They talked for a few minutes; the board member listened to the president's concerns and then explained, briefly, how a mediation process might work. The conversation ended with the board member pledging to contact the center director to discuss the matter.

The board member promptly telephoned the center director. The director, hearing the account, instantly committed the center to exploring possible service.

The center director quickly started to make telephone calls to multiple stakeholders. His goal, as he stated to each, was to explore each stakeholder's concerns and then have everyone (including the center director) assess whether using a mediation process at this point in time was an option worth considering. He assured each stakeholder that the initial inquiry and telephone conversation were confidential. He listened carefully to their respective accounts. He probed for additional information. He helped each assess their various options for resolving their concerns. He ended each conversation by asking the stakeholder for suggestions about other people the center director should contact for possible inclusion in subsequent discussions.

By early afternoon, the center director had spoken with the president of St. Augustine's governing school board; the lawyer for St. Augustine's school board and, with the lawyer's permission, Father O'Brien; the lawyers for Tony Shaw and, with the lawyers' permission, both Tony and his mother; Reverend Scott; and Reverend Davis. Each of these individuals agreed that the center director should not at this time contact Newton's chief of police, any of the identifiable student

314

leaders at the high school, or anyone from St. Augustine's parent group. The director also contacted several mediator colleagues affiliated with the center to assess their availability for and willingness to serve.

By 2:30 p.m., each person noted above had agreed to the following:

(1) They would meet that evening at the center's offices in Lyon beginning at 7:00 p.m. in a mediation session to discuss the situation involving Tony Shaw and St. Augustine and to explore possible options for addressing it. Stated differently, participants were explicitly committing themselves to participate in a mediation conference, not an arbitration hearing or some other form of adjudicatory process.

(2) Each participant would come prepared to stay as long as necessary to discuss the matters, presuming that participants or the mediators felt that progress was being made; there would be no end time dictated by personal schedules.

(3) Each pledged that no one would make any comment to media personnel or friends about the scheduled meeting before it occurred.

(4) The mediation team would consist of the center director (Caucasian, law-trained, and professionally known to lawyers representing Tony Shaw); the center board member with whom the school board president had made initial contact (Caucasian, businessman, and trained volunteer mediator with the center); and the center associate director (African American, trained mediator, previous director of youth services programs, and professionally known to both Reverend Davis and Reverend Scott).

OUTSIDE THE PUBLIC GLARE

All participants arrived at the center shortly before 7:00 p.m. They waited in the reception area. We mediators welcomed people to the center and invited them to move from the reception area to the main conference room. Standing at the door of the conference room, we introduced ourselves to each participant as the participants entered the room, shaking their hands in the process and directing them to the chair at the table where their respective "name tent" was displayed. We also encouraged the participants, before sitting down, to introduce themselves to one another and shake hands. Tony and his mother had not seen or spoken with Father O'Brien since the Monday incident. Although saying they felt awkward, Father O'Brien and Tony Shaw shook hands.

As we mediators assumed our chairs, the president of the school board stated, "It was challenging to comply with that guideline about not telling the media that we were meeting tonight. I had telephone calls from three television stations and the newspaper reporter between 3:00 and 4:30 p.m. today, asking me if I could tell them about any developments."

Reverend Davis immediately stated, "Well, they must have called me after they called you because they were still hunting for an angle."

No one said anything. An electrifyingly huge signal had just been sent: two important stakeholders in this drama had been confronted with a challenge of complying with an agreed-upon guideline. At least as measured by the fact that no one from the media had appeared at the center, each had honored the commitment to try talking with one another directly and privately.

We mediators broke the silence by thanking the president and Reverend Davis for sharing that information and then publicly commended them for adhering to their commitment to use this opportunity outside the public glare to explore possible resolution.

THE SETTLEMENT TERMS

The discussions started at 7:00 p.m. The parties met in joint session until 9:30 p.m. Everyone participated. We mediators then moved into a caucus format. At 2:00 a.m., the parties initialed terms of a complete settlement.

What were the terms? As announced in a later press conference, the terms included the following:

- Tony would take his scheduled final exams during the regularly scheduled school examination period—June 11-15—but would write them at a location either near the school or at the law offices of the board's lawyer instead of at the high school; the location, to be secured by the board president by 5:00 p.m. on Friday, June 8, would remain the same for the administration of each of the four exams that Tony would write.
- A grading review and appeal process was established, to be used in the event that Tony received a grade lower than C on any exam; the goal was to ensure that the grading of Tony's exam was consistent with those practices used for other students in that class.
- Assuming that Tony passed all of his exams, Tony would be awarded his high school diploma from St. Augustine.
- Tony would not physically return to St. Augustine High School but could participate in any senior party or other student gathering held away from the school premises.
- Tony would not attend his high school graduation ceremony.
- Reverend Davis would not organize or conduct any demonstrations at St. Augustine on Friday, June 8, or through the following week as long as Tony was taking his examinations as set forth in the agreement.

- Tony and Reverend Davis would use multiple avenues to communicate to their friends and acquaintances their belief that the controversy had been resolved satisfactorily and their commitment to take every reasonable step to ensure that the scheduled graduation ceremony would go forward without any disruptions.
- Father O'Brien, in the presence of Tony and his lawyer, would telephone the Big Ten coach on Friday, June 8, about 10:00 a.m. to inform him that the matter had been resolved and that Tony, upon successful completion of his examinations, would be awarded a diploma from St. Augustine.
- Tony, through his lawyer, would withdraw the lawsuit.
- We mediators, at the participants' request and with their participation, would convene a news conference for 11:00 a.m. that Friday morning to announce the settlement.

AN UNEXPECTED CODA

As the participants initialed the document recording the settlement terms, Ms. Shaw asked if she could make a comment. In a quiet tone, strikingly different from her strident comments earlier that evening, she said softly, "Father O'Brien and members of St. Augustine, I have been angry since this incident developed. I was angry when we started tonight. What we have agreed to tonight to fix the situation is acceptable, but it is not the way I had hoped my son would finish high school. We will move on. But I do want to thank you, sincerely, for making it possible, through your scholarship, for Tony to have received a fine education. And I want to thank everyone here tonight for making it possible for Tony to be the first person in my family to be in a position to attend college."

There was a distinct pause. People then cautiously smiled at one another and left the room.

SECOND THOUGHTS:

This controversy occurred before the advent of cell phones and the Internet. However, I do not believe that its lessons for contemporary practice are limited by that fact. There are four striking elements of this experience that, with the perspective of time, garner my interest. I think they highlight, or at least suggest, how the contemporary alternative dispute resolution field has or has not developed since its emergence forty years ago. I discuss each element below in a question-and-answer format.

(1)   Can or should cases involving constitutional issues be mediated?

Yes, of course cases involving constitutional issues can be mediated. The more important inquiry is what else is at stake and what priority, given those other concerns, does a party attach to vindicating the constitutional claim? Tony Shaw was interested in taking his exams while the coursework was still fresh in his mind, graduating from high school, and going to college. While he wanted his speech protected under the First Amendment, it was not his most important priority. The school wanted the picketing, public attention, and student tensions to subside. Most important, it wanted its graduation ceremony to proceed without protests or disruptions. All of those matters—taking exams, diploma status, graduation exercises, and demonstrations—could be negotiated.

Some commentators argue that matters involving constitutional rights are too important to be resolved in any forum other than a courtroom. This case underscores how misguided that sweeping claim is. Furthermore, the court would not have heard the case until after one week following the scheduled graduation in any event. None of the parties' other interests could be addressed or satisfied by the court outcome, and the parties' lawyers, to their credit, recognized that.

(2) Will mediation services provided through the private marketplace or civil court–annexed programs be available to help citizens resolve community controversies involving social policy?

Usually not. The private marketplace of mediators was not accessible to Tony Shaw or his legal representative; even if they had some money to pay the mediators' fees, the presumptive notion of many lawyer mediator practitioners that one party (in this case, St. Augustine) could pay a disproportionate share of the mediators' fees without jeopardizing the mediator's neutrality has no credibility in this context. Court-annexed mediators were not available because the lawsuit was filed in a court that did not have mediation programs. The case therefore reaffirms the significance of having an independent, proactive community-based dispute resolution resource available to its citizens.

How would this be helpful? While this narrative was being written during the summer of 2010, two events took place in the United States that crucially exposed an important lacuna in the development of the mediation field in our country. In New York City, information about a proposed plan to construct a Muslim community center in lower Manhattan triggered explosive citizen protests; politicians and political pundits across the country strongly expressed sharply competing positions and proposed solutions. I have no personal knowledge of any quiet, nonpublic efforts to bring the various stakeholders together for discussions; and, at least from a distance, there appears to be no credible, institutional, neutral dispute resolution resource to which any of the interested parties could turn. On the West Coast, by contrast, a different case developed. A ticker statement across ESPN stated that the wealthy owners of the Los Angeles Dodgers, mired in a contentious divorce proceeding, were scheduled to meet in a private mediation session in an attempt to resolve the issue of how to allocate ownership of the baseball club in their matrimonial settlement. To me, the discouraging lesson from these two events is that money buys access to mediation and that mediation's dominant use may be mismatched to social needs.

(3) Is mediator diversity important?

Diversity is crucial. Quite simply, neither Tony Shaw nor Reverend Davis would have participated in the mediation without, minimally, a racially diverse mediation team. They did not ask for it. They did not have to. Everyone knew that they needed to have confidence that the mediators might understand how Tony could have made the statement that he did, and there would have been no credibility with Davis's constituency without a racially diverse mediation team. Diversity in mediator backgrounds and training is also significant. People are understandably skeptical of official processes, including court procedures or alternative forums. They need to have a basis for believing that their appearance and participation in the process will not instantly put them at a disadvantage. They do not need someone to protect them or advocate for them. They simply need someone who they believe will listen and understand their perspectives. And familiarity breeds comfort and initial strands of trust. With so much contemporary mediation activity—particularly that which is compensated—dominated by lawyer mediators, we tend to minimize the urgent need to have trained mediators from multiple backgrounds.

(4) Is mediator neutrality more important than requiring parties to consider Pareto-optimal bargaining outcomes?

Yes.

Some could criticize the mediators for not insisting that the participants consider longer-lasting matters that could improve race relations, both within and outside the school community. In the rhetoric of many negotiation and mediation scholars, we focused on facilitating a resolution acceptable to the parties but failed in discharging a mediator's alleged duty to promote Pareto optimality, i.e., the point at which it would be impossible to improve the outcome of one party without impairing the outcome of the other party.

The parties made crucial choices, particularly regarding who would not participate in the conversation. They chose not to include any other students (the student council president or the student newspaper editor). They chose to exclude the Newtown police chief. They chose to exclude parent groups. They focused on addressing the eruption, tensions, and issues within a framework that they viewed as being within their capacity, time constraints, and needs.

In truth, the mediation team perhaps could have done things to prompt participants to consider the longer-lasting matters that could improve race relations. But, in all candor and without trying to be defensive, the demand for Pareto optimality seems not only incoherent at a practical level (How would one know that it had been achieved?), but, more importantly, it also posits a mediator duty for directing the conversation that disrespects party autonomy.

Tony Shaw graduated. He enrolled at the university in the fall and played on the football team. St. Augustine's June high school graduation ceremonies proceeded without incident. The parties reached their resolution by assuming responsibility for dealing with their challenge and actively participating in a process that they viewed as a justice event. Their resolution might not have saved the world, but it was warmly embraced. Helping parties secure such outcomes, I believe, is congruent with and distinctive to the mediator's role.

28.
Sisters of the Precious Blood v. Bristol-Myers

Frank J. Scardilli

LEGAL BEGINNINGS

In 1977, a case pitting a missionary group against big business practices found its way to the U.S. District Court for the Southern District of New York.

The Sisters of the Precious Blood (Sisters) sued Bristol-Myers Co. (Bristol), claiming that Bristol's sales practices in connection with its infant baby formula in the Third World were contributing to serious illness, malnutrition, and death of infants because of the unsanitary conditions often prevailing there. Frequently, the formula was mixed with contaminated water; there was no refrigeration; and the use of the formula discouraged breast-feeding, which was clearly healthier than the formula in most instances.

The Sisters, who owned 500 shares of Bristol stock, had proposed a shareholder resolution requesting that management report to the shareholders the full extent of Bristol's marketing practices of the infant formula in the Third World to alert other shareholders to what they perceived was irresponsible business behavior. The Sisters initiated the lawsuit against Bristol under the proxy solicitation section of the Securities Exchange Act of 1934, alleging that the shareholder resolution that the Sisters proposed was defeated because Bristol's stated opposition to the resolution in the proxy materials distributed to the shareholders was based on serious misrepresentations of fact.

The Sisters' lawsuit was aimed at forcing the company to craft a corrected proxy solicitation to be submitted at a special meeting of the shareholders called specifically for that purpose rather than waiting for the next annual meeting of shareholders.

The court declined to grant the relief sought by the Sisters. This case was on appeal to the U.S. Court of Appeals for the Second Circuit from the trial court's grant of summary judgment in favor of Bristol-Myers Co., which is when I was called in to mediate the dispute as the chief mediator of the Court.

UNCERTAIN OUTCOME

The first of four conferences seeking to mediate this dispute was held on July 19, 1977. As is customary, I first explored the arguments of counsel relative to the strengths and weaknesses of their legal positions on appeal. The parties seemed genuinely far apart in their assessment of the likely outcome in the Second Circuit. The issue on appeal involved some complexity because of the rather technical requirements for suits under Section 14 of the Securities Exchange Act of 1934. While generally appellees have a distinct advantage, if for no other reason than that only about one out of eight cases is reversed on appeal in the Second Circuit, the outcome of this particular case was hard to predict. Even if the district court decision were deemed technically correct, this could have disturbing policy implications because the decision appeared to create a license for management to lie with impunity whenever it sought to defeat a proposed shareholder resolution. The Securities and Exchange Commission was apparently disturbed by this implication and had advised me that it was seriously considering filing an amicus curiae brief urging the appeals court to reverse the trial court's decision.

OPPOSITE ENDS OF THE SETTLEMENT CONTINUUM

Predictably, the parties' respective positions on what might constitute a satisfactory settlement were far apart. The Sisters were adamant that no settlement terms could be discussed unless Bristol openly admitted that it had lied in its earlier proxy solicitation and that this fact had to be communicated through new proxy solicitations at a special meeting of the shareholders to be convened solely for that purpose. Bristol, of course, insisted that it had been truthful all along. It offered, however, to permit the Sisters to make any written statement that they wished at the next annual shareholders' meeting, and Bristol would simply state its opposition to the proposal without elaboration. This was unacceptable to the Sisters.

Apparently because they believed no amicable resolution was possible, counsel who appeared for the parties were very able but had virtually no settlement authority. Because it was clear that I needed parties with more authority and flexibility, I set up a second conference requiring senior counsel to attend with their clients.

DISTORTED VIEWS

The second conference was held in the middle of August 1977 and was attended by senior counsel for both sides; the inside general counsel of Bristol; and a representative of the advisory committee of the Interfaith Center on Corporate Responsibility, which was the real moving force behind the Sisters' litigation.

It soon became apparent that there was very deep hostility and profound distrust between the parties. Each was convinced that the other was acting in bad faith. It became clear that the respective parties' self-image was significantly at variance with the image each had of the other.

The Sisters had spent years accumulating data in affidavits taken throughout the world regarding the enormous peril to infants created by the indiscriminate use of infant formula in the Third World. They had witnessed suffering and death and were suffused with the self-righteousness of avenging angels. To them, Bristol was a monster that cared only about profits and not at all about the lives and health of infants. The Sisters were outraged by Bristol's insistence that it had not lied. Their distrust of Bristol was total and uncompromising.

Bristol regarded itself as by far the most responsible marketer of infant formula in the Third World, far more responsible than its three major American competitors and the giant Swiss company Nestlé. It claimed that it produced a quality nutritional product that was very useful when mothers either could not or chose not to breast-feed their infants; that it did not advertise its infant formulas directly to consumers in the Third World; and that the company policy already sought to minimize the danger of improper use by its labeling. In short, it was convinced that its business practices were both prudent and responsible. Therefore, Bristol was furious that it had been singled out as "baby killers" by the Sisters, who had so testified before a congressional committee and who had lost few opportunities to criticize Bristol in the media. It was clear the company viewed the Sisters as wild-eyed, misguided religious fanatics who were themselves engaging in a distortion of the facts as well as reckless character assassination.

At this conference, the Sisters, for the first time, insisted that they would have to be reimbursed for their litigation expenses of approximately $15,000 before any settlement could be effected. After checking with top management, counsel for management flatly refused to pay anything at all to the Sisters.

As negotiations proceeded, it became apparent that no meaningful communication could take place until each of the parties realized that its view of the other was a grossly distorted caricature and counterproductive.

COOPERATION VERSUS LITIGATION

I struck often at the theme that it was dangerous to assume that one with whom you disagree violently is necessarily acting in bad faith. Moreover, I stressed to both that I had become fully and firmly convinced that each of the parties was acting in complete good faith, albeit from a different perspective. I strove to get each to view the matter through the eyes of the other.

It was necessary to convince both sides that their interests were not nearly as incompatible as each perceived them and that the interests of each would be best served by a cooperative problem-solving attitude rather than a litigious one.

I stressed that neither party's true interest would be served by winning the appeal. A win by Bristol would not be likely to stop the public attacks in the media that so angered and disturbed them. Likewise, a win by the Sisters could mean a remand for an expensive trial with no assurance whatever that Bristol's marketing practices thereafter would be altered in any way.

I forcibly made the point to the Sisters that their insistence that Bristol admit that it had lied was totally unrealistic and that progress was impossible as long as they insisted on humiliating the company's management. I reminded them that their real interest lay in effecting marketing changes in the Third World and that they could best achieve this in a climate of cooperative goodwill with management. As long as management perceived them as vindictive, it was likely to simply dig in its heels and refuse to budge. I urged that a softening of their attitude would undoubtedly create a more flexible attitude in management.

Bristol, in turn, was forced to concede that notwithstanding what it viewed as the distasteful stridency of the Sisters, there was indeed a real moral issue to be faced, and it had a real interest in being perceived as a highly ethical, responsible company that was not insensitive to the human tragedy that could result from the improper use of its product in the Third World.

A CHRISTMAS MIRACLE

After considerable negotiation in four face-to-face conferences supplemented by numerous telephone conferences over a period of nearly six months, the parties finally agreed on the following:

1. The Sisters were satisfied that over the course of the six months' mediation, Bristol had already changed some of its marketing practices that the Sisters had regarded as particularly offensive.

2. The Sisters would be given direct access to Bristol's board of directors and other representatives of the company at various times for the purpose of maintaining a firsthand continuing dialogue on the problems of marketing infant formula in the Third World.

3. Bristol and the Sisters would prepare separate written statements of their respective views, not to exceed 1,500 words, to be presented to the shareholders in the next quarterly report of the company. This would be preceded by an agreed-upon joint preamble that would recite the background of the litigation and its resolution by the parties and confirm that the Sisters and Bristol planned to continue to exchange views in an atmosphere of mutual respect for each other's good faith.

To ensure that the statements would not be inflammatory, each side was given the right to veto the statement of the other. Agreeing on the principle, however, was easier than its implementation. Numerous drafts were exchanged; and, when appropriate, I mediated their respective versions.

The parties arrived at the final agreement on language as a result of a four-and-a-half-hour drafting session involving eight people sitting around a conference table in the courtroom on the afternoon of Christmas Eve of 1977. In a sense of relief and elation, the chairperson of the Interfaith Center on Corporate Responsibility stated, "It is fitting and perhaps prophetic that we have finally resolved our differences on how best to protect tender infants on this [Christmas] eve" when the infant Jesus was born.

SECOND THOUGHTS:

I have always had an aversion to seeing things in black and white. Therefore, what I remember most vividly about this case is how each side considered itself especially virtuous and, consequently, especially insulted by the other side's view. After a very long career as a mediator, preceded by a number of years in a private law practice, I have noticed that many people have an aversion to complexity and ambiguity. Consequently, yearning for comfortable simplicity, they often fall into the trap of oversimplification, which can distort reality, hide shades of gray and make it virtually impossible to hear compelling counter-arguments.

My worldview on these matters has been largely influenced by my legal education at Yale Law School, which examined law's impact on society, and my involvement with general semantics, which is the scientific study of the relationship between language, thought, and human behavior.

My experience with this case is a testament to my lifelong ambition: to understand the world in all of its complexity and build a bridge of understanding between people, especially those coming from different religions, different cultures, and disparate socioeconomic backgrounds.

29.

Glen Cove

Lela P. Love

A version of this story was first published in 20 CONSENSUS 1, 1–2 (1993).

BACKGROUND: TENSIONS BUILD

In 1988 tensions began to build between Glen Cove officials and the Central American immigrants (some of whom were undocumented aliens) who congregated in front of Carmen's Deli to find employment. More than one hundred men, many from other towns, would gather on a given day to seek odd jobs from landscapers and other contractors.

Local merchants and neighbors expressed concerns about disorderly and noisy behavior at this shaping point (a locale in the city where employers go to find day workers), including catcalling to women and littering and urinating in public. City officials were also concerned about traffic safety since employers would stop on a major road to negotiate with and pick up day workers. There also was a sentiment that it was illegal for those who were undocumented to seek employment.

Salvadoran workers, on the other hand, were interested in their survival: the day labor was their means of livelihood, and a shaping point was essential for finding work. Many who gathered were political refugees from El Salvador to whom a return home might mean a death sentence. There were those who felt that since the laborers serviced the lawns and country clubs of the wealthy, the effort to remove them from gathering in public was unfair.

In addition to issues about the shaping point itself, the perception among the Hispanic community that the city—particularly the police— was hostile created problems for both sides: poor channels of communication to cope with the host of problems and a lack of resources for Central Americans when they were preyed upon by criminal elements in the community (a pressing problem).

ORDINANCES PROPOSED TO DEAL WITH THE PROBLEM

Tensions heightened in 1989 when the city, in an effort to curb the size of the gatherings, successfully urged the Immigration and Naturalization Service to round up and detain illegal aliens gathering in front of Carmen's Deli. This was followed by the city's proposing first an ordinance making it illegal for groups of five or more people to assemble publicly to seek employment and later an ordinance prohibiting any "illegal undocumented alien" from soliciting work in a public or private place. These ordinances engendered a strident debate, although neither was adopted. In 1990, the city council did adopt an ordinance that prohibited standing on a street or highway and soliciting employment from anyone in a motor vehicle and also prohibited occupants of a stopped or parked motor vehicle from hiring or attempting to hire workers.

The Hispanic community and civil libertarians saw the ordinance(s) as specifically targeted against Hispanics, as well as unconstitutional. Several months after the ordinance was adopted, advocacy groups for Central American refugees filed a $3 million class action suit against Glen Cove, alleging violation of Hispanic people's First Amendment right of freedom of speech and Fourteenth Amendment right of equal protection.

LITIGATION ENSUES

After nearly two years of litigation, the parties decided to attempt to work out their differences in mediation. I had the privilege of mediating the case.

WHAT MEDIATION ACHIEVED

Two full days of mediation, spaced a week apart to give the parties time to come up with innovative proposals to address the concerns raised on the first day, were sufficient to achieve consensus on an outline of an acceptable accord. This agreement was refined over several months and adopted in late 1992, providing for the dismissal of the lawsuit and the enforcement of the terms of the agreement by the federal court.

The significant achievements of the mediation process in this case were as follows:

The parties recognized their mutual interest in improving communications with each other.

- Greater accessibility to the city soccer field for the Salvadoran community was arranged.
- The city agreed to help find alternative sites for a shaping point (including possible use of Industrial Development Agency funds) or to support alternatives to meet the Hispanic community's employment needs. The Central American Refugee Center (CARECEN) agreed to educate day laborers who congregated in public places about their responsibilities to the community.
- Relations between the police and the Salvadoran community were addressed by CARECEN's agreement to host community meetings, giving the police a platform to educate Salvadorans

about community interests and concerns and a chance to undertake such education themselves. The police in turn agreed to cultural awareness training for all city police officers, appointing a liaison to the Salvadoran community who would attend CARECEN-organized community meetings, training two officers in conversational Spanish, taking ability in Spanish into account in hiring officers, adopting a policy barring officers from inquiring about immigration status under certain circumstances, and instituting a written protocol (in consultation with CARECEN) for the police handling of situations in which a party does not speak English.

- The ordinance was amended to a form acceptable to all parties and designed to promote the city's interest in traffic safety without singling out the Salvadoran community or infringing upon constitutional rights.

Perhaps most importantly, the mediation created a respectful dialogue between the parties, which should result in an enhanced ability to confront new problems as they arise. Alan Levine, the director of the Hofstra Constitutional Law Clinic, which represented CARECEN, said, "If everyone lives up to their obligations under this agreement, it promises to establish the kinds of relationships between a municipal government and a minority population that one would hope for."

Second Thoughts:

In looking at the litigation and the subsequent mediation of the Glen Cove case, it is notable that what was being discussed in each forum was very different. The litigation focused on whether the town ordinance was constitutional and on some discrete incidents of alleged police misconduct. The mediation, on the other hand, focused on communication issues (many having to do with non-English-speaking residents), e.g., the posting of town notices for non-English-speaking individuals, the interactions between police and non-English-speaking victims of crime, and forums for town officials to communicate concerns to minority groups. The town's concerns regarding public conduct of Salvadorans at the shaping point were also addressed.

Perhaps the most exciting breakthrough of the mediation was the agreement to collaboratively redraft the ordinance itself. This outcome gives support to the notion that even constitutional issues can be mediated. Furthermore, whether a court had found the ordinance constitutional or unconstitutional, the many other issues would have never been addressed in that forum. A finding that the ordinance was unconstitutional could have resulted in the town simply enacting a new ordinance sensitive to the court's prohibition of certain language but not responsive to other issues that the mediation addressed. In any case, a litigated outcome would have left many issues on the table. Mediation resolved not only the issues that were being litigated but also many other issues that, although not causes for legal action, were nonetheless extremely important to the individuals and groups involved in the controversy. And almost all of the outcomes or agreements arrived at in the mediation required collaboration between the two sides, creating an entirely different relationship than the previous adversarial one.

Clearly, litigation with its ability to generate precedents in important arenas is critical to the public good. But this mediation, and others like it, suggests that mediation also has important, and different, public benefits to offer.

Glen Cove has enjoyed improved relations between town officials and the Salvadoran community in part, arguably, as a byproduct of the mediation. Perhaps the most important outcome of the mediation, though, was setting new precedents with respect to community interaction and constructive problem solving between a minority group and a town. Much like the difference between giving someone a fish (providing a resolution) and teaching that person to fish (enabling constructive problem solving), the latter arguably has more hope for far-reaching and long-lasting results.

30.
Newcomers and Old-Timers: Lessons We Learn

Karin S. Hobbs

A STUDY IN CONTRASTS

The Rexall drugstore on the corner still had the vertical neon sign circa 1954. Electrolux vacuums were still sold on Main Street, and the citizens went about their business as if the year were 1950. People walked more slowly, took their time, and talked with their neighbors—in person. Cell phones and laptops were by and large absent, left at home, unimportant. The local coffee shop bustled with older gentlemen in their Wrangler jeans smoking cigarettes, drinking coffee, and spending an hour or two together discussing the latest city council meeting and whether the rivers would have enough water to feed the alfalfa, the corn, and the sugar beets.

I met with the clients and their attorneys in a law office in the small Utah town, nestled in a valley surrounded by hills covered in aspens and majestic purple mountains. The clients, Harold and Jeremy, were a study in contrasts: crusty and crisp, religious and not, old-timer and newcomer. Their only seeming similarity was that they were both making their home in this rural Utah town.

THE BOUNDARY DISPUTE

That morning, meeting with both attorneys and their clients, I learned about the boundary dispute. Harold owned a building in which he operated a dry cleaning business. For over two years, he had been in a lawsuit with Jeremy, a chipper young entrepreneur who had constructed an office building next door to Harold's dry cleaning business. Jeremy's building, according to Harold, encroached on Harold's property by four inches. Harold was seeking to have the building demolished. Harold had tried to halt the construction two years earlier; but the court denied his request to stop the construction, measure the boundaries, and determine whether the building was misplaced. Now, he was red-faced and angry. When I asked his attorney how likely the court was to order the building razed, the attorney responded that demolition was the legal remedy for encroachment, but he acknowledged it was unlikely that the court would order the building demolished. Harold looked slightly surprised. I explained to Harold that in the law, it is considered a "waste" to tear down a building, so the court was not likely to do that.

"Goddamnit," Harold said, "I've served on the city council for fifteen years. I know the rules. You just can't build on someone else's ground. When we approve building permits, we look at all these issues. I was conflicted off of this one. These newcomers from out of state—they just don't know what they're doing. They haven't had much experience. They just approve things without thinking. I just don't understand why the court won't see that this building needs to come down."

I walked down the hall and talked with Jeremy and his attorney. Jeremy's attorney claimed that the building was properly approved by the city council and that there was another survey indicating that the building was not encroaching. He acknowledged that the property deeds and surveys in the area were the subject of much litigation due to the confusing development of boundaries in the area, dating back to the early settlers and their rock walls.

These were neighbors in a small community with a huge potential for continued conflict. Having worked on many property cases, I knew that they would have to hire competing boundary experts to testify regarding their inconsistent surveys. A lawsuit would only result in a win for one side and a loss for the other. The win might be a hollow victory. The court was not likely to demolish the building. The best-case scenario for Harold was probably an order of the court awarding him monetary damages. He, like many others, would have a piece of paper entitling him to money. But he would need to collect it. Explaining that fact to clients was difficult and caused them to question our judicial system. Jeremy was stretched to the limit and could not pay a judgment. His house was mortgaged, he had car payments, and he had a family to feed. The best-case scenario for Jeremy was a ruling that his building did not encroach on Harold's. But even with a win, Jeremy would encounter a mad neighbor on a daily basis.

BEYOND BOUNDARIES: MORE TO THE DISPUTE

We seemed stuck, but I didn't think we had nearly enough information to conclude the discussions. My gut told me that I just had to keep the parties talking. There had to be more to this. The parties were interested in continuing the mediation, so when Harold had to work a shift at the fire station after lunch, we reconvened there in the afternoon.

As we sat in the fire station that afternoon, we began to learn about the actual crux of the dispute. In a private session, Harold told me that when Jeremy's building was constructed, the construction project created mud puddles. Huge mud puddles. Customers leaving the dry cleaning shop with their clean clothes complained of the mud, and sometimes they unknowingly dragged their laundered items through it. Customers were taking their business to the only other dry cleaners in town. Harold was losing business.

One day, Harold had gotten mad at the general contractor. He stopped one of the workers from driving over his back alley to get to Jeremy's new building. The worker called the general, who told the worker to drive on through. So Harold put up cones, then barricades. The contractor moved the barricades and ignored Harold.

Meanwhile, in the other room, Jeremy complained that Harold's actions delayed the project, costing him thousands of dollars. Harold was rude and disrespectful to the contractor. "He tried to prevent the workers from entering the site. It was a huge hassle." Jeremy thought that Harold was just being anti-development and contrary. He assumed that Harold either did not like his new stucco building on Main Street or was jealous—or maybe just grumpy and old.

THE GENERATION GAP

As I talked with Jeremy, the contrast between the men became apparent. Jeremy was a young-thirty-something-year-old man, religious, blond-haired, and blue-eyed. He grew up in southern California and had moved to Utah three years earlier. He was a newcomer. His wife and three children depended on him to support the family. He was financially stretched owning the newly constructed building and was just barely making it. In contrast, Harold had lived in this small Utah town all his life. His family owned a farm and a cattle ranch. He was a respected member of the community who worked hard and cared about the town. He drank coffee and smoked cigarettes with the locals every morning. He was seventy-five. When he turned his farm over to his son, he opened the dry cleaning shop to keep himself busy and out of his wife's way.

I thought the only option was to have them talk. I asked Jeremy if he would be willing to talk directly to Harold.

Jeremy wondered what they would talk about. He said that Harold clearly hated him and wouldn't even look at him. "I used to wave at him in the morning, and he won't wave back," said Jeremy. "So I stopped waving, and now I ignore him, too." Jeremy noted that he couldn't afford this litigation and certainly didn't have any money to pay to Harold.

I told Jeremy to just give it a chance. "See what he has to say. If it's hard to hear, just try to let it roll off your back. I think age and experience have something to do with this."

Jeremy seemed okay with talking to Harold, so I walked down to the main office of the fire station where Harold was waiting. I began, "Well, Harold, you're a community leader in this town. I would like you to talk to Jeremy. I mean . . . maybe you are hoping to teach him something," I suggested, carefully choosing my words.

Harold looked up at me. "I DO have something to teach him," he said forcefully. I had heard that phrase before. It sounded sort of like revenge, but was it? Over the years, I had learned that this sometimes meant that one person was trying to use a lawsuit out of "principle" to teach a person to do something differently in the future. But litigation rarely accomplished that goal and was horrendously expensive, so I hoped the "lesson" was different. Harold stared out of the glass enclosure at the fire truck with his foggy blue eyes. He sat up tall in his chair. He looked energized but not angry. I thought it was a good sign, but it was hard to be certain.

CLOSING THE GENERATION GAP

I slowly walked back to fetch Jeremy from his room and brought him into the main room with Harold, thinking about how I would work with these men together. The men shook hands briefly. Jeremy sat down in one of the three folding chairs informally arranged for a conversation. They were both willing to talk. Good enough, I thought. Now to make sure that everyone stayed sufficiently calm to produce good communication.

They looked to me. I thanked them for agreeing to talk and then summed up the issues: Harold filed the lawsuit because Jeremy's building was on his property. Jeremy understood the issues and the frustration but believed that his expert would testify that the building was not encroaching. The lawyers were happy—"Well, not really happy, but they are willing," I said, trying to lighten my remarks—to take this to court. Neither Harold nor Jeremy wanted to bear the expense of litigation. It had already been very expensive, and they wanted to solve this before they spent more money. Jeremy simply did not have money to pay Harold and was wondering if there was something else he could do.

I concluded by saying in a quiet, slow voice, "And I can see there is a pretty obvious generational difference between you guys." I intentionally did not go into any more details.

"Well, Jeremy," Harold said, "I'm old and set in my ways. I don't think you should have built this building on my ground. It's just not right." He paused. "But even more than that, your building really hurt my business. What, with all the noise and the dust and the dirt, I lost customers. I still don't have 'em back. I think I might have lost half my business during your nine months of construction. My customers went to the other dry cleaners across town, and they haven't come back. Now, I need to do something to bring them back. I was thinking about printing a mailer with a 50 percent off special." His voice trailed off. Jeremy was quiet.

Harold began again, saying that he was really hoping that Jeremy would pay him something due to all the damage he had caused or for the fair market value of the ground he took. Harold looked over at Jeremy for a response. A few long seconds passed.

Jeremy looked directly at Harold and apologized, saying that he didn't realize that there was damage to Harold's business. "Maybe I could help you with some advertising," said Jeremy.

"And another thing," Harold broke in, "I think you should get involved in this community. I could help you. Around here, we work together. You oughta meet us in the coffee shop some morning. A lot a business is done there, you know. If you spent a little time, I think I could teach you a few things about this town."

"I would like that Harold," Jeremy said. Jeremy told Harold that he did feel that Harold could teach him something about the town because everyone in the town respected Harold. Jeremy then said that he just got upset the day that Harold stopped waving to him; although he tried to be friendly, he said, Harold wouldn't even look at him.

Harold said that he didn't remember that, but he did remember Jeremy's mud puddles and how his customers didn't like dragging their clean clothes through them. Harold also remembered how rude

Jeremy's contractor had been and how the contractor had ignored Harold. Harold's voice trailed off.

Jeremy asked why Harold hadn't called him. Harold said he had tried to contact Jeremy—he'd walked into Jeremy's business and talked to the girl at the front desk, assuming that she had told Jeremy that Harold had been there.

Jeremy sighed. "Oh, I guess I knew you came by. I just didn't know what it was about. And, honestly, Harold, I was a little afraid of you. I did call my contractor and tell him to keep it cleaned up. But it was hard with the snowstorms and the way it melts so fast around here in the day and then freezes at night. I'm from California and didn't know what to do. I was just hoping to get the project done. And I thought my contractor was keeping it cleaned up—as cleaned up as he could until it snowed and melted all the time. Sorry. Guess I should have talked to you, but I never knew when you would be at your business."

"Well, you really caused me to lose a lot of business," said Harold. Scooting his chair next to Jeremy, Harold handed Jeremy his profit and loss statements from the past three years, walking him through the finer points. I knew that at this point, the discussions were moving along from adversarial to problem solving.

With Harold's brusque approach rolling off his back, Jeremy looked at the spreadsheets showing the decline, acknowledging the problem but pointing out that he didn't have money to give to Harold because he had a family to support, his wife was pregnant with another child, his building had stretched him to the max, and he had been wondering how to make ends meet as it was. Almost as an afterthought, he added, "I have an extra office available for rent in my building. If I could rent it, I would be in better shape."

Harold scooted back a bit and paused, rubbing his short gray chin whiskers thoughtfully. "I have an idea. I know this town and these folks, and Mrs. Baxter's son was looking for a place to rent. . . . Maybe he'd rent from you."

Next there followed a string of "negotiations," all initiated by Jeremy and Harold themselves. Jeremy proposed that he help Harold print and mail the flyer advertising the 50 percent off special. He said that his wife put together closing baskets for new homeowners for every loan that they closed in their mortgage company and that she could add the flyer in the baskets, or they could even send it to their customer list. Jeremy asked what the flyer would cost. Harold guessed around $500. Jeremy then requested information on Mrs. Baxter's son so that he could fill the vacant office in his building and help a little more with Harold's financial situation. Harold then asked if he could park behind Jeremy's building because parking was tight behind his own building. Jeremy agreed.

I interrupted. "So, Harold, let me see if I am understanding the proposal. If Jeremy pays for the flyer and allows you to park in his back alley, does that resolve this case?"

Harold looked at me thoughtfully and paused. He noted that he did lose a lot of money, and Jeremy did have his four inches of ground. Harold then asked Jeremy if he could swing another $5,000 if he rented to Mrs. Baxter's son. Jeremy said that he would pay the $5,000 regardless of whether he rented the office space if Harold would give him two years to pay it. Harold said that although two years was a long time, he would accept that proposal because he could see that Jeremy was stretched.

A Sign of Cooperation

Then Harold added, "And I guess I should also just let you know that I was thinking about putting up a new sign on the corner. Do you have any problem with that?"

"Hmm. Well, I don't mind. I mean, I think its good. I would like to advertise on the sign if we work that in. I just don't know if I can afford it right away," Jeremy said quietly.

"Well, sure, but let me get back to you on that. I'm meeting with the sign company next week to figure out the cost and all. I want to make our corner the nicest corner on Main Street," said Harold.

As the meeting wound down and the attorneys arrived to write up the agreement, I was wondering what had happened, when it had happened, and how these guys had managed to completely turn around their relationship. I know that I believed from the beginning that they could communicate and understand each other. I firmly believe that identifying their generational gap was key. After mentioning that fact, both men seemed to go from assuming negative intent to learning the other person's perspective. From that point on, I just watched a most amazing conversation.

For years, I wondered how it all turned out for them. Then one day I drove through their town, and there it was—a sign advertising both businesses.

SECOND THOUGHTS:

This mediation occurred in 2001 when I had been in private mediation practice for only three months. Previously, I had mediated at the Utah Court of Appeals, but that was different: one side had won, and the parties were court ordered to mediate with me. I recall spending the first hour in each case getting past those hurdles. So leaving to go into private practice was great. I've mediated many cases over the years, and each one has been rewarding in its own way; however, this case had a particular impact on me.

At the time of this mediation, I had only mediated about 400 cases. If I wasn't hooked on mediation before, this case hooked me. I saw the good that could be done.

The case presented quite simply. These two men were at odds. They did not understand each other. When I began the mediation, I was concerned that the underlying lawsuit may have escalated their dispute into seemingly intractable positions. If tried, the case would be assigned to a rotating judge, so no one knew what he or she might order. The lawyers disliked the uncertainty for their clients, so they were willing to try mediation. However, they were skeptical about settlement because Harold was really mad. Despite that, the lawyers gave me the latitude to work with these men. I appreciated that. In fact, I am indebted to them, as are their clients.

I was amazed as I watched the mediation process work. I began by simply actively listening to both men in separate rooms. I could see, after a short while, that it would make a difference to both men if they could appreciate each other's perspectives. Harold seemed to believe

345

that Jeremy's act of building on his property was intentional and that Jeremy knew the construction mess caused the dry cleaning business to suffer. I believed that such a misunderstanding could best be cleared up via communication directly between them in order to maximize the opportunity for understanding and shifting of perspectives. I knew this was somewhat risky, but I figured that no one had anything to lose. The men would not resolve this case without understanding each other.

Before I put them together, though, I thought about their differences. The generation gap seemed to be a key problem in this case. I thought about how different it was to talk to my grandparents. My grandparents wanted respect and good manners. I thought Harold probably wanted respect also. There were other dissimilarities, too, that added to the communication problem, such as religion and their disparate identities in the community. This was a case in which neither side understood the other's point of view.

Moving them together in one room was slightly risky, but I noticed a decrease in tension when they sat together. My gut realized that it was good and the timing was right. I was initially concerned that Harold could be harsh, but even the remarks that may have felt a little harsh seemed in line with his gruff generational style of communicating the facts as he saw them. Jeremy had a cheery enough disposition to counteract Harold's gruffness, and he was eager to resolve the dispute with Harold. I had primed Jeremy to listen and had asked him to try to let fighting words roll off his back. For Harold, I was pretty certain that I would not be able to coach him to temper his remarks, so I really didn't try. However, I did ask him to be frank with Jeremy because I felt that Jeremy was willing to learn; Harold responded to this obvious deference to his wisdom. As I have found many times since, these two just seemed to need a forum and a bit of mediator prep to move into a productive conversation.

When the actual negotiating began, I could really see that my involvement had become very limited, which is often the most effective way to be a mediator. I figured the less I said, the better for them in the long run. They needed to solve the problem themselves. It was interesting to watch them generate options and discuss them. I knew going into the joint session that Jeremy was unaware of the extent of the mud problem and the impact on Harold's business. I did not know that Harold was thinking of the flyer, parking options, or a sign. On Jeremy's end, I knew that Jeremy was suffering financially, but I did not know the extent of his financial woes. I also did not know that he had a vacant office, nor did I know that Harold knew of a potential tenant. When Jeremy offered to buy the flyer, I was surprised but pleased. Obviously, he was trying to find principled ways to pay Harold, and that was one.

In the end, when Harold mentioned his intent to put up a sign and commented that he wanted "our corner to be the nicest corner on Main Street," the moment was magical. These two guys, newcomer and old-timer, were looking in the same direction, forming joint solutions.

Since this mediation, I have been able to duplicate this experience in cases involving boundaries, roads, and business partnerships, to name a few. Each time, it is a little different, but the men and their lawyers in this particular case clearly taught me to give all of my clients a process, to time their discussions unscientifically but carefully, to provide a key observation or two to help them see a different perspective, and to allow adequate time and space for them to arrive at their own solutions.

PART IX
Beyond Agreements

I once heard an experienced and perceptive
lawyer observe, speaking of complex business
agreements, "If you negotiate the contract
thoroughly, explore carefully the problems that
can arise in the course of its administration, work
out the proper language to cover the various
contingencies that may develop, you can then
put the contract in a drawer and forget it."
What he meant was that in the exchange that
accompanied the negotiation and drafting of
the contract the parties would come to
understand each other's problems sufficiently
so that when difficulties arose they would,
as fair and reasonable men, be able to make
the appropriate adjustments without
referring to the contract itself.

Lon Fuller, Mediation—Its Forms and Functions

31.

Failed Mediation:
A Success Story

Carl S. Kaplan and Carol B. Liebman

"Failed Mediation: A Success Story" is based on a mediation conducted by Mr. Kaplan and his partner and supervised by Ms. Liebman when Mr. Kaplan was a law student.

FAILURE AND SUCCESS: A FINE LINE

On the data sheets, this case, which we co-mediated with Jody Rosentsweig, will be reported as failing to settle, but the case was our biggest success of the fall.

THE INCIDENTS

We were about two-thirds through the opening statement and Carl had begun to explain writing up the agreement when the respondent,

Linda, interrupted with an impassioned outburst: "Agreement! There's not going to be no agreement. I'm going to settle this on the street. Her son f***ed with my daughter. I'm going to hurt her. I've done time and if I have to go back [to jail], that's okay. The only way this will be settled is on the street." We tried to calm her with some empathic responses, but Linda's anger did not subside. "Every day I look at my daughter. . . ." She started to cry. "I know I got to deal with it. I want to f*** her [the complainant] up."

After some clarifying questions to Linda and an opportunity for the complainant, Rena, to be heard, the following story emerged. Linda and Rena had taken care of each other's children in the past. Recently, Linda's children stayed overnight at Rena's house. Linda's daughter said that after Rena fell asleep, she was molested by Rena's twelve-year-old son. The daughter told her mother that he padlocked her in a room and forced her to perform oral sex. Linda reported the incident to the Child Welfare Agency (CWA). Both CWA and the police investigated but had taken no action.

Rena had filed a harassment complaint against Linda. She claimed that Linda had repeatedly threatened her, once coming to the house with a loaded gun. Another time, someone set a fire outside Rena's door; she assumed that it was Linda.

RENA'S SIDE

After an extremely tense joint session, the mediators decided to meet first in caucus with Rena, the complainant, since she had spoken only briefly in the joint session. Rena was defensive during the caucus. (What we might have done differently to help Rena trust the process is a topic for another article.) When asked what she would like in a mediation agreement, she said that she would not trust Linda to keep any agreement, so she would not sign anything. We explored her concerns a bit more and then asked her to stick with the process long enough to see what progress we could make when we met with Linda in private session. We asked her to wait and invited Linda into private session.

LINDA'S SIDE

Linda returned to the room accompanied by her twenty-year-old son, who had sat in on the public session looking glazed and uninvolved. Linda was calmer in the private session. She seemed to be struggling with a great moral problem. On the one hand, the molestation of her daughter was an evil that must be avenged, and Linda thought that she had to hurt Rena to achieve rough justice. Indeed, to Linda, hurting Rena was the right thing to do. And yet, so far, Linda had not acted, possibly because she knew that hurting Rena would result in jail time and that jail time would hurt her own children. Linda really did not know what to do. She was stuck on the razor's edge and could only howl.

As she began to retell her story, her rage returned. She asked if her friend, a calming influence, could join us. Then, sitting between her friend and her son, Linda retold her story with less anger and more sadness. Her daughter was nine years old, she told us, crying. The molestation had hurt the daughter's performance in school. The child was in therapy. Linda added that she was angry at Rena not just because of what happened to her daughter but because Rena failed to exercise any kind of parental role in the household when her daughter was there and because Rena had never expressed any sympathy for her daughter.

As the discussion continued, Linda's rage would flare up; and then, with support from her friend and a great deal of effort on her own, Linda would calm down. Finally, we asked whether Linda could sign an agreement that contained a stay-away, no-physical-contact provision. Linda responded, "I can't do that. I pulled a gun on her. I might do it again. I don't want to be dishonest."

A PLEA FOR AN END TO THE CYCLE OF VIOLENCE

At this point, as we were about to give up, the son intervened. He asked whether we could bring Rena back so that he could say something to both women. "I want to tell them this has to stop," he said. "I want to tell them that if my mother hurts Rena, then her people will come after my mother and I'll have to protect her and it will never end." He wanted to plead for an end to the cycle of violence. It was worth a try.

We went to get Rena, only to find that she had left with no explanation—she was gone.

We returned to the mediation room to break the news and wrap up, fearing that serious violence between the two women lay ahead. Linda struggled to keep her rage in check. Then the son spoke up again: "Mom, listen to me. Leave it alone. When you were in jail, Grandma took care of us. It was hard. I've only begun to get myself together, to get back in school and work toward my future." He went on to say that if Linda attempted to harm Rena, then Rena's people would try to get back at her, and he would have to jump in. The son tried to explain that any retaliation by Linda would involve whole families in a Greek tragedy, that many people could get hurt or arrested, and that his hope for a better life for himself and his young sister would be lost. Linda, who had probably never thought about the conflict in these terms before, listened and nodded as her son continued. "Mom, I've never told you how hard it was when you were away. I don't want you to go to jail again. I don't want that to happen to my little sister."

As the son spoke, Linda went through a physical transformation. We could see her body language change as she took in his words and their powerful message. She told us that she had been to a therapist for help in controlling her temper. She told us that she did not want to be the source of further harm to her daughter. She seemed to be promising her son that she would take his plea to heart.

FAILURE: NOT ALWAYS WHAT IT SEEMS

We thanked Linda for coming to mediation, thanked her friend for being there for support, and thanked the son for his wise comments. They left, and we reported the case as a failed attempt to mediate. But we were certain that despite the lack of an agreement, mediation had empowered Linda to work toward nonviolent ways of solving the conflict. We counted this case as one of our biggest successes.

Final Thoughts from the Editors:

This book ends with "A Failed Mediation" for a number of reasons.

One reason is the oft-repeated truth that an agreement—or lack of one—at the end of mediation says very little about the value of the process in many important senses. Are parties' lives better? Can they move on with their lives beyond the sometimes-suffocating aspects of being in conflict? Have they come to any different, more nuanced understanding of their situation? Can they deal, without a mediator, with the next dispute that they encounter?

Linda's dilemma was not resolved with a tidy handshake or signature on an agreement. However, she appreciated a universe of important consequences that had not previously been her primary motivator. The realization she came to was perhaps more important than any accord she could have reached with Rena that day: that her children needed her to be sane, in control of her anger, and out of jail.

Another reason that this book ends here is the principle of unknowability. As mediators, we never know the epilogues of the cases that we work on. The "failed" mediations may well transform into success stories where the parties become stronger and happier and ultimately resolve their dispute or choose to live with their unresolved dispute because of some spark of understanding that was lighted in the mediation. And, sadly, the "successful" mediations may stumble and fail down the line.

Collectively, these stories are a tribute to how impactful mediation can be. Given this potential, the stories highlight how important it is to be mindful of small things as a mediator—the setting, the food, the agenda, the vocabulary; and how critical it is to listen for the big things—what is at the heart of the matter for the parties. The book celebrates the power and potential of mediation, which is fueled by the careful and skillful work of mediators.

The Story Tellers

ABOUT AND BY THE AUTHORS

Tracy Allen is a full time neutral from Grosse Pointe, Michigan. A technologically challenged, recovering tax attorney, she mediates and conducts educational programs in connection with complex commercial disputes worldwide and is an adjunct professor of ADR processes and advocacy at Pepperdine and Lipscomb Universities. Ms. Allen became a mediator because she abhors conflict, hates to read and has an insatiable need to fix things. Her life as the only child of parents who were only children has embedded attributes critical to success in the profession: curiosity, tenacity, creativity and integrity. These traits have brought her professional recognition in *Best Lawyers* and *Super Lawyers*, and the appointment as a Distinguished Life Fellow and Past President of the International Academy of Mediators, all of which she finds humbling and astonishing. Ms. Allen's passions include snow skiing, cooking and music, particularly the classics. She remains eternally grateful to her brilliant and compassionate mediator colleagues who keep her fresh and optimistic.

Eleanor Barr has been mediating for over a decade after spending the previous decade litigating complex cases. She is a fellow of the International Academy of Mediators and has been an adjunct professor of mediation at the Straus Institute for Dispute Resolution at Pepperdine University School of Law. She spent her childhood in a suburb of New York City and her adolescence in the Midwest and has been living in Los Angeles for over twenty years. She is married to her junior high sweetheart whom she met again as an adult, and they have a daughter who has been a natural mediator since her toddler years. Ms. Barr's passion for mediation stems from her lifelong quest to understand the value of different perspectives and to seek balance in the midst of complexity and turmoil.

Lee Jay Berman has served as a full-time mediator and trainer for seventeen years. A Distinguished Fellow with the International Academy of Mediators, Mr. Berman is also a diplomat with the National Academy of Distinguished Neutrals and a dispute resolution expert with the United Nations Development Programme. He directed Pepperdine University School of Law's Mediating the Litigated Case program for seven years and then founded the American Institute of Mediation. Mr. Berman was the national chair of the ABA's Dispute Resolution Training Committee for four years and has trained judges, attorneys, and business leaders in India, Croatia, Jordan, the Netherlands, and the United Arab Emirates. He authors the popular blog *Eye on Conflict*, and lives with his wife Trish in Marina del Rey, California.

Russell Brunson has been a mediator and dispute resolution trainer since 1997 and has worked with community-based organizations, schools, universities, and justice facilities across the United States. He is currently a manager with the Peninsula Conflict Resolution Center and has been an adjunct professor of dispute resolution at Notre Dame de Namur University and Hastings College of the Law. He is interested in distance-based learning and has coauthored the Emmy award-winning *Take a Stand: Stop the Violence* interactive CD, which teaches negotiation skills to teens and adults. He has also co-created: *Out on a Limb*, an interactive website that teaches conflict resolution techniques to young children, parents, and elementary school teachers (http://urbanext. illinois.edu/conflict/); and *The Art in Peacemaking*, a conflict resolution training manual for arts educators. Mr. Brunson's passions include a lifelong quest to appreciate the complexities of communication and collaboration; biking; the Mets; tending his fruit trees; and spending time with his wife, son, and tribe of cats.

Kenneth Cloke has been a mediator since 1980 and is an arbitrator, attorney, coach, consultant, and trainer specializing in resolving complex multiparty conflicts—including organizational and workplace disputes, marital and family conflicts, and public policy disputes—and designing preventative conflict resolution systems. He is a founder and first president of Mediators Beyond Borders. He is the author of numerous books, including: *Mediating Dangerously*; *The Crossroads of Conflict: A Journey into the Heart of Dispute Resolution*; and *Conflict Revolution: Mediating Evil, War, Injustice, and Terrorism*. He is the coauthor with Joan Goldsmith of: *Resolving Personal and Organizational Conflict; The End of Management and the Rise of Organizational Democracy; The Art of Waking People Up*; and *Resolving Conflicts at Work*. When not mediating, he is writing, swimming and gardening in Idaho, or grandparenting four kids on Bainbridge Island Washington, and two on the way in Longmeadow, Massachusetts.

Charles W. Crumpton, partner in Crumpton & Hansen, Honolulu, has mediated in Hawai'i and the continental United States since 1985. His practice primarily involves personal injury, insurance, malpractice, business, employment, construction, real estate, community and public interest matters. He has taught business and conflict management at Hawai'i Pacific University, the University of Hawai'i Shidler College of Business Administration and the Viet Nam National University's Hanoi and Ho Chi Minh City Business Colleges. Mr. Crumpton has trained mediators and attorneys in mediation in Hawai'i and the US. He has served as co-chair of the Hawai'i State Bar Association ADR Section for over 15 years and has chaired development of the Hawai'i US District Court Mediation Program. He is AV-rated by Martindale-Hubbell and has been selected as a Best Lawyer and Super Lawyer in ADR by peer review since 2005. He treasures family, friends, colleagues, jazz, running, water sports, living in Hawai'i and yearly time in Vietnam.

Ben J. Cunningham is a founding partner of Lakeside Mediation Center in Austin, Texas. He has been mediating disputes professionally since 1987. In lives prior to becoming an attorney and a mediator, Mr. Cunningham's exploration of the planet earth led him to become a journalist, soldier, director of an international relief agency, big-city cop, and hostage negotiator. For ten years, Mr. Cunningham has been a member of the advisory board for graduate alternative dispute resolution programs at Texas State University. A former board member of the Texas Association of Mediators, he will serve as President of the Austin Dispute Resolution Center in 2012. Mr. Cunningham, who holds the designation of Distinguished Credentialed Mediator awarded by the Texas Mediator Credentialing Association, is a frequent speaker on topics of ADR and negotiation and a trainer of mediators.

Eric R. Galton has been a mediator for twenty-two years. He is one of the founders of the Lakeside Mediation Center in Austin, Texas. His first book, *Mediation: A Texas Guide*, won the CPR Best Book Award in 1991 and has been translated into three languages. Mr. Galton has served as an adjunct professor for Pepperdine University School of Law and University of Texas School of Law and has lectured and conducted trainings around the globe. He will serve as President of the International Academy of Mediators in 2012-2013. He is fortunate to be married to Kimberlee Kovach, one of the preeminent mediation scholars. His passions include his five children, his three year old 104 pound labradoodle named Emmy, Bruce Springsteen, Duke basketball, Texas Longhorn football, New Zealand wines, and all things Austin.

Debra Gerardi is a conflict engagement specialist and provides mediation, coaching, training, and other consulting services to health-care organizations internationally. She is the president and chief creative officer for Emerging HealthCare Communities (EHCCO); and she has provided professional services to over 100 leading organizations, including various health systems, academic medical centers, The Joint Commission and Joint Commission Resources, the WHO World Alliance for Patient Safety, and the U.S. Department of Defense Patient Safety Program. Ms. Gerardi attributes her success as a mediator, and in life, to her seventeen years of improvisation training and performing. She lives with her husband and two cats in a cozy house by the sea.

Susan M. Hammer is a mediator in Portland, Oregon. She was named the Oregon mediation Lawyer of the Year 2012 by *Best Lawyers* and was also recognized in *Top 25 Oregon Women Lawyers* and *Oregon Super Lawyers* for alternative dispute resolution. She is a distinguished fellow of the International Academy of Mediators and a senior fellow at the Willamette University College of Law, Center for Dispute Resolution. She was formerly a partner at Stoel Rives LLP. She serves on the boards of Ecotrust, Pacific Northwest College of Art, Willamette University and the International Academy of Mediators. Susan loves hiking, skiing and just being in the mountains and forests of the Northwest. She and her partner, sculptor Lee Kelly, have led several treks in Nepal and have traveled extensively in Asia, Indonesia, Central and South America.

Karin S. Hobbs has served as a full-time professional mediator since 1998, mediating personal injury, class actions, construction, contract, property, malpractice, probate and family disputes. She is known for her ability to work with emotionally charged clients and complex legal disputes. Ms. Hobbs served as Chief Appellate Mediator at the Utah Court of Appeals, founded the Dispute Resolution Section of the Utah State Bar, and taught mediation and negotiation at the University of Utah S.J. Quinney School of Law. In 2004, Ms. Hobbs received the Peter W. Billings Sr. Award for Excellence in Alternative Dispute Resolution. She has published numerous articles, including *How to Achieve the Best Results in Mediation* published in the AAA's Handbook on Mediation. Ms. Hobbs is thankful for her supportive husband, their three incredible children, and her family. She enjoys skiing, fishing, hiking, camping, traveling and the solitude she finds in her cabin in the mountains.

David A. Hoffman became a mediator twenty years ago and also practices law at Boston Law Collaborative, LLC (BLC). He teaches the mediation course at Harvard Law School. He is a past chair of the ABA Section of Dispute Resolution, and has published two books on ADR, including *Bringing Peace into the Room* (with coeditor Daniel Bowling). He is a graduate of Princeton (B.A. 1970), Cornell (M.A.

American Studies 1974), and Harvard Law School (J.D. 1984). He and his wife, Beth Andrews, live in a cohousing community in Acton, Massachusetts, where they raised three children. Mr. Hoffman's passions include his family, his colleagues at BLC, teaching, running, Pete Seeger, windsurfing, the dunes of Cape Cod, and trying to make the world a better place. Mediation has taught him that the same skills and insights needed to make us more centered, compassionate people also make us better mediators.

Jeff Jury of Burns Anderson Jury & Brenner, LLP in Austin, Texas has practiced law for 25 years and has mediated matters for 14 years. His mediation experience includes complex commercial, tort, real estate and construction matters. He teaches Advanced Dispute Resolution at Baylor Law School. Jeff, who believes that baseball metaphors apply to all aspects of life, is a "five-tool" player (dad, mediator, arbitrator, teacher, litigator) who once hit a 750-foot home run to straightaway center field on his kids' Wii video game. A recipient of the Texas Center for Legal Ethics Professionalism Award, Jeff has presented and written articles or book chapters on topics that include dispute resolution, construction law, and legal ethics. He is currently Membership Co-Chair of the International Academy of Mediators, and has served in leadership positions of many mediation and practice-related organizations. The best part of his life, however, is raising and loving his two sons.

Carl S. Kaplan participated in Columbia Law School's Mediation Clinic as a student. He is currently senior appellate counsel at the Center for Appellate Litigation, a non-profit defender organization in New York City that handles criminal appeals for poor people. Mr. Kaplan also is a lecturer-in-law at Columbia Law School, where he designed and co-teaches an externship program in criminal appeals, and was a Markle Fellow at the Centre for Social-Legal Studies, Oxford University, where he studied Internet Law. He wrote a popular legal affairs column, "Cyberlaw Journal," for the Web site of The New York Times from 1997 to 2002. Prior to entering law school, he was a writer and editor at a number of publications, including the late and lamented

New York Newsday, where he was a business features reporter. He and his wife, Pamela Mendels, a writer, reside on the Upper West Side of Manhattan. They have two children and an insane Irish Terrier.

Jeff Kichaven has been a commercial mediator since 1996 with a nationwide practice based in Los Angeles. He is a 1980 Cum Laude Graduate of Harvard Law School and a 1977 Phi Beta Kappa Graduate of the University of California, Berkeley. He has been named California Lawyer Attorney of the Year in ADR and has taught the Master Class for Mediators for Harvard Law School. He has also received a Special Award for Excellence in Mediation from the Asian Pacific-American Dispute Resolution Center. He has served on the Board of Trustees of the Los Angeles County Bar Association and the Board of Governors of the International Academy of Mediators. He is also on the Board of the Center for Civic Mediation, which provides mediation training and supervision to Los Angeles-area students, allowing them to resolve disputes through dialogue and to proceed through school without physical injury, disciplinary records or arrests.

Jeffrey Krivis is the author of two books: *Improvisational Negotiation: A Mediator's Stories of Conflict About Love, Money, Anger— and the Strategies That Resolved Them* and *How to Make Money as a Mediator (And Create Value for Everyone)*. He mediates a variety of cases, including class action, employment, entertainment, complex business, and insurance and catastrophic injury. He has taught at Pepperdine University School of Law since 1994 and serves as an emeritus member on the board of trustees and on the Straus Institute Advisory Council. Mr. Krivis is the Past President of both the International Academy of Mediators and the Southern California Mediation Association. He is a Sunday golfer and woodshed blues guitarist.

Carol B. Liebman is a clinical professor at Columbia Law School, where she founded the Columbia Law School Mediation Clinic and is the director of the Negotiation Workshop. She has mediated cases in a wide variety of contexts and is a prominent speaker and trainer on conflict resolution. Ms. Liebman is the co-principal investigator for the Mediating Suits Against Hospitals (MeSH) study and was co-principal investigator for the Demonstration Mediation and ADR Project, a part of the Project on Medical Liability in Pennsylvania (http://medliabilitypa.org) funded by the Pew Charitable Trusts. She is the coauthor with Nancy Dubler of *Bioethics Mediation: A Guide to Shaping Shared Solutions.* She is currently studying conflict resolution with her grandchildren, ages 5-11, using scholarly sources such as Harry Potter, Dodsworth, Percy Jackson and Pokemon. Liebman embraces the win-win opportunities presented in daily life except when rooting for the Red Sox to win and the Evil Empire to lose.

Lela P. Love has been a mediator since 1983, pioneering one of the first law school mediation programs in the United States at Benjamin N. Cardozo School of Law. She has mediated a wide range of disputes and trains mediators nationally and internationally. She chaired the ABA Dispute Resolution Section and initiated the first International Mediation Leadership Summit in The Hague in her chair year. She has coauthored three textbooks on dispute resolution, as well as a book on mediation with Joseph Stulberg, *The Middle Voice: Mediating Conflict Successfully.* She received the 2009 Frontline Champion Award on Mediation Settlement Day at the Association of the Bar of the City of NY and the 2010 Lifetime Achievement Award from the American College of Civil Trial Mediators. Despite promoting collaborative processes, Lela enjoys competition of all types, including horse jumping, downhill skiing, running, and Speed Scrabble.

Peter Miller became a mediator in 1986. Currently, he practices in the New York metropolitan area. He mediates primarily in the family and workplace arenas, although his experience also includes business and other disputes. He has worked extensively for the U.S. Postal Service's REDRESS program as well as other government agencies with workplace mediation programs. In addition, Mr. Miller has extensive experience in community mediation cases. He serves often as a trainer of mediation, including in programs on transformative mediation skills offered by the Institute for the Study of Conflict Transformation. This past year, with some expert guidance, he logged his family's land in Vermont—an activity in which mediation skills are completely without application.

Frank J. Scardilli, now retired, has been affectionately known as the "Dean of Federal Appellate Court Mediators," having served longer than any other appellate court mediator in the nation. For more than thirty years, he was the chief circuit mediator for the U.S. Court of Appeals for the Second Circuit. He has won that prestigious court's highest honor, the Second Circuit Merit Award, which "signifies the esteem the Second Circuit holds for his mastery of the art of negotiation and ability to solve difficult legal problems." Mr. Scardilli, a 1949 graduate of Yale Law School, taught negotiation at Benjamin N. Cardozo School of Law for fifteen years; the Frank J. Scardilli Lectureship in Negotiation, Mediation, and Conflict Resolution ensures in perpetuity that students at Cardozo are offered a course in the theory and skills of conflict resolution. He takes particular pride in being regarded as the loving and caring patriarch of his extended and closely knit family.

Jan Frankel Schau committed to a full-time mediation practice mediating litigated cases after the events of September 11, 2001. She is an exclusive neutral with ADR Services in Los Angeles, California. Ms. Schau studied international relations and diplomacy at Pomona College before enrolling in Loyola Law School. She learned the art of mediation through her personal experience raising three teenage children with her husband, Michael. She prides herself on both her creativity and an unfailing optimism, qualities that are highly valued in mediation. Most of all, she believes that everyone has an interesting story to tell, and she is ever eager to listen.

Margaret Shaw has participated in the resolution of thousands of disputes nationwide. A former civil litigator, she has maintained an active alternative dispute resolution practice for more than thirty years. She joined JAMS when ADR Associates, a firm that she cofounded, merged with JAMS in 2004. For twenty-five years she taught ADR and negotiation as an adjunct professor of law at New York University School of Law and has authored numerous articles on dispute resolution and mediation. She feels blessed to be part of the mediation community and finds humor to be both the most necessary and the most effective mediator characteristic.

Joseph B. ("Josh") Stulberg, JD, Ph.D. is the John W. Bricker Professor of Law at The Ohio State University Moritz College of Law. Since 1973, he has been involved full-time in ADR work as a national program administrator, mediator, trainer, program designer and scholar. A former Vice President of the American Arbitration Association in charge of its Community Dispute Resolution services, he is a Distinguished Fellow of the American College of Civil Trial Mediators. He is the author of multiple technical manuals on mediation processes as well as coauthor of several mediation texts, including *The Middle Voice: Mediating Conflict Successfully* with Lela Love. He served as Reporter for the Revised Model Standards of Conduct for Mediators and as Task Force Chair of the ACR Study of the 2009 Arbitration Fairness Act. An avid marathon runner and fan of any sport with a racquet, he loves listening to classical music.

Lawrence M. Watson Jr. has practiced exclusively in litigation and alternative dispute resolution with an emphasis in complex multiparty disputes, commercial problems, and construction claims. In 1988, while serving as senior litigation counsel for the Carlton Fields law firm and leading its Orlando office, Mr. Watson became one of the first civil trial mediators certified by the Florida Supreme Court. He went on to Chair the Florida Supreme Court Standing Committee on Mediation Rules and Policy for over 10 years, and is still an active member. He has received The Florida Academy of Professional Mediator's Award of Merit and the Lifetime Achievement Award from the American College of Civil Trial Mediators. An avid Florida Gator football fan, addicted golfer and a frustrated fly fisherman, Mr. Watson is also a principal in Upchurch, Watson, White & Max Mediation Group of Orlando, Florida.